James R. Downey

Abelard to Apple

Abelard to Apple

The Fate of American Colleges and Universities

Richard A. DeMillo

The MIT Press
Cambridge, Massachusetts
London, England

For information about special quantity discounts, please email special_sales@ mitpress.mit.edu

This book was set in Stone Sans and Stone Serif by Graphic Composition, Inc. Printed and bound in the United States of America.

Library of Congress Cataloging-in-Publication Data

DeMillo, Richard A.
Abelard to Apple: the fate of American colleges and universities / Richard A. DeMillo.
    p.   cm.
Includes bibliographical references and index.
ISBN 978–0-262–01580–6 (hardcover: alk. paper) 1. Universities and colleges—United States. 2. Education, Higher—Aims and objectives—United States. 3. Educational change—United States. I. Title.
LA227.4.D46   2011
378.73—dc22

                                                                    2010049657

10 9 8 7 6 5 4 3 2 1

Some other institutions and presidents will confront their problems, take a careful look, and then turn tail and run.
—Clark Kerr

Great as was the influence exerted by Abelard on the minds of his contemporaries and the course of medieval thought, he has been little known in modern time, but for his connection with Heloise.
—George Croom Robertson

Contents

Preface

In late 2006, I began writing a five-page memo on the future of my university—a simple essay that could be browsed and critiqued by colleagues. Some of what I had to say was harshly critical of the status quo, so I found myself explaining why some firmly held but absolutely incorrect beliefs about higher education were not true and how they had managed to become ingrained in the way universities operate. Five pages were not enough to do that, and my little memo began to grow. Although I have spent much of my career in higher education as a professor and administrator, it did not take me long to exhaust what little I knew about where universities came from and how they work. So, as my short memo became a white paper, I started to consult with experts. I talked to academic leaders, business executives, and policymakers. I told friends and colleagues what I was up to, and they pulled volumes from their bookshelves and said, "You must read this." Stacks of books began appearing at my doorstep. I bought an extra e-book reader just to keep track of my online purchases. What I found was a vast library devoted to both the past and future of universities: memoirs of university presidents, densely annotated histories of higher education, complex economic studies filled with charts and data, sensational warnings about how technology would affect universities, and a few deeply felt defenses of traditional academic values—virtually all of it incomprehensible outside academia.

When academics get together to talk about the future, they talk mainly to each other, but the American system of higher education has many more stakeholders than that. Over the course of months, the intended audience for what was now clearly becoming a book manuscript shifted noticeably from my academic colleagues to a more general readership—parents, students, taxpayers, elected officials, employers, decision makers at all levels—citizens who have a stake in what happens to the nation's colleges and universities and want to be informed about the forces shaping their future.

This book is intended to reach the many stakeholders in America's higher education system who are outside the academy, who are not involved in higher education on a daily basis, and whose voices are seldom heard from within. It is not a book of secrets, but I suspect that many readers will be surprised by what they read here. Some of my colleagues will be shocked that the curtain has been parted, but many more will welcome the daylight.

I resisted the temptation to write a business book for universities, although I have tried to identify the milestones that should be on any roadmap for change. I have no recipes for success. Beyond the *Rules for the Twenty-First Century* in chapter 20, there are no concise chapter summaries that can be transcribed to executive briefings. This book should be read like a novel. Each chapter reveals a little more about the forces shaping our institutions, the character of American higher education, and why some universities make good choices while others do not.

There may be no formulas in these pages, but there is a story; every university needs to figure out where it lies in the arc that takes us from a twelfth-century French monk named Peter Abelard to Apple Computer, an iconic twenty-first century enterprise. How a university identifies and confronts the challenges along the way says a great deal about the likely outcome of a perilous journey. Some institutions will follow the paths that they are on. Many will not survive the coming changes. Universities that follow a different path might survive, but they will not survive intact. They might find themselves in an unforgiving world—a competitive marketplace in which they are ill equipped to prosper. For them, prosperity will depend entirely on a new set of rules and a very different conception of the value of universities in the twenty-first century.

Acknowledgments

The many people I interviewed as I was preparing this book are for the most part identified by name. I have quoted others based on personal conversations and email messages and—when I thought that their remarks would be uncontroversial or reflected public statements they had made elsewhere—I have also identified them by name. Other events and conversations have been turned into *case study* narratives when there did not seem to be any purpose served by using actual names and places. My profound thanks go out to these individuals. All other direct quotations from sources other than personal communications are cited and appear in the endnotes.

This book would not have been written but for the Georgia Tech Threads experiment and my own "band of well-chosen professors" who were fearless in reimagining undergraduate education. There were forty of them, so I cannot thank them individually, but they were led by Merrick Furst, who articulated both the Threaded curriculum concept and the organizational vision that made it possible for the college to achieve profound change; Charles Isbell and Tom Pilsch, whose feat of curriculum engineering gave us a fully accredited program in eighteen months; Mark Guzdial, whose computational media course was the model for a new program; and Blair MacIntyre, who turned a single course into a degree program and blazed the trail for Threads. Provost Jean-Lou Chameau and president Wayne Clough cleared away bureaucratic hurdles and pushed me to think big. My fellow deans Don Giddens, Sue Rosser, and Tom Galloway gave me their generous help and encouragement at every turn.

Tom Friedman—who told me several times, "I don't know anything about universities"—put me on the right track from the outset. It turned out that Tom was underselling himself and knew exactly the question to ask: "What is the value of a university in a world that has been flattened by technology and economic interdependence?"

A number of my colleagues gave me unvarnished criticism and advice, including David Bader, Beki Grinter, Aditya Mathur, and numerous anonymous reviewers. Ellen Zegura and Dick Lipton spent many hours discussing very early drafts of this book and offered important suggestions for how to focus the manuscript. They were both generous with their time and patient with my meandering ideas. My wife Ronnie Martin read in detail several complete drafts of the manuscript; her ability to question my assumptions, hold in check my overblown prose, and tolerate hours of one-sided conversations helped turn an essay into a book.

Tom McMail was both a coach and mentor, and the many hours he put into this task went well beyond what was required to help out a friend. His late-night email was always uncomfortably accurate—especially his early feedback that I'd better figure out how to write a book for a general audience if I really wanted anyone to read it. From his position at Microsoft as university liaison, Tom was often able to see the big picture well before I did. I was most impressed, however, that he never once asked me to find a way to give Microsoft equal billing with Apple in the title.

My MIT Press editor, Ada Brunstein, slyly suggested that the "crazy white paper that I am writing about universities" might actually be more interesting than the project I was currently working on. Her gentle nudges at the beginning and her support and excitement throughout the process of writing the book were essential.

My thanks go out to all of them. Any factual errors or shortcomings in this telling of the story of universities are entirely mine.

Finally, I am indebted to the wide cast of characters who make up this story and to the historians who kept their words alive throughout the centuries. The most important of these is Peter Abelard. Although there is a five-hundred-year trail of love letters, sonnets, and poems that all trace back to Abelard's affair with Heloise, his influence on the development of western universities is only sparsely documented. There is also little known about Abelard's biographer, George Croom Robertson, beyond the brief biographical information in the memoirs of *Philosophical Remains*. He was a professor of psychology and philosophy—a position that carried the title Professor of Mental Philosophy—and was for a time editor of the philosophical journal *Mind*. Peter Abelard was one of a handful of thinkers who shaped Western ideas about education, so I was struck by Robertson's conclusion: "Great as was the influence exerted by Abelard . . . he has been little known in modern time, but for his connection with Heloise."

The idea of using Peter Abelard as a metaphor for the ancient ideal of university teaching came to me when I was well into writing the first draft of the manuscript. For years, I too had known Abelard's name only in conjunction with Heloise and the unpleasant fate of their love affair. But in the days leading up to the controversial 2002 merger of Hewlett-Packard—where I worked as chief technology officer—and Compaq Computer, the lawyers leading the top-secret due-diligence project used the code name Heloise for HP. Compaq was called Abelard. All of our internal documents said Abelard and Heloise, and we were expected to follow suit not only in public, but even in senior executive meetings where everyone was in on the secret. Parties on both sides of the merger read—with great amusement—significance into this choice of names since HP's female CEO Carly Fiorina and Compaq's male CEO Michael Capellas were not only rivals but were widely suspected to be personally unfond of each other. Fiorina, a classics major in college, had picked the names and Capellas was apparently unaware of the symbolism when he agreed to be called Abelard.

One afternoon in early 2002, I decided to dig around to see what was else was known about Abelard and Heloise, and I discovered Robertson's biography of Abelard in the eleventh edition of the *Encyclopedia Britannica*. As I was preparing this manuscript, I recalled a particularly striking passage acknowledging that even Abelard was not immune to faculty-centered hubris and that he came "to think himself the only philosopher standing the world." It was a plot twist that I could not have invented. Life was downhill for Peter Abelard from that point on, which is probably a moral lesson for us all.

Prologue

It was only midmorning, but the September heat had already slowed the ordinary comings and goings in the hotel across the plaza from the Dallas headquarters of the O'Donnell Foundation. Newly arrived guests paused long enough in the air-conditioned lobby to search for the registration desk, or perhaps for a colleague awaiting their arrival, before moving deliberately on. Mary Alice and I were early for our scheduled meeting with the foundation's executive director, and we unwisely decided to pass the hour at the Starbucks next door, sweltering in a line that stretched out the door and into the Texas sun. By the time we shuffled into the cool atrium of Crescent Court Tower, I had taken off my jacket and loosened my tie. My chief fundraiser was also wilting, but I suspected that might have had as much to do with the stress of explaining my resignation to yet another loyal advisor, benefactor, and friend. Mary Alice would, after all, need Carolyn Bacon Dickson's support when a new dean was named; my role was to reassure Carolyn that, despite a tumultuous spring and summer, leadership would be passed on responsibly.

A tall, elegant woman, Carolyn Bacon Dickson speaks quietly, with a Texas accent that has been carefully refined over the years. The physical resemblance to her brother, Atlanta entrepreneur John Bacon, is striking, but in manner and speech they are very different. John Bacon is an engineer, a spinner of new businesses who trolls university offices and laboratories looking for professors and students who share his passion for the high-risk, high-reward world of technology startups. It doesn't take John long to get wound up. His voice rises quickly as the conversation darts from business plans and angel funding to university politics, the arts, and his famous cousin, the actor Kevin Bacon. Unlike her brother, Carolyn calmly lowers her voice when she wants to be forceful.

"Oh, good," she said when we were shown into her office, "You're early. Mr. O'Donnell is still here. He wants to talk with you about the Augustine

Report." She was talking about foundation president Peter O'Donnell, who had recently coauthored a report for the National Academies of Science and Engineering, "Rising Above the Gathering Storm: Energizing and Employing America for a Brighter Economic Future."[1] It was called the Augustine Report because Norm Augustine—the retired CEO of Martin-Marietta, whose influence on important matters of national security policy was legendary and had already spanned five presidential administrations—chaired the study group that produced the report. Congress had given Augustine a remarkable challenge. They wanted him to identify "the top ten actions, in priority order, that federal policy-makers could take to enhance the science and technology enterprise so that the United States can successfully compete, prosper, and be secure in the global community of the twenty-first century."

The Augustine Committee was given only ten weeks to gather and analyze data, seek advice from academic and business leaders, and reach consensus on its ten recommendations, so it was understandable that it limited its scope. I had been pleased to see that K–12 education topped their priorities, followed by research, higher education, and intellectual property, but despite the concern for higher education, there was a gaping hole in the Augustine report—a four-year hole. Nowhere in the report about a gathering storm was there any mention of the pummeling that two thousand colleges and universities in the United States were taking. If this was going to be a defining roadmap, shouldn't it at least mention the millions of college-age students who enroll in the nation's public and private universities? They are, after all, the pipeline for the graduate programs and research laboratories that the committee chose to focus on. Augustine's committee had just assumed that the institutions needed to implement its recommendations would continue to exist. The truth was much different.

Carolyn knew this as well. She stood by quietly as I made my case to Peter O'Donnell that America's colleges were anything but healthy and that a collapsing bubble in higher education would imperil virtually all of the "Gathering Storm" recommendations. O'Donnell listened politely and asked a few questions. He was most curious about why he had not heard about these things from the five university presidents and five distinguished professors who also served on the committee. I said, "Because they are from the universities that will survive a collapse. They may even prosper from it. They are the ones who have the least incentive to recognize a problem."

We did talk about Peter O'Donnell's passion for K–12 education and high school Advanced Placement (AP) programs. He got that into the report. I had started a model program to train AP teachers in Georgia, and I told him how that was working. It would have been nice to see something about undergraduate institutions, too, but the report was essentially complete, and I didn't think I would have any impact on the final result.

As soon as we were seated for lunch, Carolyn leaned over the table, lowered her voice and said, "Rich, I want to know how you're doing." A change of leadership was underway at Georgia Tech. Not only had I announced my intention to step down, but Georgia Tech president Wayne Clough had recently departed to become the secretary of the Smithsonian Institution. Two years before that, a popular provost named Jean-Lou Chameau had left Tech to succeed Nobel Prize winner David Baltimore as president of Caltech, one of the most prestigious private universities in the world.

Clough had been Chameau's PhD thesis advisor at Stanford, and together they had been responsible for transforming Georgia Tech from a middle-tier engineering school to a first-rate university. Chameau had hired me to work the same magic for the College of Computing—to turn it into a top ten graduate program, to salvage a rapidly sinking undergraduate program, and to expand the boundaries of the field beyond traditional computer science.

The new acting president, a former dean, had been publicly dismissive of "new" academic disciplines. I ran a whole college of new academic disciplines. It did not bode well for some of Georgia Tech's most innovative programs.

Carolyn knew much of this story, but she was now asking—one friend to another—how I was doing. Mary Alice spoke up: "He's great!" We talked about the projects I wanted to complete before I stepped down in November and about the book I wanted to work on the following year. We also talked about my white paper on higher education—a few pages of pithy observations about how Georgia Tech could avoid the fate that was awaiting American higher education—which I hoped would have some impact on my colleagues as they cast about for new ways of organizing engineering education.

Then Carolyn asked, "Where will you go, Rich?" I was not going to go anywhere. Tenure gave me the freedom to speak my mind, to raise my critical voice to power. I could just return to the faculty. She seemed greatly relieved to hear that, and the conversation moved on.

"Tell me the story again," she said. It took me a few seconds to realize that she was talking about my white paper—the argument I had just made to Peter O'Donnell about the direction that American colleges and universities were heading, and how difficult it was to change course without strong leadership. I had not really thought of it as a story before, but as we lingered over our lunch, I started to imagine that American colleges and universities were the main characters in a drama: fated personalities, trapped between what they perceive to be the course of history on one side and where historical forces are actually taking them on the other. Trapped also by culture and tradition, they continue to sow the seeds of their own destruction. They follow tried and true patterns that have worked for them in the past. It is the only thing they know how to do. They can save themselves, but will they recognize the paths that lead them away from disaster? It would require them to abandon old alliances and throw in with an array of distasteful characters. Carolyn was right. It had the elements of a compelling story.

Late in the afternoon, as I climbed, tired and sweaty, into my seat for the return flight to Atlanta, I thought about my friends John and Carolyn Bacon, who spent much of their time trying to understand why universities operate as they do, and what I would like to be able to tell them about the inconsistencies of academic life. I thought about Peter O'Donnell, who, like others on the Augustine panel, was in a position to raise a warning about the state of the nation's colleges and universities, but had not been aware that there might be fundamental trouble brewing. Tenure, leaders, tradition—the very idea of who the university was there to serve—these were all topics for faculty lounge arguments. A faculty lounge is a place that does not open its doors to outsiders.

"Maybe I shouldn't be writing a white paper," I said to myself. "Maybe I should be telling the story that I wanted John and Carolyn to hear. Maybe I should be writing the book that I would have wanted Peter O'Donnell to show Norm Augustine before the Gathering Storm committee wrote its report. I should be telling the story of the fate of American colleges and universities." It was a compelling story.

I Great Visions to Lure Them On

1 Are You Teaching This Summer?

Academics believe deeply that the public does not understand the daily life of a university professor, a belief that is amplified by an innocent conversation starter at neighborhood social gatherings: "Are you teaching this summer?" University professors always seem to be busy in the summer, when classes are not in session and the most conspicuous activities on campus are related to landscaping. It is a question that betrays only an innocent fascination with a somewhat mysterious occupation. What an academic hears in the question is a hint that hours spent outside the classroom are hours not well spent: what else could justify that big summer paycheck? High school teachers "take the summer off" without pay to travel or perhaps to get a few more college credits toward an advanced degree. What in the world could a college professor do in the summer that would justify any pay at all? "Are you teaching this summer?" is the most annoying question that a professor can hear because there is no easy way to answer. It does not rank among the most important questions facing university professors today, but it is a window into academic life.

This is a book about the fate of American colleges and universities, institutions on a path to marginal roles in a much different world than they are designed for. The story of higher education begins with an understanding that it is not monolithic. It will make much of what I have to say about universities easier to understand if I explain a few things about academic life—what motivates academics, how they view each other, and most importantly, how they view anyone outside the university. The gears and levers of a modern university are hidden from public view by a curtain, and I want to help you peek behind it.

Behind the Curtain

The fate of American colleges and universities is in the hands of the people on the inside who pull the levers and turn the gears, and of those on the outside who operate huge, interconnected networks of rules and systems. Virtually everyone involved in higher education is either a professor, a former professor, or an academic professional whose career has been carefully built in the service of professors. Much of what I describe in this book therefore hinges on university professors—the way they look at the world, how they are rewarded, and how their collective decisions are shaped by a culture that few outside academic life understand. Even highly educated professionals, who have spent years immersed in university studies, feel adrift in academic waters where titles and organization charts have little meaning, administrative boundaries are notoriously confusing, and primary loyalties are often to peers with no obvious connection to the institution.

If academic life is impenetrable to the layman, it is because universities are designed to be mysterious. The mystery begins with rituals that are especially forbidding to outsiders. Universities are by definition associated with rites of passage—passage from adolescence to adulthood, from apprentice to master. European universities were originally medieval and monastic, and American institutions inherited their traditions. They adopted rites of passage that were based on religious symbols and universal beliefs, a point that Kathleen Manning analyzes in her study of cultural symbolism in universities:

Although most colleges in the United States are secular, the religious nature of institutional life remains firmly embedded in higher education.[1]

This influence is most obvious in the academic rituals like commencement ceremonies that involve scepters and other magical icons and imagery, monastic gowns and regalia, and the ritual intonation of passages that confer special status to conferees. An academic processional resembles nothing as much as monks solemnly filing into chapel for Mass. It is not accidental that literature is filled with deliberately blurred boundaries between religion, wizardry, and scholarship.

Symbolism masks the real nature—humanistic and materialistic—of modern universities, entities that produce and consume many billions of dollars annually. Modern universities are businesses—conglomerates and federations of fiercely competitive organizations run by smart, capable people with a remarkable ability to focus their attention on problems that are beyond the reach of most of society. But universities are not monolithic. The ideal of the university as a community of scholars has been effectively replaced over the last few decades by what former University of California President Clark Kerr called a *multiversity*—an enterprise that serves many public and private constituents and balances the desires of many internal and external communities.[2]

Bands of Well-Chosen Professors

Perhaps the most significant force shaping Kerr's multiversity is research, so I want to begin by talking about the difference between a research university—that is, a university that hires and promotes faculty members based on their ability to conduct independent scholarly investigations—and other institutions. The idea of a research university is ancient. In the eleventh century, the first European universities in Bologna and Barcelona, Paris and Padua attracted professors like Galileo and Dante Alighieri, who were renowned for independent, original thought. They in turn attracted students who would be trained for independent discovery and analysis. The idea took hold throughout Europe.

The European ideal of a research university was largely ignored in the United States until the middle of the nineteenth century, when a former Yale College librarian named Daniel Coit Gilman seized on the idea of forming an American institution devoted to graduate instruction and research. In 1872, Gilman became president of the University of California, but the state legislature effectively blocked his efforts "to make a respectable and responsible institution of the University of California."[3] The founding in 1874 of a new, private university in Baltimore, based on the German model, gave Gilman the opportunity he desperately sought. In 1875, Gilman became the first president of Johns Hopkins, a university endowed by its namesake, a Quaker philanthropist. Hopkins's $7 million bequest to found a hospital and university was at the time the largest philanthropic gift ever.

The Johns Hopkins trustees settled on a university that would realize the scholarly ideal of an institution devoted to the *creation* of knowledge, and Daniel Gilman became the nation's most visible advocate for the role of pure university inquiry in society:

First, it is the business of a university to advance knowledge. . . . [N]o history is so remote that it may be neglected; no law of mathematics is so hidden that it may not be sought out; no problem in respect to physics is so difficult that it must be shunned. No love of ease, no dread of labor, no fear of consequences, no desire for wealth will divert a band of well chosen professors from uniting their forces in the prosecution of study. Rather let me say that there are heroes and martyrs, prophets and apostles of learning as there are of religion. . . . By their labors, knowledge has been accumulated, intellectual capital has been acquired.[4]

Johns Hopkins University under Gilman's guiding hand was at the head of a crowd, and as more institutions embraced knowledge creation as a part of their mission, the well-chosen bands of professors acquired more influence over the day-to-day running of the university. But it was always a delicate, and sometimes confusing, balance—even for Johns Hopkins—between research and teaching the thousands of students who were pouring into colleges and universities and whose interests did not necessarily lie in the laboratory. The confusion would get more profound with the sudden appearance of dozens of new institutions. Some of the newcomers were small, privately funded schools with strong denominational ties and no real interest in original scholarship, but others, funded from public coffers, were distinctly American—inclusive, diverse, and accountable only to an ideal. None were modeled on their European forbears.

The Land Grant movement—beginning with the 1862 passage of the Morrill Act—meant that higher education in the United States was no longer reserved for the upper classes of society. Land grant colleges were created to address the nation's need for doctors, lawyers, clergy, engineers, and farmers. It would have been easy for institutions like Harvard and Johns Hopkins to adopt the European model, but not the open access promised by the Morrill Act:

without excluding other scientific and classical studies and including military tactic, [land grant colleges are] to teach such branches of learning as are related to agriculture and the mechanic arts, in such manner as the legislatures of the States may respectively prescribe in order to promote the liberal and practical education of the industrial classes in the several pursuits and professions in life.[5]

But, in fact, Harvard, Johns Hopkins, and the other private institutions of the Northeast joined Michigan, Cornell, and the newly chartered land grant colleges in embracing "liberal and practical education of the industrial classes." By the 1930s, led in part by immigration from German centers of learning, American scientists had established themselves in research universities, and institutions like MIT—under the leadership of Karl Compton, who pioneered cooperation between universities and the military—shed their "engineering school" personae for a new blend of engineering and science that would be equally at ease fighting wars and fueling economies. Professional schools of business, education, and law quickly adopted the methods and values of research: unfettered, quantitative inquiry, peer review, and independent societies clustered around the key problems as judged by the community. Medicine was easy to launch on this path because of the direct connection between medical innovation and wealth-generating products and services in health and medical fields. This was another gift from Hopkins, who was as generous to the university teaching hospital as he was to the pure sciences.

The other event that irreversibly changed the nature of research universities was the creation of the National Science Foundation and the postwar growth in federal support of university research. In the closing days of World War II, a former MIT dean named Vannevar Bush was asked by President Franklin Roosevelt to make recommendations for the continued health of the American scientific enterprise that had been so critical in the war effort. Bush was at that time president of the Carnegie Institution, which awarded research grants to scientists. His recommendation was to set up a federal agency that would in effect create a public version of the Carnegie Institution. To Bush, this was not philanthropy, but rather a strategic investment in a national asset:

Basic scientific research is scientific capital. Moreover, we cannot any longer depend upon Europe as a major source of this scientific capital. Clearly, more and better scientific research is essential to the achievement of our goal of full employment.

How do we increase this scientific capital? First, we must have plenty of men and women trained in science, for upon them depends both the creation of new knowledge and its application to practical purposes. Second, we must strengthen the centers of basic research, which are principally the colleges, universities, and research institutes. These institutions provide the environment which is most conducive to the creation of new scientific knowledge and least under pressure for immediate, tangible results. With some notable exceptions, most research in industry and Government involves application of existing scientific knowledge to practical problems. It is only the colleges, universities, and a few research institutes that devote most of their research efforts to expanding the frontiers of knowledge.[6]

Bush's recommendation led directly to the chartering of the National Science Foundation (NSF) and its unique system of unsolicited proposals and peer review. Today, NSF supports virtually all academic research in basic science and mathematics. It also led indirectly to a massive increase in government investment by other government agencies like the National Institutes of Health (NIH), the Defense Advanced Research Projects Agency (DARPA), and the Department of Energy (DOE) that today fund university research in the sciences, engineering, and information technology. At the end of the war, the federal government spent less than ten billion dollars (in 2000 dollars) for research and development, virtually none of which was for nonmilitary research. Sixty years later the government was spending more than a hundred and twenty billion dollars on research and development, forty-three billion of which was directed toward nonmilitary research.

Between 1953 and 2004, federal funding for basic scientific research—the kind supported by NSF—grew at an annual rate of 6.3 percent, nearly double the 3.3 percent average annual rate of growth of the economy as a whole.[7] Research universities adjusted their missions and priorities to accommodate their newfound wealth, but much of the burden of maintaining research operations fell on a new generation of university professors, who now had to raise money; staff, equip, and manage complex facilities; and mount marketing campaigns that could be used to justify such a large expenditure of public funds. These were highly skilled scientists who were also trained in the business of conducting research and, most important, in raising money to do it. Professors could no longer retreat to their ivory towers. A new kind of academic career was born: one that required salesmanship and management ability. It was not long before success or failure at a research university depended as much on these skills as on classroom performance or other scholarly pursuits. That was how professors were chosen.

It is no wonder that twentieth-century universities became market-focused, and nowhere did the economics of the marketplace figure more prominently than in how the bands of well-chosen professors were recruited and compensated. In order to attract and retain medical doctors, lawyers, and business school professors, universities had to offer both the freedom to practice and sufficient compensation to make academic life somewhat competitive with private sector jobs. By the same token, scientists and engineers who generated the bulk of the federal research funding could be lured away by other universities or by the many industries in which their work was highly valued. They generated income, and they demanded compensation that reflected their financial contribution.

The humanities and the arts took a back seat, and the financial stratification of universities began in earnest. By the 1990s, it was not uncommon to see yearly compensation for senior faculty in the most competitive fields top three hundred thousand dollars, effectively pricing top recruits out of the job market for small undergraduate institutions. Meanwhile, in the least sought-after disciplines, salaries stabilized at far less stratospheric levels—except for the occasional stars who could demand more—which enabled small, liberal arts colleges like St. Olaf College in Minnesota and Williams College in Massachusetts to assemble departments of mathematics, philosophy, and literature that rivaled the best research universities.

Salary differentials at major research universities became a source of campus tension. No university could maintain the fiction that it was a classless society of scholars—a band of professors—who pursued knowledge for its own sake and for whom compensation was as likely to occur in spiritual form as in dollars. But it was just one of the inconsistencies of academic life that universities had to find a way to accommodate.

Inconsistent Institutions and Class Societies

By the time the Vietnam War exposed deep social divisions over free speech, academic freedom, and the role of federal research on college campuses, multiversities—with all their inconsistencies—had effectively replaced Gilman's ideal of an American version of the European research university:

> The multiversity is an inconsistent institution. It is not one community but several— the community of the undergraduate, and the community of the graduate; the community of the humanist, the community of the social scientist, and the community of the scientist; the communities of the professional schools. . . . Devoted to equality of opportunity, it is itself a class society."[8]

The jarring idea that a university is a *class society* is important to understanding academic culture. It helps explain one of the most curious aspects of academic life: the loyalty that a professor feels toward the community of specialists in his or her particular field of study. This loyalty oftentimes is a much stronger bond than institutional loyalty. Professional and academic societies, editorial boards, and honorific organizations allow professors within a class to associate with their peers. Professional societies are a meritocracy that exists apart from traditional university ranks and titles, sometimes bestowing honorary titles like *Fellow* to reward achievement that might otherwise be overlooked by a professor's employer.

Academic ranks stratify universities into classes. There are even classes of entry-level positions. A young faculty member armed with a new degree may be hired as an instructor or a postdoctoral fellow. Neither of these positions, however, is on a track to senior, tenured faculty status. Postdoctoral positions are pure research apprenticeships. After a fixed term of employment, the expectation is that a postdoc will move on to another laboratory or perhaps to a different kind of entry level job—maybe even to a tenure track position.

Instructors are members of the teaching class. They are frequently part-time employees hired to help smooth out normal enrollment fluctuations. Increasingly, however, instructors are permanent teaching staff with uncertain career prospects. At some institutions, instructors draw salaries but are not even covered by benefits like retirement or health care. They are among the most vulnerable staff members at the university.

The most desirable academic rank for a beginner is assistant professor, a probationary rank that cannot be occupied indefinitely. A successful

assistant professor can expect to eventually be promoted to associate professor and finally to full professor. At any of these ranks, additional distinction
is possible. Yale University, for example, uses a portion of its endowment
for a Gibbs Instructor. The Gibbs Instructor is usually a budding superstar
who understands the limited nature of the appointment and is interested in
using the relative freedom offered to Gibbs Instructors to begin a research
career. Other endowments may be established to fund associate or full professors. These positions usually carry honorific titles like the "John Doe Professor of Economics," "University Professor," or "Distinguished Professor."

A Full Day's Work

Most people outside academia experience only one aspect of a college professor's professional life: classroom teaching. But because the vast majority
of American colleges and universities are actually multiversities, classroom
teaching occupies only a small fraction of a professor's workday. A typical
day might also include scholarship, service activities, and an array of administrative and management tasks ranging from personnel and financial
management to fundraising and university governance. These roles are not
always equally balanced.

At top research universities, professors are often expected to "pay their
own way"—that is, to construct a coherent research agenda that will attract not only graduate students but also the independent funding needed
to support their research programs. In return, the university offers not only
access to students and equipment but also the freedom to pursue wide-
ranging lines of inquiry. This includes, in many cases, time away from campus to consult, lecture, or serve on boards of directors—all activities that
may carry lucrative compensation above and beyond the salary paid by the
university. Not surprisingly, professors at research universities tend to channel their scholarly activity into work that has economic benefits, either
personal or institutional.

At undergraduate institutions—where research may not be required—
professors are also expected to do scholarly work, but scholarship in the
sciences and professions at a teaching university is often more difficult to
fund from external sources. Rather than pursuing big-ticket independent
research, professors are more motivated to integrate scholarship into classroom activities or research projects that can be successfully completed by
undergraduates.

Part of a typical workday at any university is spent in the classroom, either teaching general education courses or teaching more advanced upper-

division courses to students majoring in the professor's field. Unlike secondary schools, in which a detailed curriculum is prescribed by a school board, a college curriculum reflects the desires and tastes of faculty members, so a course at one institution is likely to be different from the same course at another institution. This means that professors spend a good deal of time developing and maintaining unique course materials.

Students need to be mentored and advised, and letters of recommendation need to be written for graduating students applying for jobs or graduate school. In large lectures or courses with laboratories, professors also manage teams of graduate or undergraduate assistants and are often responsible for hiring, firing, and managing instructional budgets. If undergraduate research is a component of the curriculum, a professor may be required to supervise research projects, internships, and cooperative programs.

Research universities add an additional layer of complexity to classroom teaching. Besides teaching graduate courses and seminars and developing curricula for MS and PhD degrees, which frequently involves finding ways to incorporate cutting-edge research into advanced courses, faculty members at research institutions have to train future practitioners and researchers and direct graduate thesis work. They are also more directly involved in helping to find employment for their students. Not surprisingly, research universities cannot demand the same teaching loads as undergraduate institutions. Nevertheless, a three-course teaching load at a research university can easily require sixty or more hours of work per week.

Here is my version of a story—the heart of which is the disconnect between what a university is and what the public understands about universities—that virtually all college professors know from personal experience. My first academic appointment after I received my Ph.D. was at the University of Wisconsin in Milwaukee, a large urban campus picturesquely perched on the bluffs above Lake Michigan. My office was on the top floor of the tallest building on campus, and on a clear day I could see all the way to Port Washington, forty miles to the north.

State officials would often use the university system as an example of the misuse of public funds by an elite minority who were not being held properly accountable by elected officials. Senator William Proxmire came out of this tradition and became famous in the 1970s for his frequent "Golden Fleece Awards" that held federally funded scientific research up to public ridicule, based largely on carefully selected project titles that when taken out of context made little sense to the average voter.

During one of these periods, the university came under the high-profile scrutiny of a group of state legislators who wanted to know how the thirty or so campuses of the Wisconsin system were spending the state's money. I was selected to be interviewed by a senator from one of the small northern towns on Lake Superior. He arrived at the appointed time, but things started out badly. The grandeur of the view from my office seemed to bother him, and he went out of his way to let me know it. He also let me know that public school teachers spent the entire day in the classroom, and that he expected the same from Wisconsin's public universities. He went on the attack: "How many hours do you teach?" I happened to be teaching two four-credit courses that semester, so I said "eight hours." "Eight hours!" he repeated, as he slapped his knee, jumped to his feet, and began pumping my hand. "You're the first man I've met around here who puts in a full day's work!" I didn't have the stomach to tell him that I meant eight hours per week, not eight hours per day.

Small wonder that the average professor feels adrift in a world where daily and weekly rhythms mark professional progress: customers acquired, products designed, money earned, hours worked. The beats that mark academic careers are not so conveniently spaced. Research conducted today may not be published for years, students taught will not be mature for decades, and milestones that mark institutional change are nearly imperceptible. A professor's workday is filled with several jobs, and any one of them could easily consume two or even three times the amount of the day that is allotted to it. Even the summer—when research proposals are being prepared to fund incoming students, research reports are written, and professional meetings are stacked from June to August—is not the season of long days and leisurely travel that neighbors imagine when they ask, "Are you teaching this summer?"

2　A World of Subjective Judgments

Nowhere is Daniel Gilman's influence on universities more evident than in the central role that faculty members play in operating the university, a principle called *faculty governance*. Virtually all academic affairs in American institutions are conducted through the work of faculty committees, and much of that work consists of senior professors evaluating their colleagues—at peer institutions as well as their own—for promotion and tenure. University tenure—the granting of a permanent appointment that can only be revoked for *economic exigency or moral turpitude*[1]—is a difficult concept for academic outsiders to accept. It is awarded after a lengthy period of critical analysis, although the term has been appropriated for other purposes both inside and outside academics. Tenure for secondary school teachers, for example, is often a formality, a sign of seniority that is granted upon completion of a probationary period. In higher education, tenure is anything but a formality.

Tenure in American universities is a component of a class system, which is one of the things that makes it jarring to the average person. It is ultimately about reputation. When it comes to tenure, departments of human resources are mainly silent. Modern management practices are set aside during the tenure review for a college professor. Students submit subjective course evaluations and professional colleagues attest to a candidate's reputation. It is sometimes enough for a colleague at another institution to say "this person would not be granted tenure in my department"—an outrageously subjective assessment of a purely hypothetical situation that would provoke lawsuits in most management-labor conflicts—to cause a tenure committee to vote unanimously against a candidate. But top-down authority makes almost no difference in the world of academic promotions.

The process of granting academic tenure is a distributed, self-organizing decision-making system that is difficult to steer from a central authority.

All that matters is reputation, and reputation cannot be bestowed from above. It has to be earned and recognized in bottom-up fashion, putting the very concept of tenure in the middle of the following puzzle: how do universities maintain the distributed, bottom-up independence guaranteed by tenure while at the same time making strategic choices that rise above the self-interested decisions of professors who are immersed in the world of subjective judgments?

Heroes and Martyrs of Learning

Tenure time is stressful for young professors. It occurs while they are not only establishing their academic credentials but also establishing families and financial stability. Tenure decisions and worries about tenure decisions are so pervasive that they frame most other academic decisions, even those—like how to structure a curriculum—that seem to rest on objective analysis and not the world of subjective judgments. The academic system of promotion and tenure is a tough, demanding, and sometimes cold system, but it is not random.[2] It is in some respects bizarrely collegial.

Tenure is an institutional pledge to protect Daniel Gilman's vision of a university faculty composed of "heroes and martyrs, prophets and apostles of learning." Tenure exists to protect free inquiry and classroom expression from political or other outside influence. Its purpose is to guarantee academic freedom. In research institutions and most other colleges, tenure is granted after mastery and achievement has been demonstrated to the satisfaction of layers of faculty committees, reviewers, and administrators. At elite private universities, the granting of tenure is a permanent commitment of endowment funds; therefore, there is often an assumption that tenure will *not* be granted to an assistant professor. To compensate, the six-year probationary period sanctioned by the American Association for University Professors (AAUP)—under whose guidelines[3] most institutions operate—may be extended to ten or more years. Failure to be awarded tenure at such places is common; but faculty members who have been denied tenure at an Ivy League institution frequently move on to plum appointments at other universities.

At most institutions in the United States, there are no fixed criteria that guarantee that tenure will be granted. It is not always a fair system, but innumerable court cases have attested to the legitimacy of terminating a professor's employment as a result of an unsuccessful tenure review. AAUP guidelines have been revised continually since 1925, and each revision expands the remedies that should be available to tenure candidates who are denied tenure, but even the AAUP has kept mum on exactly what obligations a university has in considering someone for tenure.

The apparatus that upholds academic freedom in American universities is due in no small measure to the 1894 trial of a University of Wisconsin professor named Richard Ely on charges of political bias in his teaching and research. Ely, an economist and sociologist from Johns Hopkins, came under fire from a new state superintendent of public education named Oliver E. Wells. Wells was a political unknown whose previous appointment had been at the grade school in Appleton, Wisconsin, where he was employed as a teacher. Wells, a Democrat, ineptly escalated a local feud over unionization to a full-blown national story involving charges that Ely taught "socialism and other vicious theories to students at the University."[4] Formal charges were eventually referred to a committee of the Board of Regents for a trial that was to include an evaluation of Ely's writings. The committee's decision, which became known at the *Wisconsin Magna Carta*, thereafter defined the American commitment to academic freedom:

Whatever may be the limitations which trammel inquiry elsewhere we believe the great state University of Wisconsin should ever encourage that continual and fearless sifting and winnowing by which alone truth can be found.[5]

Oliver Wells's attempt to silence Richard Ely was followed by many struggles between raw political will and free academic inquiry. One of the most famous was the Walter Cocking Affair. Its outcome redefined the boundary between government and higher education.

In 1941, the American state of Georgia was still a segregationist stronghold. Its three-term governor Eugene Talmadge was an enormously popular political figure who had been swept into office on the strength of a populist, free-market, anti–New Deal platform that catered to the state's one-party rule and its racially divided past. Talmadge was a strong figure who thought nothing at all of bypassing constitutional channels to gain political advantage. He owed some of his popularity to his willingness to institute reforms like lowering utility rates, which he accomplished by executive decree. He once declared martial law to fire members of the highway board and physically removed the state comptroller general from the state capitol building when he refused to cooperate. In the summer of 1941, Eugene Talmadge turned his attention to Walter Cocking, the dean of the College of Education at the University of Georgia.

Georgia's College of Education was in sorry condition when Walter Cocking was hired in 1937. Cocking's job was to raise the academic standards and national profile of the school. As a seasoned administrator, Cocking rapidly did exactly that, creating cadres of supporters and—no doubt because of his authoritarian management style—enemies. Cocking had unwittingly given his enemies, many of whom were personal and political friends of Governor Talmadge, all the ammunition they needed.

It is not clear whether Talmadge himself initiated the ensuing smear campaign, but letters—many from faculty members in Cocking's own college—began to surface that questioned his credentials, his management ability, and his commitment to maintaining a racially divided system of public education in Georgia. Governor Talmadge, who was also a member of the University's Board of Regents, accused Cocking of conspiring to racially integrate a demonstration school in Athens, Georgia, and used his influence over the other board members to have Cocking fired under a new policy of removing "those who advocated communism or racial equality."[6]

In the political firestorm that followed, Harmon Caldwell, the popular president of the University of Georgia, threatened to resign unless the board reconsidered its action. When the regents met on June 16, 1941, there was an impressive display of support for Cocking, including statements from local academic and business leaders like Emory University president Harvey Cox, who said that he was "one of the best men in the field of education in the South."[7] The only evidence presented against Cocking was an easily refuted charge from a disgruntled faculty member in the College of Education. He was reinstated by a one-vote margin, which threw the governor into a rage.

Talmadge mounted vicious personal assaults on Cocking's character and background. A favorite target was Cocking's relationship to the socially progressive Rosenwald Fund, which Talmadge publicly called "Jew money."[8] Talmadge replaced three board members with hand-picked sympathizers, and the newly constituted board met once again on July 14, this time voting to remove Walter Cocking as dean. Emboldened by his victory, the governor led a ruthless, year-long purge of higher education in the state of Georgia, which eventually resulted in the loss of accreditation for all of Georgia's "public institutions for whites."[9] The accrediting agencies, in their letters withdrawing accreditation, cited the "lack of independence" of the universities.

It was Talmadge's political undoing. He lost his bid for a fourth term as governor. His successor, Ellis Arnall, ran on a platform that included insulating the university system from political influence. The new governor enthusiastically backed a 1943 amendment to the state constitution guaranteeing the independence of the Board of Regents from interference by any branch of state government. The constitutionally established independence of the Board of Regents of the University System of Georgia remains a fiercely guarded principle in state government.

No Written Guidelines

It has become popular in some circles to conflate the subjective nature of academic advancement with political bias, using as evidence the apparently large number of university faculty at top-ranked universities with progressive views. This is not a recent trend. Senator Joseph McCarthy's hunt for communists in the 1950s targeted academics and creative artists, among other professions. Although charges of bias in tenure decisions have been given recent publicity[10]—possibly emboldened by successes in demonstrating gender bias at some major research institutions[11]—real evidence for political bias is lacking. Even studies that aim to prove bias find no corresponding definitive evidence of political bias in academic decision making.[12]

Bias is different from fairness, however, and to many it seems unfair that the requirements for promotion are vague and subjective. If tenure reviews are by and large unbiased, why not write down specific guidelines, so that every candidate can have a fair and equal shot?

In many countries with strong public universities, professors are civil servants, an employment status that insulates them from subjective processes like tenure review. At first blush, this does not seem like a bad idea. After all, government bureaucracies also have an interest in protecting the important processes of state from undue political influence and granting a measure of independent decision making to career professionals. In the United States, there has been sustained resistance to applying this idea to colleges and universities, with good reason: the willingness of government to manipulate organizations run by political appointees has been demonstrated repeatedly. When universities—particularly public universities—are swept under a political umbrella, the temptation to make conformance to political ideas a standard of conduct is irresistible, as Oliver Wells and Eugene Talmadge demonstrated.

The Walter Cocking Affair was on my mind one morning in late 2005, when I cohosted a delegation of academics from Iraq. The Iraq War violence was still considerable, but the new government was trying to put together the pieces of an economic recovery strategy, and restoring normal operations to Iraq's decimated universities was a critical component of that strategy. The delegation consisted of deans and other administrators from six of the country's largest institutions, all of whom had trained outside the

United States. Their purpose in the United States was to absorb as many examples as they could of academic and administrative practices in the expectation that many would be applicable to their home institutions.

I was asked to speak about our promotion, tenure, and retention processes, but I could see their discomfort growing as I spoke. One by one they stopped taking notes and laid down their pens. I paused, and the leader of the delegation, a provost from Baghdad, quietly asked, "Where are the standards for tenure written down? How do your faculty members know when they have satisfied the requirements?" At American research universities, there is no list of written requirements that, once satisfied, qualifies a candidate for tenure. This strikes many people as fundamentally unfair. My Iraqi colleagues were clearly disturbed by our practices and made it clear that such an approach would never be tolerated in their country.

But in a modern research university, the criterion for granting tenure is demonstrated impact; therefore, the only requirement that matters is *demonstration of impact*. For the most part, there are no written guidelines for *how* to achieve impact; it simply has to be demonstrated. Guidelines are rare because written tenure criteria are likely to become threshold requirements. In that case, tenure becomes an exercise in what my colleague Sue Rosser, now provost at San Francisco State University, once called "teaching to the test," that is, structuring a professor's probationary period not around contributions to knowledge, but rather toward satisfying a predefined set of criteria such as number of papers published or research grants obtained. "Tenure at most universities," Rosser, a former dean, once said to me, "is a lifetime commitment on the part of the university, and it should not be granted as a right of employment or an obligation of the employer." A civil service, with its emphasis on seniority and entitlement, is the one thing that American research universities want to avoid. They often point to lagging research productivity in countries where university professors are part of the civil service as evidence of just how bad an idea it would be.

I found it particularly ironic that our Iraqi visitors drew the line at written requirements for academic promotion and tenure. They, after all, were from a nation that had just emerged from decades of the most brutal, controlling political climate imaginable. Written requirements to define academic success were a Talmadge-like invitation to steering the type and quality of university inquiry.

Academic Freedom, Noble Causes

In a strange twist of fate, the freedoms guaranteed by tenure were put to the test in the 1960s at the institutions where the traditions were strongest. The

Vietnam War was the occasion for academics to exercise their rights to free speech in the classroom. Many professors were longtime activists whose opposition to the war and to the politicians waging it grew out of deeply held political convictions rather than scholarly research.

Sometimes activism spilled over into violent protests, like it did in Madison, Wisconsin, with the 1970 Sterling Hall bombing of the U.S. Army Mathematics Research Center (MRC), where I had an office in the late 1970s. Despite the appearance of "Army" in the name of the center, there were no green uniforms around Sterling Hall. My colleagues were for the most part pure mathematicians with virtually no connection to the Vietnam War.

But harsh political speech in classrooms on the other side of campus had whipped up radicals like David Fine and Leo Burt. Fine edited and Burt wrote for the campus newspaper, *The Wisconsin Daily Cardinal*, and both of them used the *Cardinal* and the cover of free speech to promote violence among student protestors. Fine was convicted for taking part in the Sterling Hall bombing and served three years in federal prison as a result. Leo Burt fled to Canada, where he simply vanished. The few remaining MRC researchers at Wisconsin from the Vietnam era are still bitter that the bombers used academic freedom as a launching pad for an attack on academic freedom that killed and maimed five professors.

Although there is a popular association between academic freedom and liberal politics, the truth is that the guarantees of tenure have protected both ends of the political spectrum. Nobel Prize–winning Stanford physicist William Shockley used his stature as inventor of the transistor to promote an overtly racist theory of eugenics, while Linus Pauling came to symbolize liberal, antiwar politics.

Pauling, a California Institute of Technology (Caltech) chemist was twice a Nobel Laureate. Horrified by the spread of fascism in Europe in the 1940s, he actively aided the war effort. He won the 1954 Nobel Prize in Chemistry for his work on the nature of chemical bonds, but he also became increasingly public about his pacifist political views. His work to stop aboveground nuclear testing earned him the 1962 Nobel Peace Prize, but he was denied a U.S. passport for travel to Stockholm to receive the prize. It was an embarrassment, but the episode deterred neither his activism nor his scholarship. Linus Pauling remained an influential lifelong advocate for nuclear disarmament, even as he pursued an unorthodox and ultimately discredited theory about the curative benefits of massive doses of Vitamin C.

Political fashions change, and it is not always possible to keep the rapidly shifting forces for and against academic freedom at bay. Clark Kerr's updates to his lectures *The Uses of the University*[13] chronicle his support

of and later disillusionment with the Berkeley Free Speech Movement
that eventually branded him a tool of the military-industrial complex.
Realizing the importance of federal funding for research projects that
might have military application, Kerr was responsible for promoting
defense-oriented research at the University of California and for defend-
ing the right of professors to carry it out. It was a principle that Kerr
used to uphold the nature of the multiversity as a community of diverse
stakeholders.

Antiwar demonstrations no longer disrupt college campuses. Disputes
about academic freedom are resolved quietly. Right-wing and left-wing politics have equally uncomfortable perches for engaging students. It may be a
weakening of resolve, but American higher education has drifted from the
principled stance of prior generations. In recent years, some institutions
have bowed to public pressure to reach into tenured ranks to punish speech
that would have been protected a generation ago. Such episodes have not
provoked widespread protests about the erosion of academic freedoms. In
fact, these setbacks seem minor compared to the many prerogatives that
faculty members enjoy as universities have become more focused on the
central role that professors play in operating their institutions. Although it
was invented to guarantee academic freedom, tenure now serves a different
purpose. It has become the major building block for the faculty-centered
university.

The Faculty-Centered University

"How many hours do you teach?" and "Are you teaching this summer?"
provoke the same reactions among professors. I have conducted an informal poll of my colleagues, and they report to me that these are by far
the two most annoying questions asked of them by friends and relatives.
It is strange that a profession that goes to such great lengths to cloak its
comings and goings with secrecy and ceremony should have such a strong
reaction to questions from outsiders who are understandably naïve about
academic practices. Some have—perhaps unfairly—characterized this as
self-absorption; but scholarly pursuits, which are largely inwardly focused,
can easily lead us professors to a certain sense that we are aliens in a strange
land when we step out of our professorial roles. College professors are, to
a degree not seen in other professions, focused on themselves, and their
institutions are centered on them.

This is Daniel Gilman's other great legacy for American colleges and universities, and its importance cannot be overstated, for it colors all aspects

of how the modern university interacts with the rest of the world. While Johns Hopkins was being chartered, the University of Virginia with its Jeffersonian traditions of democracy and equality was developing an alternative to the Johns Hopkins culture. Frederick Rudolph's characterization captures the essence of the two opposing world views:

A most striking difference was the way in which Johns Hopkins developed as a faculty-centered institution. The University of Virginia had revealed a more than ordinary attention to faculty in its planning and recruitment, but central to the Virginia experience was a democratic philosophy as expressed by Thomas Jefferson. The institution in Baltimore, however, saw the faculty, its needs, its word, as so central to its purpose that Gilman insisted that the faculty be given only students who were sufficiently well prepared to provide the faculty with challenging and rewarding stimulation. Nothing could have been more remote from the spirit of the old-time college, where the teachers were theoretically busily engaged in stimulating the students.[14]

American universities are faculty-centered. They are designed so that important decisions are made by elite bands of well-chosen professors whose focus is on the prevailing components of the multiversity: faculty research, faculty careers, and faculty tenure. It is for this reason that a faculty-centered university is at a fundamental disadvantage in the twenty-first century. Its value to students erodes and, in a competitive era, it is at a severe disadvantage.

We will see that as faculty-centered universities turn their attention inward toward the needs of professors and their profession, they become protective, rigid, and inevitably irrelevant. Some will be affected more profoundly than others. This process may leave many institutions—those with the brands and resources to set their own agendas, for example—largely untouched. Outside these favored few, however, it will have a lasting effect, including on the two thousand or so public and private universities that live hand-to-mouth and rely on shrinking subsidies and that enroll 80 percent of the nation's 14.8 million college-age students.

There is a global explosion in both the demand for higher education and in the number of institutions that can meet the demand. In any marketplace with abundant choices, the winners are those with competitive brand, price, or value. American colleges and universities are finding it increasingly difficult to compete in any of these dimensions. Most will never be able to establish the kind of brand recognition that would give them unassailable advantages. They are extravagant in their use of resources, and the resulting inefficiency gets passed along to students as higher costs. But above all, they are faculty-centered. They do not understand the value they provide.

Without dramatic changes in how higher education is conceived and delivered by the nation's colleges and universities, their fate is predictable: they will continue on an accelerating path toward the margins of a global marketplace in which they are particularly ill-suited to compete, a marketplace that might be willing to sacrifice core principles like academic freedom. This book is about why this is so and what might be done about it.

3 The Smartest Kid in Class

David Baltimore was thirty-seven years old when he was awarded the Nobel Prize for Medicine. He was at the time the youngest Nobel laureate in history, but his prodigious talent had also attracted attention at an early age. His autobiography credits a summer internship—at the celebrated Jackson Laboratory in Bar Harbor, Maine—for his early passion for biology.

He was still in high school that summer. In the middle of his undergraduate years at Swarthmore—a time when even the brightest science students are struggling with differential equations and molecular biology—Baltimore attracted the attention of George Streisinger, a scientist who himself had gained attention at a young age when he won the worldwide race to be the first to clone a vertebrate.

As an MIT graduate student, Baltimore distinguished himself from his classmates and came under the influence of a series of increasingly important mentors, including Jerard Hurwitz, one of the discoverers of the enzyme that produces RNA in cells. His course was set: as a very young man, Baltimore became a star and a collaborator of Nobel Prize winners like Salvador Luria.

By age thirty-four, Baltimore was a full professor at MIT. Two years later, he was awarded the Nobel Prize for medicine. His earliest experience with science taught him not only to be the best student and educator, but also how to direct research in high-energy academic environments, coordinating the work of students and collaborators. It also taught him how to seize leadership opportunities—sometimes at considerable risk to his professional reputation.

He was appointed director of MIT's famous Whitehead Institute, and seven years later, he was named president of Rockefeller University. Perhaps because of his very visible early successes, Baltimore was a target for ambitious competitors, and as a result, his career was plagued by investigations of what proved to be unfounded accusations of scientific misconduct by some of the scientists who worked in his laboratories.[1,2] He held his post at Rockefeller University for two years before returning to the MIT faculty.

He was appointed president of Caltech in 1997 and held that position for nine years. Baltimore was responsible for the explosive growth in the biomedical sciences at Caltech, an institute whose research reputation had been built largely on a legacy in the physical sciences that included eleven Nobel Laureates. Student, teacher, or president, David Baltimore spent most of his life in classrooms, and by all accounts he was the smartest kid in every one of them.

Searching for the Right Leader

David Baltimore is fearless and visionary, and has been in the spotlight throughout his career. Sometimes he invited attention with outspoken positions on matters of public policy, like the federal government's response to the 1992 SARS epidemic;[3] sometimes the attention was the unwanted by-product of high-profile investigations. According to astrophysicist Kip Thorne, who led the Caltech presidential search, it was Baltimore's ability to articulate a vision and direction "in a period of change—changing relations to the federal government, changing ties to the private sector, and a growth in biological sciences at Caltech—while maintaining our traditional strengths"[4] that attracted their attention in the first place.

American universities love to hire leaders like David Baltimore, accomplished and tested men and women who are able to communicate where they intend to take their institutions. In good times, they are able to articulate aspirations. In bad times, they are the best problem solvers around. They are often the best salesmen, which helps when they need more resources. Best of all, they are not afraid to be roughed up—it is how their careers have been built. Unlike most academics, they have been leading for a long time, and they are completely comfortable doing it.

If there is a looming crisis in American higher education, and leaders such as David Baltimore are at the helm, why are colleges and universities not acting with more urgency? If higher education is approaching a crossroad, why haven't the smartest kids in class anticipated it and set course for a new, more promising direction?

At a Crossroads

You can look back through the centuries and see the road that our institutions of higher learning have traveled. This journey starts with the twelfth-century monk Peter Abelard, who—through a combination of genetics and clever marketing—managed to attract students to schools that were the forerunners of the first great European universities. Abelard was not alone; there are many important figures along the path to modern universities, including Thomas Jefferson, who was perhaps more than any other American figure responsible for steering postrevolution universities—with their entrenched views of classical education—toward the institutions that we see today.

The first half of this book describes the road ahead, blocked by global economic and political forces that we are now just beginning to understand. Half of the world's population has joined the modern economic era in the last ten years alone, and—with raised aspirations—they see higher education as the key to better lives. But they also might have a very different conception of what it means to be a university. That has always spelled trouble. The history of higher education is filled with disruptive shifts in which universities that were out of step with student expectations and cultural demands were pushed aside by more nimble institutions. The colleges and universities that want to continue unchanged along their current path will find that they cannot. They will be left by the wayside.

There are also roads to the left and right. To the left is a failed model of higher education: a destructively competitive, needlessly expensive, hierarchically regulated, mass-production approach to education, whose self-satisfied but rigid methods are especially ill suited to global demands for specialization and access. The road to the left leads to ruin.

The road to the right I am calling *Apple*. The Apple Computer Company is an icon of American design, but Apple—and its growing site for downloadable college courses, iTunes U—is also a metaphor for a new conception of higher education. This road leads to a new value system that represents universal access, open content, and reliance on new technologies. The road to the right is the only path to choose, but it cannot be traveled without preparation.

Letting the Smartest Kids Choose a Path

University leadership in the United States is for the most part unaware that the crossroads is ahead. Few of today's leaders have serious plans in place for choosing a path, either left or right. The obvious question is how so many smart people could miss what seems to be an inevitable crisis. If a modern university is a classroom, the smartest kids in class are in charge of where the classroom is heading, but they are not well prepared. To the contrary, they seem to be poorly equipped to make the strategic choices, believing instead that the path ahead is going to be clear for some time. The way that university presidents are chosen and rewarded virtually guarantees it.

If you were to simply count the hours, it turns out I have spent most of my life in classrooms, and there was always a smartest kid in class. Usually, I was not the smartest, but I always knew what kept the smartest kid at the top. The smartest kids in class were the most competitive, but they also had friends, and they were the most likely to influence their classmates. This behavior was reinforced year after year by parents, teachers, and coaches. They were adaptable but were able to focus. They did not seem to mind ambiguity, but they made good choices. They took risks, but they seldom guessed wrong. The smartest kids were capable of working very hard, and they ended up at very good universities studying medicine, law, or science, although many others wound up in politics, finance, or engineering.

Not all of the smartest kids ended up in leadership positions. Nor did all the leadership positions go to the smartest kids in class. CEOs, newspaper editors, and Supreme Court justices are sometimes amazingly average people whose leadership skills seem to have emerged from nowhere. But the leadership of virtually every major university in the United States comes from that select group of kids who were once the smartest in class. The system is rigged to make sure that happens.

It is a significant fact of university life that leadership is handed to men and women with remarkable skills, because university presidents have enormous influence over the future of their institutions. David Kirp's exhaustively researched book *Shakespeare, Einstein, and the Bottom Line*[5] compiles case studies of dozens of university presidents who changed the paths that their institutions were on. William Durden rescued tiny Dickinson College from a near-death spiral of "plummeting enrollments, declining student quality, dwindling endowment." MIT president Charles Vest started a revolution when he proclaimed that classroom lectures and materials, the very things his star-studded roster of professors thought they were valued for, would be made freely available to anyone who wanted them from MIT's Web site.

No one who knew either man has been surprised by the magnitude of their achievements. William Durden was impressively successful in many careers inside and outside academia, and Charles Vest distinguished himself at every stage of the academic ladder. For every Durden and Vest, there are a dozen other leaders who transformed their institutions, staved off disaster, or whose influence on the course of higher education was profound, so it is stunning that Clark Kerr says of the current generation of university leaders that they "have no great visions to lure them on, only the need of survival for themselves and their institutions."[6]

Opera and Football Equally

To those outside academic circles, the career path that leads to a university presidency seems mysterious, but every step along the way is evolutionary—designed to select a specific set of skills. Success in the undergraduate classroom leads to admission to the best graduate schools. Success for graduate students draws the attention of the most demanding professors who are able to guide them to eye-catching doctoral dissertations and the postdoctoral appointments that are the most fertile ground for future academic leaders. These are also the environments that put them in close personal and professional proximity to other students who are similarly positioned, thus beginning a network of connections that will be valuable years later as they begin to exert broader influence.

Assistant professors are promoted to tenured professorships in a long, grueling, competitive process that culls out many who are equally smart by focusing on a scholar's ability to break out of the insular cocoon that academic life so readily provides. Future leaders are drawn from the small pool of those who can demonstrate the value of ideas in a cycle that leads to publication, research grants, influence, more students, and more publications. Full professors become presidents of professional societies or editors of journals. Some are comfortable in seats of power and become advisors in government or industry. Some are selected to lead their colleagues and become department heads, deans, provosts, or presidents.

Despite all this careful grooming, the magnitude of the task of running a modern American university necessarily overwhelms many of the smartest kids in class, precisely because few of the skills needed to rise to the top of the academic administrative pyramid have much to do with the skills that a president must somehow acquire:

The university president in the United States is expected to be a friend of the students, a colleague of the faculty, a good fellow with the alumni, a sound administrator with the trustees, a good speaker with the public, an astute bargainer with the foundations and the federal agencies, a politician with the state legislature, a friend of industry, labor, and agriculture, a persuasive diplomat with donors, a champion of education generally, a supporter of the professions . . . a spokesman to the press, a scholar in his own right, a public servant at the state and national levels, a devotee of opera and football equally, a decent human being. . . . No one can be all of these things. Some succeed at being none.[7]

The fate of a university is in the hands of the smartest kid in class—someone who has been painstakingly selected from among all the other smartest kids who have made it to the top of the academic pyramid for the specific leadership traits valued by selection committees and boards of trustees. These are the very people who should be most likely to see a looming crisis if there were one.

Three Ways to Miss a Crisis

To be fair, many of the leaders I mention later foresaw both crises and opportunities. Their responses were responsible for some of the great innovations in higher education. The abandonment of the outmoded, rigid, classical university curriculum and rise of the modern research university came about in that way. The role universities should play in the innovation-commercialization-wealth creation cycle was not obvious until visionary university deans and presidents defined it.

Michael M. Crow at Arizona State University (ASU) peered into the future and decided to prod his university to be the *New American University*. Nam Pyo Suh realized that the aggressively intelligent, incremental style that marked his success at MIT and NSF was not the answer for his new university, the Korean Advanced Institute for Science and Technology (KAIST), as it sought to rise among the world's engineering programs.

But most presidents did not—and still do not—believe in a coming systemic crisis. If university presidents are the smartest kids in class, it is fair to ask, "Why?" or even more pointedly, "What do you know that the folks who run things don't know?" The answer to that question is rooted in how university leadership is created, rewarded, and sustained. In academic life, as in business and government, it is very unlikely that existing leadership—especially successful leadership—will recognize disruptive change and, in those rare instances when it is recognized, be able to do anything about it.

First of all, successful university presidents are stuck in what Harvard's Clayton Christensen calls *The Innovator's Dilemma*,[8] a fact of business life that keeps leaders focused on the execution of strategies that have succeeded in the past and makes them vulnerable to disruptions that are not yet a threat. As I discuss in more detail later, there are a few ways out of the innovator's dilemma, but they all involve a sort of irrational step: abandoning the carefully constructed and productive methods of the past for untested and not widely accepted approaches.

Second, the downside of selecting from among the smartest kids in class is that university presidencies are for the most part held by a remarkably homogeneous group of people who tend to pass the same concepts, biases, and views of the future around a tribal campfire where the next generation of leaders submits to review by its elders.

Finally, the hierarchical nature of reputations in higher education—although it gives tremendous freedom to the institutions at the top—dooms those presidents farther down the hierarchy to institutional envy, mimicking patterns of behavior that are not particularly well suited to their institutions and, therefore, are likely to lead them down the wrong path.

A Homogeneous Group

Outside of the few remaining monarchies and monolithic political parties, university presidents are perhaps the most homogeneous group of leaders in the world. The presidents of forty-eight of the American universities that have been consistently ranked among the top fifty over the last century received their doctorates from another one of the top fifty. Two institutions alone—Harvard and Yale—account for nearly 30 percent of sitting presidents at top-ranked institutions. The pattern is repeated the farther down the list you go. If you are the president of a major university in the United States, you have without question been the smartest kid in every classroom from kindergarten to graduate school. That is the candidate pool for virtually every presidential search in the country.

What skills do these exceptional individuals share? Because they have earned doctorates from and joined the faculties of the most prestigious institutions, they are not only clever, articulate, and able to please their teachers; they also have a prodigious ability to focus with single-minded precision on a singular and very difficult question, often to the exclusion of complicating contexts or downstream applications of their inquiries. Academic life not only rewards solitary pursuits, but also places a premium on criticism, helping to push to the top those who are best at promoting their own points of view, often to the detriment of friends, colleagues, and others, who hold what are therefore less worthy points of view.

Academic biographies—especially in the sciences—are filled with stories of stars who are not only distrustful of methods and techniques they did not create themselves, but are also actually disdainful of lessons that could be drawn from related fields. Many prefer instead to invent everything that needs to be invented to solve the problem at hand. Fearful of committing themselves to courses of action, they are often suspicious of strategy. They have been rewarded for solving problems in isolation from distracting contexts. That is the applicant pool for university presidencies. Homogeneity shows. Speeches, strategic plans, and inaugural addresses are all opportunities for a president to explain a unique institutional vision, but—as I discuss in Chapter 9—it seldom happens. The best, most tested course is to promise to be a good steward. It is a generic promise that varies little from institution to institution or generation to generation.

Boot Camp

Harvard's School of Education runs a well regarded and highly selective "boot camp" for new university presidents. Aimed at providing deans and provosts (and the occasional lawyer or politician) with the tools to help them make the transition to the top leadership post, the Harvard boot camp zeros in on the roles and responsibilities to which new presidents would not have been exposed in their prior academic positions. At the top of the list is how to deal with university culture and tradition, followed closely by fundraising, governance, financial management, and communication skills.

New presidents are exposed to methods for identifying and recruiting effective administrators and theories of academic leadership. The life of a president is qualitatively different from other administrators in terms of the demands it places on personal lives, so the boot camp includes seminars on how to handle the pressures of having the entire campus rely upon your skills and judgment.

Way down at the bottom of the list is—time permitting—strategic planning. Strategy is a hot topic in business circles, but it is less highly regarded in academia. Rather than a substantial discussion of the many modern approaches to strategy in rapidly evolving business environments, the Harvard boot camp, according to marketing materials, focuses on "the president's role in the design and implementation of strategic planning efforts." No wonder new presidents are left to draw their own conclusions about the unique needs of their institutions and about what the job might entail if the ground shifts:

John Russell, president of McCurry University, knows the presidential balancing act well. . . . Many college presidents started their career as faculty, Russell said. [Abilene Christian University President Royce] Money rose from the ranks of the college's faculty, and he said he sees himself as a sort of "chief teacher" in his role as president. . . . Russell agreed, saying that many college presidents see themselves as teachers "on a little different stage." "Much as a faculty member is more than a transmitter of knowledge, the college presidency involves more than the transmission of policy," Russell said.[9]

The term "teacher in chief" captures nicely a president's role relative to faculty culture and governance, but does little to chart the course that a chief executive might have to take in steering the organization through difficult or uncertain conditions when flexibility and intelligent response are needed. A boot camp teaches new presidents what to do inside the box, but not what to do when they have to think outside of it to solve big problems. Royce Money was one of those presidents who quickly figured out what to do. Under his leadership, Abilene Christian University became an agile risk taker, embracing technology and new business models while much larger, much richer universities were still arguing about whether there was a problem to be solved.

The Dilemma

Homogeneity might also be another reason that university presidents aren't alarmed: higher education in the United States is hierarchical. At the top of the hierarchy are prestigious private colleges and a few highly selective public research universities. Their courses were set long ago, and short of complete economic collapse, they can survive or even thrive by carrying out new and improved versions of tried-and-true models that have worked in the past. At the other end of the hierarchy are institutions like proprietary universities that are themselves disruptors. They are not alarmed because disruption favors their new business models. Everyone else has to choose one path or the other. Why aren't university presidents alarmed? From his post in California, Clark Kerr saw American community colleges and comprehensive universities—not the research universities—absorb the large influx of postwar students, and he knows precisely the dilemma facing most university presidents:

The elite institutions in the United States remained elite; some even more elite in their admission standards. The rest of the system absorbed the impacts of this enormous historic development. In the course of doing this the rest of the system also accommodated all those new lesser professions and occupations that would have also diluted the universities. In particular, the one-time teachers colleges became comprehensive colleges and universities with a vast added array of occupationally oriented programs. The community colleges and the comprehensive colleges and universities took on, even eagerly, the impacts of universal access to higher education.[10]

If the presidents of the most prestigious universities don't really have much to worry about, there is little incentive for a president of a university that aspires to greatness to behave any differently. To get to the top of the hierarchy, an up-and-coming university must look and act like one of the institutions above it. If there is alarm among presidents, it is probably because some have noticed that "most successful new policies in higher education have come from the top [of the university],"[11] and they have come to the realization that they have to play a different game. They cannot compete with the richest, most prestigious universities. They have to choose a different road.

Presidents are the smartest kids in class and are the ones most likely to change their institutions in distinctive and unique ways, to create innovative business models, and to creatively destroy outmoded processes and traditions that are either not valued by the new generations of students or cannot be paid for by any realistic growth forecasts. That is why Clark Kerr sounds so desolate when he writes about coming to the conclusion, late in his career, that presidents are not the ones to undertake big challenges— they are encouraged to turn their backs on big problems.[12] The smartest kids in class are rewarded for whistling past the graveyard.

4   The Twenty-First Century

From 1994 to 2008, Georgia Tech's tenth president, G. Wayne Clough, led the transformation of his alma mater from its traditional role as a good, but undistinguished regional engineering school to its current stature as a national and international powerhouse, ranked seventh nationally among all public universities and eighth in a global ranking of technical universities. Achieved mainly on the strength of a strategy for developing its research capabilities, the university's evolution largely ignored its role as an undergraduate institution until quite late in Clough's tenure. Then Georgia Tech began to behave strangely. It endowed chairs in the humanities, invested in the performing arts, and expanded international campuses and programs. It made massive investments in new fields like biotechnology, computer science, and public policy.

Thomas Friedman declared in his book, *The World Is Flat*, that:

the Georgia Tech model recognizes . . . that the world is increasingly going to be operating off the flat-world platform, with its tools for all kinds of collaboration. So schools had better make sure they are embedding these tools and concepts . . . into the education process.[1]

Clough was fond of saying that the Georgia Tech mission was to define the concept of a twenty-first-century technological university, a vision that has guided the university for a decade or more. Georgia Tech would seem to be a university that despite the conflicting demands placed on its bands of well-chosen professors and the difficulty of engaging university leadership in transformational change has seen the crossroad and has made choices. But the kind of introspection that it would take to explain even in broad terms what a twenty-first-century university might look like never occurred. Many on campus openly worry about that lapse.

I Will Define It

Many other universities have raised their aspirations during the last ten years. Columbia University embraced distance education to reach students who would not otherwise have access. Carnegie Mellon University established an international network of campuses focused on technology training. Rensselaer Polytechnic Institute—after a generation of neglecting research—has emerged as a place for invention at the intersection of emerging disciplines. London's Imperial College used the wealth of its patent portfolio to create the most innovative venture capital fund in Europe. Arizona State University is aiming to be the "New American University" with its massive expansion and international reach.

The rush to define the twenty-first-century university is driven by a combination of political and economic factors. It is fueled, above all, by *enabling technology curves*, the growth-driven law of the Internet era that describes the annual doubling of capability and capacity for equal costs. Paradoxically, mainstream universities—where much of the technology originated—have been slow to embrace these technologies, even as they became ubiquitous in other sectors of the economy.

Dan Reed, former head of the National Center for Supercomputing Applications (NCSA) at the University of Illinois and now the chief high-performance computing evangelist at Microsoft, has a theory about why this is so. Reed points out that universities are focused on acquiring the highest-performance technology that can be produced, even though they realize that the number of users who can actually make use of all that extra capability becomes smaller and smaller as performance—and therefore cost—increases. This means that—to the few faculty members in mainstream universities who determine which next-generation technology to acquire—value equals cost. But today's supercomputer is tomorrow's laptop computer, as the technology curves push prices for computing capability down, until what used to be an expensive asset that could attract an elite few professors becomes a commodity, available from exactly the same mass-market, low-cost vendors used by home consumers. It turns out that in the inverted economics of cutting-edge academic research, the elite academic users are not very interested in spending just a little bit of money. This is the *computer in the cathedral* syndrome, a key component of the coming crisis that I will describe in part II.

Like Georgia Tech, many universities have tried to redefine themselves. Many have aspired to be models for what higher education will be like in the future. The answer for many institutions seems to be: "The New American University will look like me. I will define it."

But exactly what will the university of the twenty-first century look like? Will it look like a twentieth-century university—classrooms, lectures, labs, libraries, departments, degrees, Saturday football—with new layers of technology, entrepreneurship, professional marketing and branding campaigns, and trendy programs? Few colleges will be able sustain this vision.

Under Pressure

The business proposition for higher education is under pressure from increased global competition, raised student expectations, and spiraling costs. Responding to any of these pressures requires institutional change that is hard for most institutions to achieve. A university that controls costs may have to forego an expensive new facility that would make it easier to compete for the best students. The number and kind of athletic programs may have to be weighed against other spending. Influential alumni may have to be told that their priorities are not paramount. Faculty recruiting committees may have to concentrate on candidates with less stratospheric research credentials who will contribute more to undergraduate education. Alarmingly, there is little discussion of—in fact, there is much resistance to—the kinds of changes in the status quo that would allow such institutions to be competitive in the future.

Sustaining an ambitious vision is made difficult by global trends that will determine who wins and loses the race to create the most successful, innovative, and influential institutions. Many universities realize that their world has become more competitive. There is a new focus on international rankings like the *Times of London Higher Education (THE)*,[2] QS *Asian University Rankings*,[3] or the Shanghai Jaio Tong (SJT)[4] rankings, even though such rankings capture perceptions at a moment in time and notoriously lack validation. The *Times* Top 100 World Universities are geographically diverse, but they are almost without exception very traditional institutions, offering traditional degrees prescribed by curricula and courses that have changed very little during the last hundred years. Between 1990 and 2002, the number of human beings who joined the modern economic world doubled, and their conception of higher education is not necessarily the same as THE 100 institutions. As each new billion joins free market economies and open societies, the definition of education is repeatedly jolted because the newcomers have different notions of what is valuable.

With his December 2006 presidential decree, Costa Rican president and Nobel Laureate Oscar Arias Sanchez created an *Executive Office of the Presidential Initiative Peace with Nature* and made science a policy priority and an economic tool.[5] Costa Rica is a nation with ethnic homogeneity, high rates of literacy, ecological treasures, and no standing army. Investment in Costa Rican universities is driven in part by a desire to advance the awareness of Costa Ricans of the role that nature and biodiversity play in defining the country's future in a region known for political instability and an inability to turn natural treasures into national wealth.

In a 2007 meeting, Oscar Arias told me that Costa Rica plans to lead by using its natural assets to bolster strategic scientific investments in areas like biodiversity. This leadership will not necessarily start in the universities and colleges, many of which struggle for international recognition. President Arias's expectation was that the more prestigious universities of the United States and Europe would learn how to collaborate with Costa Rican scholars at the in situ laboratories of the Central American ecosystems. Costa Rica was prepared to capture the economic benefits of this research for its own citizens, bucking a decades-long pattern of risk-averse Central American investors sending dollars to the United States but ignoring domestic financial and technological infrastructure. The effects of this strategy are dramatic. Government agencies that a decade ago were aimed at reinforcing a well-entrenched system of promoting and maintaining the status quo and led by sleepy bureaucrats are today headed by economists who seem to have been plucked from Sand Hill Road, Silicon Valley's famous venture capital conclave.

The Costa Rican story is repeated a dozen times. The trend today in Latin America, Africa, India, and emerging Asian powerhouses like South Korea is toward a reinvented system of higher education that is tailored to national ambitions.

Lessons

This book is ultimately an essay about value. Much of what American universities think of as value has little meaning to the rest of the world and can only be achieved at unsustainably high costs. The institutions that will thrive in the coming century are the ones whose offerings are in demand in a world where there are abundant choices for higher education. Those that don't seriously reexamine their value will have a hard time surviving, because prospective students will find that it can be done better and cheaper elsewhere. And they will choose accordingly.

Instability threatens most colleges and universities in the United States. Once-reliable sources of revenue are either drying up or being divided among many more institutions. Underlying value propositions are eroded from above and below. Costs rise for most institutions as they continue on a go-it-alone path when newer, smaller, and more nimble competitors collaborate to offer equivalent services at lower prices.

If they expect to survive, American universities must, over the next generation, apply the three principle lessons of the expanding global economy to their own operations:

1. *Focus on value*   Universities have to come to grips with the central value problem in higher education—the value locked in a university degree depends on the skills and aspirations of the student. To focus on that value, a university has to figure out how to deliver it with reasonable cost and competitive quality. The universities that thrive will be the ones that have both compelling value and a way of personalizing it.

2. *Focus on costs*   Traditional universities are profligate spenders, a problem that can be addressed only by controlling costs in ways that make higher education uncomfortable:

a. *Deskilling*   Mainstream universities use inappropriate skills to deliver value in an age where an equivalent classroom experience can be obtained for free.

b. *Better use of physical plants*   The economic framework of running a bricks-and-mortar business does not scale well with massive increases in size, but the reward structure in mainstream universities actually penalizes institutions that are careful in their acquisition of physical assets.

c. *Better use of materials*   Increasingly costly materials and services are rejected in a marketplace when they exceed what customers are willing to pay for. Universities are drawn toward purpose-built courseware, equipment, and infrastructure. They reward vendors for avoiding efficiencies of scale and quality available to most large enterprises.

3. *Establish reputation*   Universities have become accustomed to a hierarchy in which a few institutions at the top are pursued by many at the bottom. It is a comfortable system for the universities that agree to let their success be defined by whomever they are chasing, but leads to chaos when there are many new institutions—all setting their own rules. Enduring reputations will be established by those universities that set their own agendas. It is a daunting prospect for many.

For most institutions, applying these lessons will not be a simple matter. Commonly held—but incorrect—beliefs will have to be abandoned.

Leaders will have to leave their comfort zones. Those of us who are stake-holders will have to demand that choices be made. Critics of this approach argue that this leaves the task of sorting out winners and losers to the mar-ketplace, but that is the new global reality for American higher education. In the end, the winners will be those institutions that can redefine them-selves and find the unique value that they provide. No longer entitled to a position that guarantees survival, every university will have a different vision of success.

II An Abundance of Choices

5 It Takes a Lot to Get Us Excited

The business model for American universities is under assault, virtually guaranteeing that prosperous twenty-first-century institutions are going to look and behave differently than their predecessors. Most observers agree with the Delta Project on Postsecondary Education Costs, Productivity, and Accountability that American universities are in for dramatic change:

America faces a growing crisis in public postsecondary education, as an unprecedented fiscal meltdown plays out at a time of growing consensus about the urgent need to nearly double levels of degree attainment. Instead of taking steps to develop an investment strategy to reduce access and achievement gaps, we are moving in the opposite direction: reductions in state finances, increases in tuition, cutbacks in enrollments, and reductions in courses and programs students need to succeed.[1]

In the public mind, universities are havens for tradition where change happens rarely and—when it does happen—slowly. This is an image promoted by the institutions themselves, but there is a veneer of truth. Universities change only when market forces make it impossible to continue business as usual, and even then change seems to need a brave trailblazer to show the way. We are "moving in the opposite direction" largely because there have been few great experiments in higher education for at least fifty years.

Twenty years ago, when I was preparing for a sabbatical year at the University of Padua in Italy, I was asked to brief the rector (the elected head of the university) on a proposed new course of study in software engineering. I was perhaps too enthusiastic, because at the height of my sales pitch he interrupted me to say "*Con calma, professore!* This is Galileo's university, and it takes a lot to get us excited here!" The great danger is believing that change is impossible. There were few layers of subtlety to the rector's message: university leadership is often tied to the past, and therefore it is not always in control of change. It may take a lot to get leadership excited, but that doesn't slow the onrushing problems.

Entrenched leadership is only part of the problem. The same curtain that uses symbolism and ceremony to cloak daily life in a university also casts its finances into shadow, an unfortunate combination for institutions that would benefit from openness and transparency. According to the Delta Project:

a much bigger impediment [to change] emerges in the form of conventional wisdoms about college finance, truisms about costs that aren't based in fact. The power of these myths is that they are held uncritically by people inside and outside of the academy, from presidents and trustees to governors and legislators.[2]

The relationship between how universities do business and how priorities are set is not a simple one. I explained in part I how the many—often conflicting—forces that shape a university also make it difficult to question fundamental assumptions about value and cost. Universities seem to need some nudging to part the curtain, cut ties to the past, or create financial transparency. They need to get excited. It might help—when you hear "it takes a lot to get us excited"—to understand just what that means.

Ranking, Reputation, and the Rise of Private Universities

It has been a hundred years since Edward Slosson ranked universities by reputation,[3] identifying the elite undergraduate institutions in the United States. The 1910 landscape for higher education is almost unrecognizable today. America was small and rural. It was rare for an eighteen-year-old to attend college, and fewer than a half million did. Land grant universities were still an experiment, and research universities were vastly outnumbered by a hodgepodge of undergraduate colleges. Public funding of academic research—which had little impact on the way institutions were organized—was unheard of. It would be another fifteen years before the 1925 publication of Raymond Hughes's reputational ranking of research universities.[4] At the beginning of the twentieth century, it would have been impossible to predict the earthquakes that would alter the shape of higher education during the coming decades.

Of the top nineteen institutions ranked by Hughes, nearly half were public universities. More than a third of the institutions on Slosson's list were public. The largest school in either ranking was Columbia University, with more than 6,700 students. Public universities were prestigious, uncrowded, and well funded. They were independent in ways that private institutions—often dependent upon denominational support—were not. It took a century for upstart private universities to erode the reputation of public institutions.

Table 5.1
Changes in Reputational Rankings 1910–2009

Ranking	1910	1925	2009
1	Harvard University	University of Chicago	Harvard University Princeton University
2	Princeton University	Harvard University	
3	Yale University	Columbia University	Yale University
4	University of Pennsylvania	University of Wisconsin	California Institute of Technology Massachusetts Institute of Technology Stanford University University of Pennsylvania
5	Stanford University	Yale University	
6	Columbia University	Princeton University	
7	Cornell University	Johns Hopkins University	
8	Johns Hopkins University	University of Michigan	Columbia University University of Chicago
9	University of Chicago	University of California–Berkeley	
10	University of California–Berkeley	Cornell University	Duke University
11	University of Michigan	University of Illinois	Dartmouth College
12	University of Wisconsin	University of Pennsylvania	Northwestern University Washington University
13	University of Illinois	University of Minnesota	
14	University of Minnesota	Stanford University	Johns Hopkins University
15	NA	Ohio State University	Cornell University
16	NA	University of Iowa	Brown University
17	NA	Northwestern University	Emory University Rice University Vanderbilt University
18	NA	University of North Carolina	
19	NA	Indiana University	
20	NA	NA	University of Notre Dame

In the 2009 edition of *U.S. News and World Report*[5] (*USNWR*) ranking of national colleges and universities—the much-debated but widely quoted reputational survey of universities—not one of the public institutions ranked by Slosson or Hughes made it into the top twenty. The University of California at Berkeley came the closest. It is ranked twenty-first. The *USNWR* ranking lists nine universities that did not make it to Hughes's 1925 list. Some did not even exist in 1910. All are private institutions. None of the institutions ranked in the top twenty in 2009 are among the top twenty in enrollment. The largest is eighth-ranked Columbia, whose 24,000 students make it the twenty-first largest campus in the United States. Large, public universities have given way to small, private institutions, and that shift has changed where money is spent in higher education.

During the last hundred years, higher education in the United States has become stratified. American universities come in three varieties. The *Élite* institutions that end up on top of these rankings are at a tremendous advantage as they compete for students, money, and global prestige. To some other universities, reputational ranking is irrelevant; these institutions operate as *For-Profit* entities. The marketplace determines success or failure. Most colleges and universities lie in the *Middle*, a land where the resources of a top-ranked school are just out of reach, a region where they find themselves unable find better ways of using what money they have to become more competitive. In American higher education, wealth flows to the top and bottom strata, but not the Middle.

Élite universities are the most desirable and selective. They happen also to be the richest. They are by and large private universities with large endowments. Harvard, with its thirty-five billion dollar[6] endowment before the market collapse of 2008, is at the top of the endowment heap. It is followed closely by Yale (twenty-two billion dollars) and Princeton (fifteen billion dollars). No other Ivy League school even comes close, although most have endowments that top five billion dollars.

The endowment at the University of Texas is in excess of fifteen billion dollars, by far the largest among public universities. Of the seventy-five schools with billion-dollar endowments, twenty-two are purely public institutions. Cornell University and Pennsylvania State University are public-private hybrids; others, like the University of Virginia and the University of Michigan, have led an independence movement among public research universities, declaring themselves free of the most onerous bureaucratic and administrative requirements imposed by state government. They lose some state funding in the process, but they are betting that reduced operating costs, endowment income, and autonomy in setting tuition are enough to offset lost public funds.

A growing number of public institutions see this approach as the path to survival because the gap between public and private universities will continue to grow for the foreseeable future. On one side of the gap are billion-dollar institutions that use their endowments to increase their reputational lead over the Middle. They offset the increased spending needed to stay ahead by passing costs on to students in the form of increased tuition. On the other side are institutions that plow every penny into a cost structure that keeps the lights on and the classrooms full, relying on automatic increases in subsidized budgets from states or churches to fund initiatives that are supposed to increase the productivity of their faculty and the learning outcomes of their students. This is an economic bubble, and it is every bit as real as the dot-com bubble of the 1990s and the real estate bubble of 2008. If it collapses it will be dangerous, but the higher education bubble affects schools on opposite sides of the gap differently.

By the time student demand levels off—around 2017—American colleges and universities will enroll twenty-five million students, up from fewer than fifteen million today. Only five million will attend private institutions, a much smaller increase than public universities will experience. Public and private institutions alike will see their revenues increase to match this demand, but not all revenues are equally useful—especially for institutions in the Middle with aspirations to join the Élite.

A private research university may receive upward of 60 percent of its revenue from the tuition and fees paid by students. The rest of its income is divided among research contracts, licenses on patents and software, interest earned on endowments—including gifts and investments income—and restricted revenue from hospitals, dormitories, and other services. The funding pyramid for public universities is exactly the opposite. Costs at public and private research universities are not dramatically different, but a typical public institution receives only about a third of its revenue from student fees and tuition. The rest comes from the other income sources, with state funds offsetting the smaller tuitions charged by public institutions.

Not only do private research universities have a smaller increase in enrollments to look forward to, but they essentially have nothing to risk, because tuition and endowment income cover 80 percent or more of their per student revenue. Public universities that eschew public support have to come up with a way of meeting the increased demand of an additional ten million students. Even universities that choose to keep their subsidies will find themselves falling further behind as states tighten their budgets and pass funding cuts along to public education.

The unfair advantage that a private institution has is its endowment. There was a brief period that peaked around 2001 during which it looked as if private giving to public universities would continue to grow, allowing public institutions in the Middle to make the kind of investments that would allow them to achieve their aspirations—broadening the scope of their programs and acquiring the kind of in-depth expertise that characterizes the Élite—but that spurt is over. Today, the per-student revenue at a public research university is slightly more than six hundred dollars, about the same as it was in 1987, measured in 2005 dollars. Twenty percent of the revenue at a private university comes from endowments and gifts, compared with less than 1 percent at public colleges and universities. This disparity is even more pronounced in nonresearch institutions.

Distinguished by Breadth and Quality

Endowments allow investment, capitalization, branding, and marketing. They are the balance sheet for higher education, and it is difficult for any institution to advance very far without a strong balance sheet. Endowments are important, but their importance is not always a function of sheer size. Universities find ways to make private gifts and endowments stretch or to combine them with other sources of income to fund projects that would be impossible to pursue otherwise.

Caltech's endowment is $1.9 billion—sizeable but not in the very top tier of private institutions. But Caltech has a very small student body, and its endowment per student is nearly a million dollars—not far behind Harvard's $1.4 million per student.

Georgia Tech's billion-dollar endowment places it near the top of public universities, but it is used mainly on capital investment projects, leaving little room for investment in new programs, scholarships, and personnel. On the other hand, the state of Georgia—through a billion-dollar agency called the Georgia Research Alliance—provides endowment-like support to its public research universities in sufficient quantity to steadily advance the university system's reputational ranking.

Many members of the *Top 75*—the seventy-five universities with billion-dollar endowments—also belong to the Association of American Universities (AAU), a private club for universities that consider themselves "distinguished by the breadth and quality of their programs of research and graduate education."[7] Therefore, it comes as no surprise that the Top 75 includes the schools that bring in the most research funding. In fact, healthy endowments and large external research programs go hand in hand.

Caltech's Jet Propulsion Laboratory brings in more than a billion dollars annually. The overhead on a billion dollars in research at Caltech generates cash that is approximately equivalent to the interest on an eight-billion-dollar endowment. Although Johns Hopkins's $2.5 billion endowment would be relatively modest by Ivy League standards, the university benefits from its medical school and Applied Physics Laboratory, which generate more than $1.4 billion in external research support— nearly twice the annual research expenditure of the next most productive university.

Medical research is pricey, so the AAU contains a large number of universities' medical schools, but there are plenty of universities without medical schools in the Top 75 that still manage to spend five hundred million dollars annually on sponsored research. MIT's annual expenditure is more than six hundred million dollars, and once the income from laboratories and institutes that are loosely affiliated with MIT's academic programs are added, that figure climbs to more than a billion dollars.

When the results of university research are commercialized, annual research spending can easily turn into cash that can be retained and used just like endowment funds. When a University of Wisconsin chemist named Harry Steenbock realized in 1923 that exposure to ultraviolet light increased the vitamin D content of milk, he also recognized the potential of his discovery for preventing childhood rickets. The university's track record at turning research into commercial products was not encouraging, so Steenbock set up a separate corporation called the Wisconsin Alumni Research Foundation (WARF) to collect patent royalties and funnel them back into the university to seed still more research. Vitamin D and other patents generated enough cash to keep Wisconsin in the top tier among public universities. WARF was just the beginning; soon, many other universities followed the Wisconsin lead.

European research universities lag their American counterparts in commercialization because they had a slower start, but also because intellectual property is often viewed with suspicion by European professors and administrators. The most successful commercialization office in Europe is at Cambridge University. But Cambridge generates less than two million pounds in license revenue, an amount that would not place it among the top twenty American institutions. There are, however, some innovative commercialization efforts in Europe. London's Imperial College goes one step beyond the

WARF model to generate commercial value from their patent portfolios. Imperial College "spun out" a publicly traded venture arm called Imperial Innovations. A mixture of public and private funds, Imperial Innovations manages a hundred million British pounds, which it uses to sell patents and form companies, and thereby to create wealth for all its shareholders, including the university itself.

It is no accident that some of the largest university research operations are located at land-grant universities and state university systems. Supporting the public education mission at this scale requires substantial annual state budgets to cover many of the costs of undergraduate education that cannot be directly recovered in tuition and fees. In reality, few of the public universities in the Top 75 are beholden to their state budgets. Top-ranked public research institutions like the University of Michigan rely on the state for less than 20 percent of their operating revenue. Things are different farther down in the Middle, where an emerging research university can receive 40 percent or more of its budget from the state legislature.

In 2009, when most public research universities were hit with budget cuts that jeopardized their aspirational strategies, a small number of institutions, including the University of Michigan, were able to rely on steady research income and a large endowment to weather the 2008–2009 recession with priorities and operations intact. Other universities balance complicated funding portfolios to augment budget dollars with gift funds, license revenue, and research income. The top public research universities are able to use this strategy to keep their reliance on state funds under 20 percent of total expenditures.

Many public research universities would be able to cut their reliance on state funds even further if they could set their fees to compete with Élite private universities, but raising tuition is a contentious public policy matter in most states. Because it is tied to public access, the governing boards in most states set resident tuition far below what could be charged in an open market, an effective discount that artificially inflates the need for state funds. The University of Texas and several other highly ranked public institutions often find that their hands are tied when it is time to attach a market-based dollar value to the state contribution to the educational enterprise. If undergraduate tuition at these universities was allowed to float to market rates, the public would be at best a marginal stakeholder. Reliance on state budgets puts public universities at a severe disadvantage. When state budgets are squeezed, public universities are faced with a choice between with cutting programs and raising tuition, both of which are politically unpopular.

Some use public anger over rising fees to pressure state legislators to loosen the purse strings for higher education. Arizona State's Michael Crow handled a 21 percent budget cut for fiscal years 2009 and 2010 by eliminating or combining colleges, schools, and academic departments while simultaneously raising tuition. A large tuition increase, however, would have imperiled the university's objective of meeting the burgeoning enrollment demand, so ASU also increased its scholarship funds, a move that drew the support of students and the praise of local politicians and leaders.

Despite their success in amassing and managing large funds, institutions in the Élite and some in the Middle have not embraced a simple concept: markets are very good at determining both value and pricing. The very idea of higher education as a marketplace, operating under market forces and without excessive regulation, causes some anxiety among traditional universities—even in the face of evidence that students will pay a premium for what they perceive to be value in higher education.

A Large Number of Capable Students

Élites are at one end of the reputational spectrum. At the other end are *proprietary universities*—For-Profit institutions. They are not exactly a new breed of university, but they have throughout the last generation become a potent factor in the competition for both students and dollars. Not surprisingly, the growth of corporations that can profitably deliver educational services has raised suspicions in traditional academic ranks. There is concern that the public good served by traditional universities is now entangled with political and economic forces in an unregulated marketplace and is therefore at risk. But regulation has little to do with it. India, for example, strictly regulates higher education at federal, state, and local levels . . . sometimes with disastrous consequences.

The untapped potential of India's literate poor—many trapped in horrific urban slums—has been an easy target for an alliance of entitled teachers, negligent regulators, and self-interested legislators and politicians, enabling unscrupulous operators of schools and colleges that promise jobs in technology, education, and medicine. These are fields that are especially prized in India because they offer a pathway to the middle class. For decades, Indian government officials were willing partners in schemes leading to worthless degrees that qualified recipients for no jobs, but even the revered, government-funded system of universities that once offered such promise to Nehru's postindependence India have been in decline under the watchful eye of the bureaucracy that was created to protect it.

Nandan Nilekani's blueprint for Indian renewal seems to focus particular anger on the state of India's traditional universities:

Our education system has become inert and incapable of adapting to a rapidly evolving economy, and even its best central institutes—arguably Nehru's most enduring legacy to India—are in danger. Their weaknesses have become particularly critical with the rise of the knowledge economy, and as India's legions of youngsters enter institutions that seem less and less capable of giving them what they need.[8]

The well-regulated but essentially fraudulent licensing of poor quality storefront universities in India, often in preference over much higher quality foreign universities, was enabled during the last decade by regulatory legislation like the Chhattisgarh Private Sector Universities Act, which led to the licensing of hundreds of privately funded universities. Most of these lacked basic infrastructure or the ability to deliver useful instruction.

There were 108 private universities in the central Indian state of Chhattisgarh prior to the passage of the Private Sector Act, but in the year following its passage, 112 new universities were established, most without campuses, libraries, or even faculty offices. The disarray in Indian higher education was aided by government bureaucracies that overly valued local participation, promoted nationalism, devalued foreign participation, and tolerated systematic corruption in the form of payments and kickbacks.[9]

The expansion of the Indian higher education system from 636 colleges at the time of Indian independence in 1947 to ten thousand today was led by a level of private investment in for-profit institutions that is five times the government's investment in legitimate programs, creating an expanding but essentially worthless system that promoted "intellectual and social slums."[10] The worst abuses of the storefront operations were curbed when the Indian Supreme Court struck down the Private Sector Act. In its place, an overly burdensome system of licensing for new universities was established, putting India at an immediate disadvantage relative to its Asian neighbors. Overregulation, for example, made it virtually impossible for local Indian governments to partner with foreign universities, a strategy used effectively in China and other parts of Asia to construct high-quality institutions by building on a combination of foreign and local investment.[11]

The new Indian university initiatives announced in 2009 after the victory of a reform-minded government swept out old taboos about partnerships. Newly appointed minister of Human Resources Kapil Sibal plans to build a staggering twenty-seven thousand globally competitive universities during the next decade.[12] Sibal's idea is to grow the percentage of high school graduates who attend college from 12 percent to 30 percent. At that rate, India can only begin to compete with Western countries that send up to 70 percent of their high school graduates to colleges and universities. Even so, Sibal's plan amounts to three hundred million new students to be enrolled in new institutions that are each about the size of Birla Institute of Technology (BITS)—a highly selective college in the Rajasthan town of Pilani in northern India that annually ranks among the best engineering schools in the world.

Like BITS itself, the new institutions will be funded in part by private corporations. They will feature collaborations with non-Indian scholars who will take up residence in the new campuses that are springing up next to the great research labs operated by Tata, Microsoft, and IBM. Some of Sibal's new campuses will look more like the gleaming new institutions in Shanghai than the crumbling affiliates of the traditional Indian institutes. Many more will be not be recognizable as college campuses at all. Unlike BITS, which adopted the trappings of a twenty-first-century university on its own, the new universities will be forced to be lean, collaborative, global, commercial, and free from the most onerous trappings of regulation because that is the only way the country can afford high-quality education for an additional three hundred million students.

Americans have long used the trappings of regulation—accreditation, federal financial aid programs, and reputational surveys—to stop the most flagrant abuses of worthless schools, or at least to confine them to narrow fields that do not seriously imperil any public interest. But there are better alternatives than regulatory control for promoting a high value system of higher education. In reality, the problems facing American colleges and universities today have nothing to do with regulation.

American higher education is in trouble because an alarmingly small— and shrinking—portion of the public believes that colleges and universities are worth the expense. In business terms, this means that the American public is for the first time questioning the value received for dollars invested in higher education. If American higher education had paid attention to the marketplace, both the penalties for failure and rewards for success would be easier to explain to the public and to policy makers.

A market-based system should, for example, reward the production of degrees that are consumed by the economy in the form of jobs, and penalize the production of graduates who cannot find employment. Incredibly, this kind of reform does not need government regulation to succeed. AAU institutions, for example, could get together and decide to incorporate market-based quality measures like employment rates and quality of job offers for new graduates as a condition of membership. The idea of collaborating to define a new economic template rather than having one imposed by a central authority seems to be catching on in some parts of the world.

Universities in the European Union—long thought to be among the most inflexible and bureaucratic in the world—have begun rewarding member institutions in just this way. This is a radical departure for Europe's top-tier universities, which have only recently begun acting in concert as the signers of Europe's Bologna Accords,[13] an agreement among forty-six nations that makes it easier to compare both the content and quality of bachelor's and master's degrees. The Bologna process is inextricably linked to employability—not surprising for a continent that has been plagued for decades by high rates of unemployment that drain scarce national resources—but there is a more fundamental shift at work, too.

The Scottish Funding Council—the government agency that distributes money to universities—rewards institutions that offer "work-related" learning experiences[14] and have exceptional success rates in placing their graduates. The challenge in Scotland is to harmonize what is clearly vocational training with a new system of academic standards that emphasizes quality and achievement. This is a difficult task. British academic traditions are not attuned to tailoring educational requirements to the needs of the job market. American institutions, on the other hand, have a long tradition of blending academic requirements with on-the-job work experience in the form of work-study or internship programs.

Work-study programs are a kind of financial aid, but they have been embraced by some institutions as a competitive advantage because of the real-world training that graduates receive. The market benefits are more pronounced in fields like engineering that already have a strong vocational component, but the effects are significant nevertheless. The growth of *service learning* programs—courses and projects aimed at community service—across a broad sweep of American institutions is evidence that universities are capable of learning from successful programs like work-study and correctly reading the requirements of a changing workforce. But despite a strong track record, these programs are curiously decoupled from degree requirements and curricula. Work-study programs are frequently administered by financial aid officers. Service learning programs are generally organized under student activities or the office of the dean of students. They are seldom incorporated into degree requirements, and as a result there are few financial incentives for an American university that offers job-related training.

The contrast between U.S. institutions and the tens of thousands of new institutions in India and China is even starker. A considerable fraction of the new universities in India are focused on careers, such as information technology, that will experience the highest growth rates during the next ten years. China's new investments in higher education include nearly sixteen hundred new universities that specialize in software engineering. Incredibly—and despite leading U.S. Department of Labor forecasts of job growth since 2001—software engineering is an academic degree that scarcely exists in the United States. One might expect that degrees in software engineering—a field that trains students in the technology and economics underlying the software industry—would be front-and-center as American colleges focus on producing graduates with the most promising employment prospects.[15] But in fact the exact opposite is true.

All aspects of information technology struggle to gain respectability in the American academic spectrum. Computer science is so far removed from the academic center that secondary schools offering AP examinations and courses in the field do so only in the vocational arts, the track that is used to prepare students who are not college-bound. So low is computer science on the academic totem pole that the National Collegiate Athletic Association (NCAA) does not even recognize computer science credits for its scholarship players. Much of the global academic world seems to be struggling, not with whether, but with how much to embrace the changing economy of Tom Friedman's flat world. Traditional American colleges and universities, on the other hand, seem to have a kind of immunity from market forces that shape daily life for the rest of us.

Distrust of market forces is embedded in American academia. Nowhere is this distrust more clearly on display than in the way that mainstream universities have ignored the lessons that could have been learned from accredited, but For-Profit universities as they gobble up students who willingly pay a premium, not for an educational "experience," but rather for a degree that enhances employment prospects.

Mainstream universities can get away with this kind of economic and cultural disconnect because they are faculty-centered. They are run by and large to suit the preferences of their faculty members in all things related to academic matters, a model that would be disastrous for proprietary universities. For-Profit institutions have to focus on students, because that is their main source of income. They are student-centered. It is, therefore, not surprising that mainstream universities underestimate the threat that the student-centered For-Profits pose to their value proposition and eventually to their business model.

For-Profit colleges receive no gifts and therefore have no endowments to spend on scholarships, infrastructure, or named professorships. They have almost no external research funding. What they do have is revenue. The University of Phoenix—the largest private institution of any kind in the United States—enrolls more than three-hundred thousand students at ninety-five campuses and one hundred and sixty-five smaller learning centers. It is accredited nationally, and it is possible to transfer credits between Phoenix and traditional nonprofit colleges. It has a football stadium, although it has no team (the Arizona Cardinals professional football team plays in the University of Phoenix stadium, publicity that costs the university well more than a million dollars per year). The University of Phoenix is owned by the Apollo Group (APOL), a public company specializing in delivering higher education to working adults. In 2007, the Apollo Group earned $408 million after taxes and depreciation on revenues of $2.7 billion. Its $2.3 billion expenditure on operations is comparable to the operating budget of any member of the Top 75. The Phoenix balance sheet shows that the school ended 2007 with $339 million in unrestricted funds. To generate that much cash in a good investment year, a traditional university would need to have $7.3 billion under active management, an amount comparable roughly to Columbia's endowment.

Phoenix enrollments grow on average by more than 10 percent per year. For a successful, private, for-profit institution—a conservative steward of resources that uses its cash wisely—enrollment growth is a good thing. Growth increases revenues and profits, which in turn allow it to develop even more sophisticated and attractive services and programs, but it does increase costs substantially. What kinds of services? In addition to online and remote delivery, proprietary institutions can create student-centered ecosystems that traditional universities have been slow to match.

Some public universities have watched carefully. Western Governors University is an online university, founded by a consortium of governors of western states, that has adopted many of the operational efficiencies of the For-Profits. It is efficient enough in its operations to begin a new semester every two weeks. This kind of efficiency pervades the For-Profit learning experience: value that translates directly to prices that students are willing to pay.

Traditional universities charge fees based on hours spent in the classroom, a pricing scheme that makes sense for neither the universities nor their students. Although real-estate costs can be high, classroom usage represents a negligible component of overall instructional costs. Except for the marginal costs of depreciation, supplies, heating, and lights, all of the other expenses associated with a classroom are fixed. A classroom is an asset and filling it with students increases its utilization—classroom hours measure asset utilization.

Nearly all of a university's real costs are labor-related. The cost of a student enrolled in any course is determined by the fraction of a professor's time—or the time of other personnel like teaching assistants and administrators—that the student consumes during the semester. This demand is determined by a student's individual needs, not by a one-size-fits-all number representing credit hours. The more attention a student needs, the more professionals are required. The salaries of those professionals and rapidly rising administrative costs are the real costs of classroom instruction.

For most students, a fee structure based on fixed enrollment-based tuition is the least attractive way to price their education. Credit-hour pricing assumes that each student places equal demands on an instructor, but in reality the incremental cost of an average student is negligible. Exceptional—exceptionally bad or exceptionally good—students are rare, but they account for an inordinate share of the labor costs of offering a course. There is ample evidence that exceptional students might be eager to pay for additional services, provided that the base price for taking a course reflected its true market value. In many cases, that base price is close to zero.

Here's an example. Carolyn is in her mid-forties, a British empty-nester who commutes between her London apartment and the Silicon Valley condo that she shares with her retired executive husband. Carolyn and her husband are both well-connected to university communities in Great Britain and Northern California—access to the best professors in America and Europe is a matter of a simple phone call to a personal friend. Carolyn has, throughout the years, developed a finely tuned sense of when an academic is operating at the top of his profession or when—in her terms—he is just "winging it." When she decided to return to a local university in London to refresh her skills in economics, it was with a sense of purpose: she wanted to help run her husband's consulting business, but she did not necessarily want to follow a degree program. Shopping for courses online seemed like a good idea, so she found a financial accounting course that was being offered by Open University (OU), an online university chartered by the British government. Open University's one hundred and eighty thousand students make it one of the largest universities of any kind in the world. It has a flexible fee structure that allows most local residents to pay only nominal tuition, and even that can be reduced by various discounts.

After a few weeks, she realized that the course was actually part of a new certificate program. "I wasn't too sure about taking a course online, and I didn't want to have to follow a program," she told me, "so I looked around

London for something I could attend part time." There were many alternatives at reputable local business schools, so she picked one that was nearby, paid her fees, and enrolled. But after her first two class meetings, she noticed that "the instructor was using lecture materials that I recalled seeing at OU. I remember going home one night and printing the online lectures so that I could compare them. They were exactly the same! The live instructor wasn't nearly as good, and I was paying five times more!"

Her first thought was that she did not want to waste the—now double—tuition she had paid, but "after awhile I got really angry. When you're paying thousands of pounds for an executive program, you expect that the instructor would have done more work than downloading his classes from the Web."

"I withdrew from both programs," she told me. "We were spending the winter in California, and one day I found a series of twenty OU lectures on iTunesU. The class was all about finance, hedge funds, and the banking crisis. It was much more specialized than the ones I tried in London, but it was what I really wanted to learn." And, best of all, from Carolyn's standpoint: "It was free and had a lot of the elementary material from the financial accounting courses anyway." Carolyn had established the base price for what she wanted to learn about accounting: zero.

A curriculum is a lumpy pattern of challenges. Most of a student's coursework does not require much more than regular attendance in class, adequate performance in classroom discussions or on projects, and passing examinations. Most students are not challenged in most of their coursework, so they do not ask for special attention from a professor. Occasionally, a student hits a lump. A lump may be a course in which an exceptional student, who wants to excel, uses an inordinate amount of an instructor's time to increase mastery of a subject. A lump may also be a course that is especially challenging to a student—one in which tutoring or remedial sessions are needed.

Exceptional students—either exceptionally bad or exceptionally good—are rare. In the twenty-year period from 1973 to 1993, I taught 1,037 students in thirty different courses at four universities. Aside from regularly scheduled office hours, less than a hundred of those students showed up in my office to ask for additional help. Nineteen of them were exceptionally good students who were either in graduate school or were preparing for advanced study. Most of them went on to do great things in their chosen professions. The remaining students were struggling with the material, and I suspect that my help was of little value to them. There may have been many more students who were helped by my teaching assistants or paid a tutor and did well enough to avoid scheduling a special appointment with me, but they did not substantially affect my workload.

Less than 10 percent—five students per year—of the total number of students I taught during that twenty-year span encountered lumps. In other words, 90 percent of my students needed only the textbooks, my lectures, and an answer or two to clarify an especially difficult point. They did not encounter many lumps. I suspect that the vast majority of my students—like Carolyn—would have gladly paid for additional services, if the base price for my courses was even close to the additional value they received by having me available to them above and beyond the classroom time or scheduled office hours: zero. But they were all charged identically.

In effect, they were charged as though the entire curriculum were very lumpy, but virtually all of the services paid for by tuition and fees are generic services—not useful to advanced students who need a more challenging pathway and not helpful to challenged students who need intensive mentoring. Pricing like this is fair to neither the students who encounter few lumps and therefore demand fewer services nor the exceptional students at either end of the spectrum. Pricing for services is just one of the business innovations that online universities have stumbled upon, and it makes their value proposition hard for traditional campus-based education to match.

Although many in mainstream higher education see proprietary universities as an annoyance, a market force to be regulated, contained, and above all not to be taken seriously as institutions of higher learning, the For-Profits not surprisingly see it differently. According to University of Phoenix president Bill Pepicello:

Our philosophy for serving students is the same as Harvard or Ohio State, and that is we're mission-driven. The mission of, say, Harvard is to serve a certain sector of the population and their mission is not to grow. And that's true of higher education in general. The reason the University of Phoenix exists at all is that all of those various [universities] and their missions did not provide access to a large number of students who are capable and wanted access to higher education. And that's our mission.[16]

With their ability to scale to match demand, deliver consistent value for market prices, and place graduates in attractive first jobs, For-Profits are clearly poised to attract what Peppicello sees as a large number of capable students—not only the nontraditional students who are shopping for part-time degree programs, but the increasing numbers of applicants for traditional institutions who prefer the learning experience, price, and employment prospects of an institution that is run like a business.

Most of these students lie in the target market for the Middle, and they tend to be the most attractive applicants—self-motivated and success-oriented. They are frequently "on their own" from a financial point of view and are willing to pay for services that provide value. The top For-Profits are adept at securing financial aid for these students. In short, the overlap between the Middle and the For-Profits should concern leaders of traditional universities.

Little competitive data exists to compare target markets for the For-Profits and the Élites; however, Phoenix estimated that in 2000, there was a 15 percent overlap with traditional universities.[17] That is a large portion of a market for the Middle to give up without a fight, especially as an even larger percentage of their most desirable applicants are also up for grabs as the number of alternatives in higher education explodes.

Harsh Realities in the Middle

Between the Élites and the For-Profits lie the institutions in the Middle— the two thousand remaining accredited colleges and universities in the United States. These range from the frankly narrow schools like the Institute of Transpersonal Psychology to the smaller campuses of the large state-university systems that must compete for fixed and increasingly stretched resources.

Many of these schools are strategically placed in important, sometimes surprising, value chains. The California Polytechnic Institute in San Luis Obispo was at one time the single largest supplier of graduates to the Hewlett-Packard Company. Rensselaer Polytechnic counts a disproportionately large number of senior executives among its alumni. Canada's University of Waterloo is the largest single source of software engineers for Microsoft. City University of New York has been a gateway to middle class careers for generations of new Americans. Land grant universities in the Midwest established agricultural and engineering experiment stations to channel innovation to millions of farmers and small business owners, leading to financial self-sufficiency in rural regions that otherwise risked being passed over by waves of economic development that benefited urban areas. The distances in the western United States are spanned by colleges with regional missions to educate teachers, miners, and farmers.

For the most part, these institutions, like most universities in the Middle, survive hand-to-mouth without large endowments and with little research funding. Top applicants—who are the ones most likely to win scholarships and fellowships—do not typically enroll in the Middle as a first choice.

Financial aid—when it is available—comes out of scarce institutional resources.

There are rare instances of progressive public policy innovations that work to benefit some institutions in the Middle. In 1993, the state of Georgia used lottery receipts to establish the HOPE scholarship, a system-wide scholarship that pays 100 percent of the tuition to any of Georgia's thirty-six public colleges and universities for any resident high school student with a B average or greater. The result was predictable: a larger fraction of the top students who would have received partial scholarships from other schools enrolled in the state universities. Free tuition is a very compelling reason for staying in the state. The national rankings of Georgia's colleges have risen steadily since the introduction of HOPE.

But for most of the Middle, business is stark and simple. It is the institutional equivalent of living paycheck to paycheck. Expenditures must balance a potentially unstable mix of heavily discounted income. Large increases in enrollments can quickly overwhelm budgets in which money in one spending category cannot be used to handle the increases. On the other hand, large drops in enrollment decrease income, decreasing an institution's ability to pay for less efficiently used administrators, instructors, classrooms, and laboratories.

The detailed financial scenarios differ from institution to institution, but the facts underlying their common plight are remarkably similar: universities in the Middle pursue aspirations that are subsidized by public funds, sponsored research, endowments, or church support. Large tuition fluctuations in either direction create revenue gaps that can only be filled by lowering aspirations or increasing subsidies. Those subsidies are shrinking.

The Middle is not homogeneous, and throughout the years many attempts have been made to describe colleges and universities so that policy makers can target programs and resources to the institutions that will benefit most. For three decades, the Carnegie Foundation for the Advancement of Teaching—an independent research center chartered by Congress in 1906—has kept track of 4,391 institutional missions and profiles, classifying institutions by academic programs, enrollments, location, and governing entities. The Carnegie Classification identifies not only the 84 Doctoral/Research Universities (DRU) and the 287 Baccalaureate Colleges in the Arts in Sciences (Bac/A&S), but also distinguishes between the 96 research institutions with very high research activity (RU/VH) and the 103 universities with only high research activity (RU/H). It is a complex and ubiquitous index of higher education, but it carries with it a hierarchy that has financial implications.

AAU members tend to end up higher in the Carnegie Classification than nonmembers, and because nontuition, nonstate revenues flow disproportionately to these institutions, university presidents find themselves under enormous pressure to define their institutional missions to conform to a profile that is more like RU/VH than one of the 84 Doctoral-Granting Institutions that have "limited emphasis on doctoral research" or the 345 Master's Colleges and Universities with large programs (Master's L) that have aspirations to join the doctoral club.

The Carnegie Foundation classifies 267 universities in the Public Master's category. These are institutions that are solidly in the Middle, and from 2002 to 2006, they lost 0.3 percent of their share of the college market, while For-Profit universities gained 2.4 percent. Losing market share at a time when the overall higher education market increased by 10 percent means that a Public Master's institution that wants to continue its climb up the hierarchy has to make some strategic choices. On a per-student basis, a typical institution in this category receives 39 percent of its overall revenue from student fees, but that has to cover 46 percent of the overall cost for that student. The difference is an amount that has to be subsidized by other sources of revenue. The largest subsidies come from public funds (36 percent, on the average). When those subsidies disappear, the remaining costs of educating a student at the same quality level have to be spread across other revenues.

Public Master's institutions have, in fact, seen their subsidies decrease. From 2002 to 2006, the public contribution per student dropped by 15 percent. Student fees have risen by less than 10 percent, leaving a gap that has to be filled somehow. Some sources of income like theaters, athletics, restaurants, housing, and parking either operate at a loss or with such thin margins that they cannot be used to help out. Gifts, endowments, grants, and contracts are the backstops when enrollments decline, but gifts and endowment income account for less than 2 percent of overall revenue, much less than the 5 percent of expenses that go to scholarships and fellowships.

It falls to state and federal grants and contracts to subsidize the educational enterprise. University officials are left pondering a choice between increasing unsubsidized tuitions and fees, or decreasing the quality of instructional services. The trend in recent years is to do both. No wonder that Public Master's institutions want to become Public Research universities, where half of the per-student income is derived from endowments, gifts, grants, and research contracts. It is institutional envy.

The framers of the Carnegie Classification are aware of the envy effect, and have developed more sophisticated tools that make it harder to interpret a classification as an assessment of quality, but it is nevertheless the basis for widely followed reputational surveys like the annual *U.S. News and World Report* rankings. Other classifications are available, but they all tend to sort out winners and losers. In 1958, Theodore Caplow, a sociology professor at the University of Minnesota, and PhD student Reece McGee published *The Academic Marketplace*[18]—a book that systematically explored academic culture and practice in American colleges and universities. One of their conclusions—that teaching is undervalued in mainstream universities—has been the basis for many initiatives aimed at the quality of classroom instruction.

Caplow and McGee developed their own classification of colleges and universities—one that is closer in spirit to how an academic calibrates his own career prospects:

Major League
Minor League
Bush League
Academic Siberia

The effect of these labels on institutions in the academic hinterlands was enormous, and—like the Carnegie Classification—caused a shift in academic behavior and even the vocabulary of institutional planning. Because resources flowed to the top of *The Academic Marketplace* pyramid, university leadership had to attract faculty members who could rescue them from Siberia, and that helped to propel hundreds of colleges and universities in the Middle to meet the demands of faculty members who would be helpful in moving institutional reputations. In an echo of the discussion of faculty-centered universities in part I of this book, the Caplow and McGee interviews identified the "two fundamental concerns of academic men [sic]—their working conditions and their performance ex cathedra."[19]

Even though the Carnegie Classification is not, strictly speaking, a ranking, university professors in the Middle have another reason for paying close attention to it: faculty pay is highly correlated with where an institution is in the classification. Universities have learned throughout the years that there is a cause-and-effect relationship between Carnegie Classifications and salary dollars. The AAUP publishes salary data for the nation's colleges and universities in a hierarchy that mirrors the Carnegie Classification. At the top are the Category I institutions that offer doctoral degrees. At the bottom are the "Two-Year Institutions without Academic Ranks" of Category IV. The high, medium, and low salary ranges for Category I universities lie above the corresponding ranges for the Category IIA schools that offer at most master's degrees, and the gap is even wider with the Category IIB colleges that offer only baccalaureate degrees.

One strategic pathway for universities in the Middle is to enroll talented students who are able to pay the full, unsubsidized cost of their education without financial aid. Talented students enable professors to compete for state and federal funds, and because they pay higher fees and do not need financial aid, they place virtually no burden on budgets. Public universities have for years differentiated in-state and out-of-state tuition, but requiring higher fees for nonresidents does not substantially change the overall profile for the Middle. Carnegie Public Master's institutions, for example, attract the same price-sensitive students whether they are in-state or out-of-state. Nonresident tuition from American students is not a significant source of new revenue.

School officials in less developed regions of the world know this. It is easy to find Web sites that counsel high school students from Asia and the Middle East on which regional campuses of which state universities are the best bet for them. Student visas are generally granted only when an incoming student demonstrates financial self-sufficiency, so the deal that some admissions officers make with themselves is to "top off" the enrollment targets with international students who can pay their own way in years one and two but are unlikely to remain in the country after graduation, in the event that they stay to finish their degrees.

On paper, these students frequently excel, but of course the paper trail reflects only what is recorded. What is missing from the record is any indication of how well they will do in an American classroom, how easily they will integrate themselves into a foreign cultural circumstance, or even how well they are able to communicate with teachers and classmates. The record does not say whether a student will be a highly qualified, culturally flexible, and capable individual or the Afghan student Ibrahim described in Ron Susskind's *The Way of the World*.[20] Ibrahim was culturally assaulted by virtually every aspect of daily life in suburban Colorado and was eventually rejected by the very school in which he most wanted to succeed.

Student quality is a complicating factor for business models in the Middle. Highly qualified students attract scholarships, grants, and fellowships, which relieve pressure on internal budgets. Highly qualified students also attract the kind of faculty members who shine in classrooms with bright, engaged communicative students. Creative and energetic faculty members mean academic programs that over time build a university's reputation, attracting better students—the kinds who are more likely to bring financial aid and, some years down the line, alumni donations. Creative faculty members also mean more success in generating sponsored research funds. That's why the Middle and the Élite compete so fiercely for these students. It is not a fair fight, and the situation approaches some equilibrium only because there are limited positions for entering freshmen at the Élite institutions and limited financial aid to help offset the cost of tuition.

Bread and Butter

In 2007, Representative Peter Welch (D-VT), motivated perhaps by public anger over the ballooning endowments at the Ivy League and other Élite colleges on the one hand and the rapidly rising tuition costs at those same institutions on the other hand, introduced an amendment to the reauthorization of the Higher Education Act that would have required universities to spend 5 percent of their endowments annually. At the same time, the U.S. Senate began reviewing tuition, financial aid, and endowment spending patterns at top institutions with an aim toward providing tuition relief to families.

By early 2008, a wave of financial reform had swept through the Ivy League, resulting in expanded financial aid programs. Dartmouth wiped out tuition altogether for students from families making less than $75,000 dollars per year. Cornell capped at $3,000 dollars the maximum amount of loan debt for families making less than $120,000 per year. According to Richard Vedder, director of the Center for College Affordability and Productivity, the effect of these changes is to allow public universities to compete with the Ivies:

These new initiatives are for kids from families that the ordinary American would consider pretty well off, people making $100,000 a year . . . these [kids] are the bread and butter of schools like the University of Virginia and the University of Michigan . . . [who are the] ones being killed because they can't compete with [the Ivies] dollar for dollar.[21]

The recession of 2009 forced some of the Ivy League schools to modify their strategy in order to generate substantial tuition income from wealthier families, but the overall dynamics are relatively unchanged.

I have spoken with dozens of deans, provosts, and presidents from universities in the Middle—including those that are poised to make the jump to Élite status—about the impact of these changes on their university's ability to recruit top students who could not otherwise afford a Stanford, MIT, or Harvard education. With very few exceptions, I was told me that they did not "expect it to have any effect whatsoever." In some cases—even among institutions with a growth strategy that demands increasing success in competing for this same group of students—the response was "I am not concerned about it." The message is the same one that I heard from an Italian rector many years ago: "It takes a lot to get us excited."

At all levels of the traditional academic hierarchy, there is an underlying assumption. It is the same for the most Élite private institutions and the most humble public community colleges: *when faced with a choice, students choose our institution because we know what their alternatives are and we believe we can compete as successfully in the future as we have in the past.* It is an assumption that is being called into question daily. Mainstream American colleges and universities do not know their competition today, either because the new institutions have arrived on the scene too rapidly and in such quantity that academic planners have not been able to catch up or because the new institutions have been previously dismissed as irrelevant to the educational goals of their students. It is competition that needs to be taken seriously, if for no other reason than this: the bread and butter of mainstream universities is being taken from them in plain sight and sometimes with their cooperation.

6 The Computer in the Cathedral

This is the story of how it became a policy of the federal government to encourage universities to divert funds from education to support an industrial policy that was not otherwise sustainable. Anyone who doubts the willingness of a modern research university to spend whatever is required to keep its "martyrs and heroes" focused on the creation of knowledge needs to spend a few hours in quiet contemplation of the cathedral in Barcelona, Spain, that is devoted to it.

The north campus of Universitat Politècnica de Catalunya (UPC) is tucked into a garden that lies on one end of Avinguda Diagonal, a wide thoroughfare that runs past Barcelona's architectural treasures, La Rambla, and the city's public beaches to the commercial shipping district. The two dozen buildings are a mixture of graceful Mediterranean styles, modern steel and glass boxes, and hastily constructed structures whose capacity is already exceeded as UPC tries to accommodate a dramatic increase in students and programs. The north campus is the seat of the university's administrative services, including the Rectorat.

A visitor to the north campus arrives at the entry gate on Avinguda Diagonal and walks along parking lots and city streets to a garden path that leads to the schools of informatics, telecommunications, and engineering. Someone who has business with the rector continues along the path to a fountain at the base of a broad staircase on which is perched the four-story Rectorat. In a city renowned for its architecture, when compared to the grand scale of Columbia's Low Library the Rectorat is a modest home for a university administration, but it is certainly comparable to Duke University's gothic Allen Building or the columned Greek Revival building that also overlooks a fountain and houses the upper administration of Purdue University. It so happens that UPC's Rectorat is literally the rectory of a church, Torre Girona. Inside the church is one of the world's most powerful supercomputers. It is called Mare Nostrum.

Figure 6.1
The Barcelona Supercomputing Center.
Image reprinted by permission of the Barcelona Supercomputing Center—Centro
Nacional de Supercomputación.

Monks and Chants

We walk up the stairs to the entrance of Torre Girona, with its pink facade
and tower that rises above the Rectorat. The door opens, and Mateo greets
us. The entry foyer is cool and dark. We can barely hear the large fans outside that move the chilled air. More noticeable is the background music:
Gregorian chants and medieval motets, played through speakers hidden in
the architectural detail of the chapel. Before passing through a metal detec-
tor, visitors to Mare Nostrum must surrender their purses and briefcases to
a contingent of security guards who inspect the contents. Security check-
points are generally bustling, noisy facilities, but at Mare Nostrum, security
screening is carried out quietly, almost reverently. Instructions are given in
hushed tones. Chanting monks are what you hear.

Mateo introduces us to Francesco, a graduate student at UPC, who will
give us a guided tour of Mare Nostrum before our meeting later in the

day with Mateo and his staff. Like graduate students all around the world, Francesco is wearing sandals and—because the air conditioning is very effective—a hooded sweatshirt. The sweatshirt is brown and ties at the waist. Francesco has given this tour often enough to know the effect of pulling the hood over his head, casting his face into shadow except for a glimpse of wispy beard. Francesco holds the door open and ushers us into the heart of the church—a monk showing worshippers to their seats at the start of a Sunday High Mass.

Even jaded technologists are not prepared for the experience of seeing Mare Nostrum for the first time. In the nave, dominating the space from the ceiling twenty feet above our heads to the basement, visible through iron grates that make up our suspended walkway, is a lighted glass cube that contains a dozen or more black monoliths. They seem to float in space, weightless and powerful. The cube hums, and the low-frequency vibrations are transmitted to the iron walkway, so that you can literally feel the power of the computer.

Francesco leads us around the cube to a stone stairway that leads to a dark choir loft high above the sanctuary. For the first time, we see the entire computer, encased in glass, filling the church, conduits carrying chilled water and cables connecting it to the outside world.

I turn my attention to Francesco once more as he turns up the lights in the loft to reveal not rows of seated monks, but an easel on which rests a large, blue poster that reads:

BSC
Centro Nacional de Supercomputación
Welcome to the Barcelona Supercomputing Center

Later that afternoon, seated around Mateo's conference table in his small director's office in the modern glass and steel building that is home to the administrative offices of BSC, I know we are back in the world of mortals surrounded by modern European workspace furnishings, fluorescent overhead lights, and warbling office telephones. Mateo begins:

In March 2004 the Spanish government and IBM signed an agreement to build one of the fastest computers in Europe. In July 2006 its capacity has been increased due to the large demand of scientific projects.

Mare Nostrum is a supercomputer based on PowerPC processors using IBM's BladeCenter architecture, Linux, and a Myrinet interconnection. Mare Nostrum has forty-four racks and takes up a space of 120 square meters. These four technologies configure the base of an architecture and design that will have a big impact in the future of supercomputing.

The show is over. It is time to talk numbers. It is time to talk about the most expensive university laboratories in the world. But we have been properly prepared, because we have experienced Mare Nostrum as it was intended to be experienced.

Exascales and Petaflops

Academic science demands extreme capabilities to make progress. When the $4.4 billion Superconducting Super Collider (SSC) project was awarded to Texas in 1988, it was to be the world's largest high-energy particle accelerator, capable of producing the elusive Higgs boson—a hypothetical subatomic particle whose existence would help explain the origins of mass in the universe. The circumference of the main ring of SSC was to have been more than fifty-four miles—much larger than Europe's Large Hadron Collider, its closest competitor, whose fourteen trillion electron-volts would have made it 30 percent smaller than SSC.

When the SSC project was canceled in 1993 amid conflicting protests over costs, national priorities, and American research competitiveness, research scientists took a different approach. Science has always been supported by two pillars: theory and experimentation. If the construction of ever more expensive physical laboratories was beyond the appetite of the American public, then perhaps science needed a third pillar: virtual laboratories based on ever more powerful supercomputers.

Supercomputing became the third pillar of science, and experimental work moved quickly into computer modeling for protein folding, high-energy physics, combustion, and climate modeling. The commercial success of Google—which amassed tens of thousands of computers and disk drives to enable the quick analysis of massive amounts of data—brought academic attention to bear on search and the new technologies of the Web. Scientific discovery in the third pillar needs technologies that are measured not in miles or electron-volts, but rather on a scale that is unfamiliar to most people. To high-performance computer specialists, it is a world of exabytes and petaflops. That is how the power of a supercomputer is measured.

Mare Nostrum is at the present time the sixtieth most powerful supercomputer in the world. Six of the ten most powerful computers are owned and operated by the U.S. Department of Energy, mostly in the national laboratories that are located in places like Los Alamos, New Mexico; Oak Ridge, Tennessee; and Livermore, California. Only two of the top ten are operated by universities. The University of Tennessee's National Institute for Computational Sciences is so intimately connected to Oak Ridge National

Laboratory that is scarcely known to be a university research center. The Texas Advanced Computing Center (TACC) at the University of Texas is number nine on the list. TACC is centrally located in the university's research campus in Austin and makes use of the university's status as an elite research institution to draw engineers and scientists from around the world.

At least fourteen of the top fifty computers are manufactured by IBM. The exact number is uncertain because the Chinese computer company Lenovo also sells supercomputers, and in 2005, IBM sold part of its computer business to Lenovo. Some recent Lenovo supercomputer sales—despite public avowals—may actually use IBM technology.

Other supercomputer vendors include companies that are unfamiliar to the general public: Cray, SGI,[1] Bull, and Appro are good examples. With the exception of IBM, the American manufacturers at the top of the Top 500 List—the constantly updated ranking of the five hundred fastest computers in the world that followers of the high-performance computing market use to keep track of bragging rights—survive by furiously swimming upstream in a river that is flowing rapidly in the opposite direction. Hewlett-Packard (HP), a company that—along with IBM—dominates the market in high-performance computers, places only five machines among the fifty fastest. At least two of those are computers that were designed by Compaq Computer, the company that merged with HP in 2002 and that had previously purchased Digital Equipment Corporation and Tandem Computers. Both of these companies had run into financial trouble, in part by investing heavily in a supercomputer marketplace that did not reward their investments.

The language of supercomputers is dominated by an intimidating vocabulary of "tera," "peta," and "exa." In the international system of units, the prefix "tera" means trillion, while "peta" denotes a quantity that is a thousand times larger: one quadrillion. For example, a light year is approximately 9.4 petameters. In the notation that scientists use to help cut down on the number of zeros they have to write, a *peta* is 10^{15}, that is, a one followed by fifteen zeros. A thousand petas is one quintillion or 10^{18}, an *exa*. These numbers seem unimaginably large, but they describe the scale of modern supercomputing.

To describe the power of a supercomputer, designers use the number of *floating-point operations per second* (*flops*) that the computer is capable of performing. These are the familiar addition and multiplication arithmetic of everyday life, carried out on numbers with many decimal places rather than whole numbers. A computer that is capable of more flops can do more of the essential mathematics that a scientist needs to get the job done. Technology has just pushed past the petaflop boundary, making more problems accessible. A physicist who uses a teraflop supercomputer—one thousand times less powerful—to model the fundamental chemical behavior of DNA molecules, put it to me this way: "I am at the limit of what I can perform in my lifetime with this machine. If I have a petaflop computer, I can run one more experiment before I die."

Scientific experiments produce enormous quantities of data, and all the flops in the world would not matter if there were no data to calculate with. The storage capacity of supercomputers is measured in *exabytes*. Just like your personal computer at home, supercomputers measure memory capacity by counting the number of characters or *bytes* that can be stored. Computer storage requirements are growing exponentially. If it were possible to capture all of mankind's spoken words since the beginning of history, it would take approximately four exabytes of storage. Thanks to supercomputers in business and science, the world is producing an exabyte of data every day. Just one new high-energy physics instrument—the Spallation Neutron Source at Oak Ridge National Laboratory—will account for one tenth of 1 percent of the global total increase.

With petaflop computers operating at exascale, computational scientists can conduct and analyze experiments on computers that would be impossible in real life. Biologists foresee the day when the growth of individual tumors can be mapped and predicted from analyzing DNA samples. Long-range weather predictions of climate scientists are currently limited by how many calculations they can carry out per day. A transition to petaflop computers would enable climatologists to precisely map the course of tornados and hurricanes hours or days earlier than is possible today. There are so many applications of supercomputing that petaflops and exabytes per mega dollar has become a standard way of measuring scientific progress.

The question is how many of the most expensive and extreme supercomputers are needed to ensure that American university research labs remain among the most well-equipped in the world. The answer to that question is tied to how many academic institutions can afford to actually make use of a high-performance computer exclusively dedicated to their needs.

The health of the computer industry is tied to volume. As Microsoft's Dan Reed pointed out, the number of users who can effectively make use of computing power decreases rapidly as computer performance increases. What that means to a computer manufacturer is that a supercomputer design has to "scale down" so that smaller and less expensive versions of the machines can be sold to many more users. HP and IBM invest heavily in designs that are usable in data centers that serve millions of users—not necessarily users with the most extreme demands, but those that nevertheless need significantly more computing power than might be available from desktop servers and workstations. As a result, all but two of the supercomputers ranked 300–400 in the Top 500 are sold by Hewlett-Packard and IBM. HP and IBM sell their most powerful computers to financial services companies, Wall Street investment banks, engineering companies, and biomedical companies.

SGI and Cray are scarcely present from position 250 on, yet their computers require the most sophisticated engineering and are therefore the most expensive to develop and manufacture. The entire worldwide market for supercomputers—defined as any high-performance server that costs more than half a million dollars—is only a little more than three billion dollars annually, a drop in the bucket for the nearly one trillion dollar information technology industry. This means that—in an industry that plows between 3 and 6 percent of its revenue into the research and engineering needed for product development—somewhere between $100 and $200 million would be available annually across all vendors to develop the next generation of supercomputers, were it not for federal subsidies. Tiny Cray, with less than 4 percent of the total high-performance market, spends by itself more than a quarter of this amount on research and development (R&D). This leaves the other 75 percent to be divided among at least twelve other manufacturers, three of which (HP, Dell, and IBM) are able spread their research and development costs among hundreds of products and services, overshadowing in R&D expenditures alone Cray's $200 million revenue.

Balancing Act

How is this seemingly impossible financial balancing act carried out? The U.S. government has a strategic interest in maintaining the flow of the highest-end supercomputers to intelligence, defense, and law enforcement agencies, and it is willing to underwrite the research expenses of companies like Cray to do so. DARPA alone provided $500 million to Cray and IBM to develop a commercially viable supercomputer, a fraction of IBM's R&D budget, but an effective doubling of Cray's. Universities long ago figured out that they could help by convincing funding agencies like DARPA and NSF that their needs would also be served by access to the most powerful computers. This would make life easier for federal budget writers. They would be able to spread the costs around because there are so many congressional districts with universities that—they argue—would be more productive and innovative if only they had a large computer sitting in the basement, waiting for biologists, climate change scientists, and cosmologists to use it for a fantastic new discovery that would enhance institutional and individual research reputations.

The organizing force for supercomputing was DARPA—the same Advanced Research Projects Agency of the Department of Defense where the Internet was born. Its portfolio of scientific projects with national security implications demanded increasingly more computing power at increasing cost from computer manufacturers like IBM, Cray, and the now-defunct Control Data Corporation. The commercial and academic communities were tightly braided, and when scientists said that a lagging supercomputing industry put unacceptable limitations on scientific capabilities, DARPA responded with new waves of investment. Much of it went to companies like Cray. By 1983, Cray was the industry leader, but its total base of supercomputers was only forty-six machines, and most of those were installed in National Labs and secure government facilities where access by academics was limited and expensive. Only three universities operated high-end computers that fell under the accepted meaning of supercomputing. Concerned that American professors would leave domestic laboratories for Europe or Japan where access was relatively cheap, the Defense Department decided to act.

In the early 1980s, Japan was a growing technology powerhouse, and its many government-sponsored initiatives posed an economic challenge for the United States. The consumer electronics industry was already under assault, but the Japanese National Superspeed Computer Project represented an even greater threat in the eyes of the American supercomputing community. If the Japanese captured the supercomputer market, strategically critical technology would be in the hands of foreigners. This was an unacceptable outcome to DARPA. But DARPA was not the only federal agency that had set its sights on university access to these powerful machines:

In 1982 and 1983 . . . three other federal organizations initiated comparable steps to address the supercomputer problem. The National Science Foundation (NSF) working group on computers in research suggested establishing ten university research centers with network links to other schools. A panel of the Federal Coordinating Council for Science, Engineering, and Technology (FCCSET) recommended that federal agencies design and establish supercomputer centers and networks of their own for long-term needs. The Panel of Large Scale Computing in Science and Engineering (known as the Lax Panel) sponsored by the National Science Board recommended a coordinated national program to increase access to supercomputers.[2]

It took only a year before federal dollars began flowing to NSA, NSF, and DOE to create supercomputer centers. NSF created university supercomputer centers at Princeton University, the University of California at San Diego, the University of Illinois, and Cornell University. A fifth center was actually a consortium of universities led by the University of Pittsburgh and Carnegie Mellon University. The idea was that NSF would provide startup funding for purchasing powerful computers, which the centers would in turn make available to scientists and engineers.

When I took over the directorship of the computing research division at NSF in 1989, the National Center for Supercomputing Applications (NCSA) at the University of Illinois was already one of the crown jewels in the NSF program. Led by a visionary scientist named Larry Smarr, it had been among the first to install a supercomputer—a Cray X-MP/24—and open its doors to the national community of supercomputer users. Smarr's unique insight was that supercomputers were very good for making pictures of physical phenomena, an area known as *scientific visualization*. Realistic motion pictures of atomic activity involved in photosynthesis, the evolution of stars, and the transmission of cardiovascular disease were beyond the reach of even the most powerful laboratory instruments, but Smarr's stunning photographs were relatively cheap to produce once the computers were properly programmed. It made a good argument for continued investment in the NSF centers.

Smarr was also a canny businessman. When one of his programmers, a young engineer named Marc Andreessen, came up with a clever way of "browsing" through thousands of pages of text and graphic material—a technology called *Mosaic*—the university recognized the potential impact on the new World Wide Web and released the Mosaic browser under terms that were unheard of for proprietary software. NCSA allowed Mosaic to be used freely for any noncommercial purpose. Silicon Graphics founder Jim Clark approached Andreessen about forming a company to commercialize the technology, and NCSA readily agreed to release Andreessen and four other programmers who had been involved in the development of Mosaic to form the company that would later be known as Netscape Communications. The economic impact of NSF's investment in supercomputing thereafter became part of every briefing on the value of the supercomputer centers, the kind of argument that is important in Washington, where congressional minds tend to wander during budget briefings that stray too far into science and mathematics.

But even in 1989, the supercomputer centers were on shaky ground. I found myself arguing as much for effective utilization by the universities as for increased budgets to support their operations. They all had their own cathedrals, but as former UC–San Diego director Sidney Karin observed:

There is no such thing as an NSF (Supercomputer) Center and there never has been. There should be. What there are, in the words of Ed Hayes, then comptroller of

NSF, are "NSF ASSISTED Supercomputer Centers." . . . NSF has neither provided suf-ficient funding nor has it provided any other kind of support when centers found themselves in one sort of difficulty or another. In my direct experience, and to my direct knowledge of activities at other centers, NSF funding has been inadequate to provide the direct support of what used to be called the base program. Each center has raised funds from industry partners, state governments, local universities, and foundations.[3]

One of the earliest casualties was the John von Neumann Computer Center (JVNC) at Princeton University. Princeton seemed like the ideal set-ting for an NSF center. It was the birthplace of modern computers, and the center's namesake, John von Neumann, is widely credited with inventing the model on which virtually all computers are based. Princeton itself was to computer scientists as close to a cathedral as is possible in the secular world, so locating one of the most powerful machines in the world there made perfect sense. JVNC made a number of unfortunate decisions. It chose to work with a company called ETA, a Control Data Corporation spinoff. Control Data had been an early leader in supercomputing, but had fallen on hard financial times, and ETA was a way of preserving some of Con-trol Data's technology. It was a disastrous move. ETA had limited funds to underwrite such an ambitious installation, and the JVNC technology was never fully functional.

JVNC's location did not help, either. Rather than locate the facility in the "cathedral," Princeton chose an industrial site far down New Jersey's traffic-clogged Route 1, almost guaranteeing that even the nearest univer-sity customers would be discouraged from making a trip to the facility. Even by the meager standards of New Jersey's industrial office parks, JVNC was at a disadvantage. The facility was inadequate for housing permanent research staff. The campus research climate was much more vibrant, and so research-ers chose to stay in their offices rather than travel to JVNC.

These were not fatal flaws, however. The fundamental difficulty with JVNC was its economic model. Princeton committed to share some of the costs to support JVNC, an absolutely critical funding component, as Sid Karin points out. In contrast to NCSA, Princeton was never committed to operating JVNC as a facility. In fact, center operation was originally the responsibility of a company called Zero One, but it was never a happy relationship. By the summer of 1989, JVNC had terminated its relation-ship with Zero One. Responsibility for operating the center fell directly on Princeton, a requirement that had not been anticipated when the univer-sity signed its cooperative agreement with NSF in 1985.

There is a reason that the vast majority of the most powerful data centers in the world are operated by government agencies: they are enormously expensive places that need hundreds of support staff, unique physical facilities, and power in quantities that rival what a small city uses on a good day. Those are operational expenses that would go well beyond the purchase price of the computer itself, if it were possible to set such a price.

There is no such thing as a "list price" for a supercomputer. Each machine is a unique feat of engineering that uses components and designs in which vendors have invested hundreds of millions of dollars. A university that wanted to win an NSF bid for an advanced supercomputer had to take into account not only the price that a manufacturer was willing to sell it for, but also the associated operational costs. The situation has not improved over the years. Negotiations over computer pricing are still intense.

If NSF issues a $30 million call for proposals for a petaflop supercomputer, a university needs to be able to purchase the computer for less than thirty thousand dollars per teraflop, a figure that is well below typical engineering costs of forty thousand dollars or more. A vendor trying to win such a bid has to decide how aggressively to price its technology, knowing that there is a good possibility that it will lose money if the system is unexpectedly expensive to engineer or install. A university that wins such a bid must plan to spend double on operating the computer, and that does not include the initial costs of building or renovating a facility and providing it with sufficient power, air conditioning, network connections, and security.

A good university negotiator might be able to get a 30 percent discount, but that still leaves a $20 million gap to be filled if the proposal is selected by NSF. This gap is filled with a contribution that the university makes to the project called *cost-sharing*. For normal NSF grants, universities had adopted the practice of documenting cost-sharing by recording all of the nonstandard costs associated with the research.

For example, if a professor needed a one-course teaching load reduction to have time to conduct research, the cost of offering that course was added to the cost-sharing budget, even if the reduction involved a course that was never offered. Cost-sharing budgets existed on paper, but seldom resulted in extra expenditures on the part of the university. Of course, university auditors could never admit that, so cost-sharing was dutifully added to every NSF budget to show that the university was bearing its share of the project expenses. To many, cost-sharing sounded like a form of kickback. Congressional committees noticed that the practice of taking into consideration the amount of money that a university was willing to pay—even if it was money that was intended to cover a portion of the cost of research—was not in the spirit of NSF's peer-reviewed system of funding the most meritorious proposals, and in 2004 outlawed the practice altogether. But that did not stop the practice of soliciting cost-sharing for supercomputer centers, and for a supercomputer center that needs to fill a $20 million gap in its budget, the cost-sharing commitment made by the university is anything but a paper commitment.

NSF supercomputer center awards are not, technically speaking, grants. They are a form of contract called a *cooperative agreement,* and it is in the nature of a cooperative agreement that all of the participants will contribute to the success of the effort. They are exempt from the cost-sharing prohibitions that govern most NSF grants. JVNC was funded under a cooperative agreement that required Princeton to contribute $3 million for five years as "leverage" to the NSF funding. Princeton apparently never took its obligations seriously. Its paper contributions left JVNC management scrambling for state and private support to keep the operation afloat financially. In the end, JVNC raised $300,000, less than 10 percent of the total funding proposed. Funds were woefully inadequate and, at the end of 1992, JVNC ceased operations.

Pyramid

Except for a relatively few graduate students, most students never come in contact with a supercomputer center, and aside from the high-profile professors that it might attract, the very existence of a supercomputer on campus adds very little value to classrooms. That is why it is hard to find an educational expense category for supercomputer operations in university budgets. As a result, most universities fund supercomputers in much the same way as they fund other auxiliary services like hospitals, theaters, and parking—that is, as a money-making venture. It is not an unreasonable model, as auxiliary services can add as much as 5 percent to a university's bottom line. In 2006, auxiliary services at public research universities accounted for 26 percent of total revenues but only 22 percent of all expenses. The profile at private universities was similar. However, operating a supercomputer center is not the same as collecting coins from parking meters.

An additional supercomputer center cost-sharing expense of $20 million calculated on a per-student basis changes university finances dramatically. At a twenty-thousand-student public research university, a thousand-dollar per-student increase in expenses to offset center operations—unless subsidized by a new source of revenue—would amount to a 9 percent reduction in spending on instruction and other education expenses, the only spending category over which universities have some control. The impact on private institutions would be similar, although—because tuition costs almost balance education expenses—endowment funds would be put in jeopardy if a center did not generate revenue as anticipated.

That is why so few Élite universities bother with supercomputers in the Top 500. There is not a single Ivy League institution in the Top 100 list (see table 6.1). Aside from Tennessee and Texas, all of the top fifty academic supercomputers are installed at institutions like the universities of Tokyo and Tsukuba in Japan, Moscow State University in Russia, and King Abdullah University of Science and Technology in Saudi Arabia, where state subsidies are large.

There are twenty-six universities in this list, many of which are not highly ranked in reputational surveys. However, these universities, plus a few new NSF supercomputing centers, are near the top of another academic pyramid. They operate facilities in support of a valuable scientific enterprise, and they are by and large subsidized by government and industry to provide those services.

It is a balancing act, but like many tradeoffs in a multiversity, visionary leaders often take on risks like these to pursue a larger vision. For many, it is a *Field of Dreams*[4] vision: "if we build it, they will come." Supercomputer centers are cathedrals built to attract professors and research funding. Even if they contribute little value to students, they are pathways to enhanced reputations.

Below the computers in the Top 500, far down in the base of the pyramid, are 239 other academic supercomputers. Not cathedrals, perhaps, but multimillion-dollar chapels. Like the reputational hierarchies, where behavior at the top cascades down the hierarchy to schools in the Middle, the balancing act at the top of the supercomputing pyramid is repeated hundreds of times by institutions that are far down in the base and that— despite their dreams—have little chance of moving up. For those universities it is a balancing act without a net, sustainable only at the expense of academic programs.

An ambitious—but not unusual—center at one of these universities is actually a loosely knit collection of ninety computers that average less than a teraflop in capability, each purchased by the university to support the research of a single professor at a discounted price that nevertheless can amount to a half million dollars or more. Because they support ongoing research projects, the computers run continuously, which adds a thirty-two-thousand kilowatt-hour load to the institution's energy bill—an added

Table 6.1
Top University Supercomputers

Rank	Site	Manufacturer
3	National Institute for Computational Sciences/University of Tennessee	Cray Inc.
9	Texas Advanced Computing Center/University of Texas	Sun Microsystems
30	National Institute for Computational Sciences/University of Tennessee	Cray Inc.
63	CLUMEQ—Université Laval	Sun Microsystems
67	University of Minnesota/Supercomputing Institute	Hewlett-Packard
70	Rensselaer Polytechnic Institute, Computational Center for Nanotechnology	IBM
71	University of Southern California	Dell/Sun/IBM
73	NCSA	Dell
79	Clemson University	Dell/Sun/IBM
105	Texas Advanced Computing Center/University of Texas	Dell
107	Ohio Supercomputer Center	IBM
163	Louisiana Optical Network Initiative	Dell
175	Texas Tech University	Dell
183	Harvard University—FAS Research Computing	Dell
222	Arizona State University HPCI / Translational Genomics Research Institute	Dell
230	Compute Canada/WestGrid/UBC	Hewlett-Packard
239	University of North Carolina	Dell
252	University of Oklahoma	Dell
273	Clemson University Computational Center for Mobility Systems	Sun Microsystems
277	Purdue University	Dell
278	Brigham Young University	Dell
288	University of Alaska—Arctic Region Supercomputing Center	Cray Inc.
305	Northwestern University	IBM
322	SHARCNET—University of Western Ontario	Hewlett-Packard
382	Columbia University	Hewlett-Packard
426	Columbia University	Hewlett-Packard
436	Caltech	Dell
452	Indiana University	IBM
462	RQCHP/Compute Canada	SGI
468	Holland Computing Center at PKI (Nebraska)	Dell

expense of more than a million dollars per year. High-volume air condition-ing needs for these systems can easily double that amount.

Expenses mount quickly, especially when professors each demand a similar, new, and completely autonomous facility, and an institution finds itself in a mad scramble trying to operate a half-dozen centers. It is often money that—despite faculty demands and promises—is not well spent. At one university, a very senior physics professor—armed with offers from competing institutions—wrangled a million dollars from his provost to purchase a teraflop computer. The vendor—needing a university installa-tion as a reference customer—was willing to deeply discount the price of the as-yet-untested technology. The professor drastically underestimated the effort in installing, tuning, and operating the machine with his current research staff. To the embarrassment of the university and the vendor, the equipment stood idle for many months and became usable only after new staff was hired. In the interim, the professor utilized shared computers at other institutions, but continued to argue that "the only way to do my research is to have complete control of my own computer."

Another professor rejected any attempt to measure how efficiently his $5 million supercomputing laboratory was being used, preferring instead to operate his facility off-campus at greatly inflated lease and energy prices. His claim, "My research uses every available second of computing power on this machine," was somewhat undercut when a university audit showed that the computer was also used for his personal email.

If centers like these contributed to the educational mission of an institu-tion in the Middle, it would be possible to balance the expense of acquiring and operating a new computer with other needs, but that happens only rarely in faculty-centered universities, where professors like to be in control of their own laboratories. As a result, even an inquisitive university admin-istrator has a difficult time determining how well utilized these investments really are.

Keeping up with the pace of technological change is not for the faint of heart. The pyramid, unfortunately, does not stand still, and today's highly capable computers can quickly fall out of the top of the pyramid. One university—with programs ranked near the bottom of the *USNWR* annual rankings—briefly made it to the Top 100 list on the wings of a special congressional authorization—an *earmark*—that subsidized a $10 million purchase. A hiring flurry followed, but—aside from a few federal contracts, also arranged by interested congressmen—research funding was slow to materialize. As the university slid further into the middle of the pyramid, the few professors who had been attracted by the advanced technology fled to other universities. This is not an isolated instance of university priorities gone astray. It is rather an often-repeated pattern of under-the-table deals between the federal government and university administrators to erode the ability of institutions to invest in their educational programs. So great is the desire to leap-frog up the reputational ladder that congressional blocs form to trade university supercomputer funding commitments for votes on future earmarks.

To maintain just a middle-of-the-pack position, a supercomputing center has to renew its investment on a three- or four-year cycle. When added to the multimillion-dollar fixed costs of real estate and electricity, just keeping afloat is almost as expensive as running an NSF supercomputing center, especially for universities that are not at the top of the pyramid. It is all subsidized by internal funds.

There is occasionally, in the 239 supercomputers that are spread across the dozens of universities locked into the middle of the pyramid, a high-performance computing facility that also supports academic programs. Those institutions would not agree that funds are being diverted from more pressing educational needs that offer value to their students—and most would not agree that maintaining their positions was a result of relenting to pressure from influential professors to maintain private laboratories. They would be right, but they would all agree that maintaining supercomputer centers without direct federal and industrial subsidies is an expensive proposition, and the ability of most of those institutions to offset those expenses with research contracts and gifts has not kept pace.

Academic supercomputing initiatives that had their origins in the pressing national needs of the 1970s have turned, in effect, into an industrial policy to support an industry that is not sustainable at its current size. Higher education has become a willing partner in a policy that diverts increasingly scarce resources from existing categories to fund facilities that add little to the student experience. Fortunately, it is not the only way that science in American universities can continue to thrive. There are other ways to ensure the continued availability of cutting-edge technology for science's third pillar.

There is no financial price tag for an alternative approach, but there are cultural barriers. The faculty-centered university has to abandon the dreams of another campus cathedral and enthusiastically embrace new models based on shared resources. But supercomputing is not the only reason that universities build cathedrals. There are other pressures to build monuments.

7 Do No Harm

Clark Kerr's multiversity is a multicultural society, so it is not surprising that outside the chilly supercomputer data centers, lawyers and administrators who have never set foot in a modern physics or biology lab compete furiously to build—with the help and encouragement of the U.S. government—other monuments to institutional ambitions that have little to do with education. Sometimes those ambitions are financial, and at a faculty-centered university, naked finance is confusing. It affects the ability of American universities—with their machinery for innovation that is the envy of the world—to compete effectively when there are suddenly abundant choices for the kind of university-based invention that attracts entrepreneurs and investment. It is the very scenario that Norman Augustine was trying to avoid in *Above the Gathering Storm*.

Picking Winners

On a visit to a top-ranked engineering department in 2005, I noticed that the hallways were unusually quiet. Every once in a while, I spotted a knot of graduate students hanging around the entrance to a laboratory that was run by a professor who I knew. "Where's Bill?" I asked, expecting to hear "He's in class," or "He's travelling today." There are a hundred reasons that Bill would not be in his office, waiting for me—an unannounced visitor—to knock on his door. That day, Bill was not in the building because, as one of the students announced, "He's at his company on Mondays and Tuesdays." I spied the students of another colleague at the end of a long hall: "She's spending the week at Google. They're going to buy her company." Mike, the head of the department, later told me that half of his faculty members were either on leave or starting companies that would take them away from campus on a regular basis. "It's a hassle for me," Mike said. "I have to find people to teach their courses." That was a manageable task, because "there are twenty companies within thirty minutes of campus filled with people who would love to teach a course every once in awhile." The real problem, it turned out, was that "junior faculty members are confused about what they should be doing. There's a lot of pressure to start a company, but they are worried that their research will suffer, and they won't be promoted at tenure time."

When I got back home, I looked up recent tenure decisions. I could not find a single instance where Mike's department had failed to promote an assistant professor who also had a successful startup. If you are a newly hired PhD, spending your time with some of the dozens of venture capitalists whose offices dot the landscape around campus is evidently effort well invested. It was not always that way.

In 1973, Stanford professor Stanley Cohen and University of San Francisco biochemist Herbert Boyer published a paper that described how to splice together strands of DNA to genetically engineer new molecules,[1] a technology called *recombinant DNA*, or rDNA. The potential of rDNA to launch a multibillion-dollar industry to synthesize insulin and hundreds of other drugs and medical products was clear to Cohen and Boyer, but they were not interested in making money from their invention. Nor were they interested in applying for a patent on rDNA, even though such a patent would stand in the way of anyone who wanted to use gene splicing for commercial purposes and could be worth hundreds of millions of dollars. Stanley Cohen and Herbert Boyer were pure academics, and they had no intention of commercializing rDNA.

Besides, many thought that it would be impossible to patent rDNA, because it would be construed as a *life form* and therefore unpatentable under then-current patent law. Inventions had to involve the manipulation of physical objects or methods for structuring activities in the physical realm. Mathematical formulas, physical laws, and the manipulation of life were explicitly excluded by patent law. At any other university, that would have been the end of the matter. But not at Stanford.

By the early 1970s, Stanford already had a forty-year history of marrying academic research and industrial innovation. When Frederick Terman—the man who is known as the *father of Silicon Valley*—stepped down as Stanford's provost in 1965, he left behind a legacy that made it hard for Stanley Cohen to keep saying "No." Terman had been a professor of electrical engineering, specializing in electronics. He wrote the definitive textbook on how to use vacuum tube technology in the design of radios. Along the way, Terman attracted students like William Hewlett and David Packard, who saw how the same technology could be used to create entirely new electronic devices. Terman not only helped them form their own companies, but personally invested in them.

Shortly after World War II, Terman was named dean of engineering. He persuaded Stanford to lease a portion of its considerable real estate holdings to some of the growing number of high-tech firms that had sprung up around Palo Alto, eventually leading to Stanford Research Park, home to—in addition to Hewlett-Packard—Eastman Kodak, General Electric, and Lockheed. One of those companies was Varian. Varian, which, like Hewlett-Packard, was launched by Stanford students, was one of the first companies to bring a university laboratory invention to market.

Terman's office of research administration had successfully patented and licensed the klystron, a vacuum tube amplifier invented by the Varian brothers, Russell and Sigurd. Stanford's share of the license revenue from the klystron patent was about $2.5 million. This was a substantial amount of money, but it was a rare licensing success. Most of Stanford's inventions were clumsily handled by a New York company called Research Corporation, which also managed patents and licenses for four hundred other research institutions.

Research Corporation acted like a traffic cop, standing between university inventors and government agencies that had supported the research. A university submitted an application to Research Corporation for evaluation. If the invention was thought to have commercial potential, the inventor would receive notification after six months or so that Research Corporation had issued a license that would allow the use of the new technology for government purposes, while simultaneously granting the universities the right to license the technology for commercial purposes. The job of Research Corporation was, in essence, to pick winners and losers in the marketplace. Stanford's agreement with Research Corporation had resulted in royalties that altogether totaled $4,500. The University of Wisconsin and a handful of others had already grown tired of the poor performance of third-party clearinghouses like Research Corporation and had set up new entities like WARF to commercialize university technology. Stanford decided that it needed a new approach to licensing faculty inventions.

When Bill Miller, Terman's handpicked successor, hired former Ford engineer Nils Reimer in 1968 to help out with technology licensing, it is not clear he knew what he was getting into. Stanford's new licensing specialist knew that he did not want to continue turning over idea after idea to a faceless bureaucracy in New York whose track record on dozens of patents was eclipsed a hundred-fold by the single klystron patent. Klystron was a winner, selected by Fred Terman because he had detailed technical knowledge of the patent's subject matter, and because he had personally coached the inventors.

Reimer vowed to introduce Stanford to a new kind of technology licensing organization, an Office of Technology Licensing (OTL). OTL was founded on a few principles, and first among these was the belief that OTL should "do no harm" to Stanford's core mission:

This includes *never* taking an action to cause delay of open and unfettered publication of research results, notwithstanding that patent rights are diminished by publication in advance of patent filing. . . . Another harm to academic principle would be the diversion of the primary focus of the faculty member on teaching and research and the student, on learning, to the pursuit of royalty dollars. Technologies of the greatest financial potential have consistently emerged from the pursuit of new knowledge rather than from research directed to commercial application.[2]

Reimer did not want to establish just another university patent office run by attorneys: he wanted to actively market Stanford inventions and divide any royalties equally among the inventors, their academic departments, and their academic deans. By 1973, Nils Reimer's OTL had revolutionized licensing on the Stanford campus, and Reimer was already planning a national organization for university technology managers to promote the Stanford method.

Nils Reimer knew how to talk to a top-notch intellect like Stanley Cohen. He understood Cohen's devotion to academic research and to his students. Reimer had Cohen's trust. Cohen knew that Reimer had more than a lawyer's understanding of his research and was trying to ensure that the potential of rDNA was not lost, but time was running out. The U.S. patent code provides for a one-year grace period between public disclosure in a published paper and the filing of a patent application. The year was almost up. On November 4, 1974, with only a week to spare, Cohen and Boyer filed a patent application and assigned the rights to Stanford University.

It takes six years for the U.S. Patent Office to grant a patent. By 1976, Boyer had turned his full attention to commercializing gene splicing and founded Genentech, the company that launched the biotechnology industry. Even though the patent had not yet been granted, other biotech companies—Merck, Lilly, and Amgen among them—followed suit. This was the start of a new high-tech revolution, as a flood of companies licensed the technology and began applying it to the production of drugs for treating diseases ranging from HIV/AIDS to diabetes. From 1974 through 1997, the rDNA inventions generated $35 billion in sales of 2,442 products, manufactured by 468 companies. The universities' share of the license revenue was $225 million.

It was a risk for all involved. The Cohen and Boyer patent could have been held hostage if the patent office ruled that the subject matter was not patentable, but in June 1980, the U.S. Supreme Court ruled 5–4 that what was patentable included "anything under the sun that is made by man."[3] The rDNA patent application was approved six months later.

Ten days later, on December 12, 1980, the U.S. Congress passed a bill sponsored by Indiana Democratic Senator Burch Bayh and Kansas Republican Bob Dole. The Bayh-Dole University and Small Business Patent Procedures Act of 1980[4] bears the intellectual imprint of university licensing experience from Wisconsin's WARF to Stanford's OTL, nearly sixty years later. Bayh-Dole cleared away the confusing detritus of bureaucratic rules and conflicting regulations by granting to recipients of government research funds the ownership of inventions that come out of that research. Most universities that relied on Research Corporation to broker their pace of innovation found themselves free to imitate Stanford's success. Almost overnight, the number of university technology licensing offices exploded to more than three hundred.

The intention of the Bayh-Dole Act was admirable: increase the public access and benefits of federal dollars spent in university research. In reality, however, Bayh-Dole altered the value proposition for American institutions. University administrators, eyeing the $200 million windfall produced by the Cohen-Boyer patents, pounced on technology licensing as a new source of revenue.

Nils Reimer's national organization—the Association of University Technology Managers—fostered the set of principles he instituted at Stanford. Unfortunately, those principles are rarely honored in major research universities today, and to many who valued those principles, Bayh-Dole became as much a vehicle for stifling innovation as promoting it. Reimer's "do no harm" credo has been trampled, as priorities and funding have diverted the mission of dozens of colleges and universities toward the short-term goals of generating license revenues.

One of the first of Reimer's principles to be tossed aside was "Don't behave opportunistically."[5] Bayh-Dole contains a "use it or lose it" provision that many universities interpret as a duty to commercialize. Any institution that does not take steps to develop practical applications for an invention runs the risk that the government will step in and reclaim ownership. Bayh-Dole compels universities to look for commercial winners. This leads to prioritizing research—not as envisioned by Nils Reimer, according to the pursuit of basic knowledge—but according to its likelihood to produce wealth in the marketplace. There are dozens of ways to misread the Bayh-Dole act, and each one takes university licensing further away from Reimer's Stanford vision, which had more to do with the public service ideals of the university than with generating much-needed income for education and research.

Inflated Expectations

Every licensing office is filled with faulty financial analyses that lead professors and administrators alike to unrealistically inflated expectations. For some, this is bureaucratic self-preservation: OTL staffing depends on budget allocations that can be justified by offsetting license revenues. Forecasts for future growth lead to raised expectations but also to more budget positions—in many cases, these are positions carved out of academic and research programs. The case, although naïve, is easy to make: for many university inventions, a fundamental patent grants a virtual monopoly to the university, so an OTL manager really only has to argue that among the university's portfolio are a few gems that will dominate some as-yet-unrecognized market.

Raised expectations often lead to more pressure on OTL officers to behave opportunistically, the very thing that Reimer abhorred. A Stanford alumnus, frustrated that the OTL was negotiating low royalty rates and not charging license fees at all to nonprofit organizations, wrote to Nils Reimer:

You've got a patent; you can dominate everything here. Why are you charging such a low royalty? You know Stanford could use the money. Charge a higher royalty.[6]

It is too easy to infer from the performance of the top license revenue-generating institutions that the potential value of patents justifies spending scarce resources emulating the Stanford model. Columbia University receives more than $135 million in patent royalties, placing it near the top revenue generators. Many administrators and professors—looking at such success stories and longing to launch the next commercial success—can overlook the fact that 94 percent of Columbia's revenue comes from just five patents. Even if university technology licensing offices were experts at picking winners and losers in the commercial marketplace—and they are not—the best they could hope to achieve is the 80/20 split of private equity funds: 80 percent of the returns are generated by 20 percent of the investments.

Few universities have the wherewithal to keep the pace and quality of investment needed to achieve even this level of success. University innovation is much farther down in the investment food chain. A typical raw idea in a university laboratory—even a very good idea—has little commercial impact until the layers of product development, market research, and management have been in place for some time. That takes much more money than the original research investment, and still the failure rate is high.

Nils Reimer's own organization estimates that many OTL offices barely earn enough in royalties to cover their costs. John Hurt of the National Science Foundation tracks the return on intellectual property (IP) rights:

Of 3,200 universities, perhaps six have made significant amounts of money from their intellectual property rights. IP rights should be pursued as a means for interacting with industry rather than as a means for raising revenue from commercialization.[7]

Even very good universities struggle. In 2001, reflecting the height of the Internet boom in Silicon Valley, the University of California took in $74 million dollars in licensing revenue. The licensing office and programs, however, cost $69 million. Observers wonder whether there would have been a better way to pursue $5 million—a way that was better aligned with the aspirations of the faculty and the expectations of its students.

Others see a benefit to the larger society in promoting the kind of innovation that Bayh-Dole is intended to stimulate, citing a large spike in patent applications as evidence that the public investment in university research is being returned to the public in the form of new products and services. According to some researchers, the data to support that claim is slim:

NSF data on patenting does not support this contention: there is no sharp break in the rate of university research, publications, patent, or startups around the time of the Bayh-Dole Act, which took effect on July 1, 1981. . . . While there has been a fairly steady increase in the ratio of university patents to university research dollars . . . there is no notable change in the slope of that line from 1965–1988. Much of the discussion of Bayh-Dole's effects has been carried out without the benefit of any corroborating data.[8]

Part of the problem is that the Bayh-Dole Act, fueled by expectations of large returns, encourages universities to adopt a culture of ownership by protecting intellectual property with legal fences, encouraging professors and students to quickly figure out ways to turn laboratory ideas into viable businesses, and discouraging the kind of collaboration that it takes to define and move real markets.

Commons

Bayh-Dole encourages ownership of small ideas, because—except for those rare inventions that stand at the intersection of what is possible and what is needed in a marketplace of billions of people—laboratory inventions solve only a piece of a problem. Many industries figured this out many years ago, creating large swaths of technologies that are freely shared in cross-licenses that prohibit individual companies from locking up key inventions with restrictive patents.

Companies agree to such unlikely sounding arrangements because they know that they cannot afford to shoulder 100 percent of the investment needed to create all of the components needed for market success. They need to create what Michael Heller in his book *The Gridlock Economy* calls *a commons*,[9] in which all competitors are free to take what they wish and create their own value. When universities focus excessive attention on ownership rights, they create an *anticommons* from which even collaborators are excluded, blocking progress for everyone:

> Often we think that governments need only create clear property rights and then get out of the way. So long as rights are clear, owners can trade in markets, move resources to higher valued uses, and generate wealth. But clear rights and ordinary markets are not enough. The anticommons perspective shows that the content of property rights matters as much as the clarity. Gridlock arises when ownership rights and regulatory controls are too fragmented. . . . Making the tragedy of the anticommons visible upends our intuitions about private property. Private property can no longer be seen as the end point of ownership. Privatization can go too far, to the point where it destroys rather than creates wealth.[10]

So strong is the impulse to maximize ownership that it may become the overriding goal in academic intellectual property agreements. I was a relatively new dean when my college won a competitive contract with Microsoft to establish an Institute for Personal Robotics Education (IPRE). Microsoft had decided to make a multimillion-dollar award to change the way that college freshmen learned programming. In an effort to attract more students to computing, entering freshmen would be allowed to choose an introductory course that taught them how to program small, personal robots rather than traditional computers. Microsoft would supply the software and provide funds to renovate existing space. Georgia Tech would develop the robots and the curriculum, building on Microsoft's technology. It was an innovative concept that excited faculty members and students. I anticipated great demand, so I was appalled when contract negotiations went almost immediately astray. At the first meeting, the Georgia Tech OTL representative threatened to walk out and cancel contract negotiations before work had even started.

Microsoft had a reputation in some circles for tightly negotiated contracts that benefitted the company to the detriment of their university partners, but this time they had sent us a new kind of contract proposal. They were claiming no rights at all. In fact, they encouraged the sharing of all research results as widely as possible. No delays on publication. No reviews by Microsoft lawyers. Professors and students were allowed to file patent disclosures on any IPRE invention, but there was no requirement to do so. IPRE was to be a commons. The only thing that Microsoft asked was the right—along with everyone else—to take inventions that were in the commons and incorporate them into their own products, and this was unseemly to OTL. The idea that Microsoft would actually be able to make money out of ideas that it had helped to create was so repugnant, so at odds with the idea of maximizing Georgia Tech's ownership, that OTL was willing to stop the project in its tracks.

I saw where these meetings were heading. IPRE was very important to me, so I immediately escalated the matter to the Institute's OTL director. "Look," I said, "I spent years on the other side of the table negotiating commercial contracts, and I know reasonable commercial terms when I see them. Your job is not to get in the way of larger university goals; it's to help us make sure this project gets launched properly, because it is important to my college, to Georgia Tech, and to the field."

The first thing I asked for was a different negotiator for our side. I set a six-week deadline to negotiate the contract, and sat in on every meeting and conference call until I was convinced that the process was on track. IPRE was launched two months later and was a great success, but everyone involved was exhausted. No administrator—regardless of his commitment to a project—can afford to pull against the weight of a university bureaucracy forever. I could only imagine what the effort would have been like at another university. Georgia Tech has a very good technology licensing office. Built on the Stanford model by former Stanford staff, it is widely considered to be a model of industry-friendly licensing. It is small wonder that hundreds of less friendly OTLs, all aimed at maximizing both their ownership and their short-term returns, create a climate that many companies find chilling.

R. Stanley Williams—my director of nanotechnology research and a valued advisor when I was with Hewlett-Packard—has been an outspoken critic of the way American higher education has interpreted Bayh-Dole and the anticompetitive measures they have put in place to deal with industry collaborators:

Typically at present, negotiating a contract to perform collaborative research with an American university takes one to two years of exchanging emails by attorneys, punctuated by long telephone conference calls involving the scientists who wish to work together. All too often, the company spends more on attorneys' fees than the value of the contract being negotiated. This situation has driven many large companies away from working with American universities altogether, and they are looking for alternate research partners.

Large U.S.-based corporations have become so disheartened and disgusted with the situation [negotiating IP rights with U.S. universities], they are now working with foreign universities, especially the elite institutions in France, Russia, and China, which are more than willing to offer extremely favorable intellectual property terms.[11]

Stan Williams knows what he is talking about. A former UCLA professor, Williams is tasked with building the next fundamental technology for HP based on the science of molecules and materials that exist only at the scale of one billionth of a meter. It will be a trillion-dollar market, but he knows that HP cannot create it alone. Williams tells Congress on a regular basis about the negative impact of Bayh-Dole on this kind of collaboration, and he says it with the same force and conviction that he used when he walked into my office one morning in the fall of 2000 and fired a warning shot to which American universities have yet to respond:

Many high-quality foreign universities are very eager to work with American companies, and by keeping attorneys out of the discussion completely they have streamlined processes to allow a successful negotiation to take place in literally a few minutes over the telephone. It is possible to specify what one wants to a professor at a university in China or Russia and then issue a purchase order to obtain a particular deliverable. The deliverable is received and verified to be satisfactory before the American company pays for it, and in this case the American company owns all rights to the deliverable and the process by which it was created.

American colleges and universities—at the urging of the federal government—are not only diverting funds to technology licensing offices that ultimately drain education and research resources, but are also weakening their global advantage at the very time when foreign universities are awakening to the need for open innovation. At a 2007 Association of University Technology Managers (AUTM) meeting attended by 1,700 technology licensing professionals, former Senator Birch Bayh urged members to fight any erosion of Bayh-Dole. In fact, his message was to expand and strengthen the act and to export it to Germany, Japan, and Ireland. The message was received. AUTM lobbied the U.S. Department of Energy to enact licensing regulations that are stricter than Bayh-Dole would have required for a new initiative that will be jointly funded by industry and government.

American universities do not have a stranglehold on innovation. In Asia alone, there are a dozen innovation hubs that combine close university collaboration with sources of capital and expertise to seed new ventures.

Those universities understand that their role is not to build another cathedral. Rather than enriching themselves, they have a mission to help create a community of successful entrepreneurs, to enrich entire nations. It is an attractive message for American researchers. An American biochemist who spends half of her time at Singapore's biotechnology hub told me that "emigration is a real possibility. I am Asian, so I feel completely comfortable over here [in Singapore]. I can bring my best students. I don't have to spend half my time writing grant proposals. I can work with the same companies that I work with in Cambridge, and best of all, I am not hassled when it comes time to decide what to do with my research results."

This is a time when there are abundant choices in higher education, and American universities are behaving as if they are entitled to a monopoly on creativity and invention. If Stan Williams is right, then this is a strategy that makes American institutions less competitive.

8 The Factory

The structure of mainstream American universities was decided in the early twentieth century, well before the great influx of students to public institutions, pressure for academic specialization, and growth of research that shaped higher education after World War II. No other modern enterprise has been as untouched by changes in markets, demographics, and economies as the American institution of higher learning.

At the end of the American Civil War, shortly after the passage of the Morrill Act, barely sixty-three thousand students were enrolled in widely scattered colleges and universities. University attendance was rare: only 1.3 percent of all 18- to 24-year-olds enrolled in postsecondary schools of any kind. University enrollments grew by a staggering 22,600 percent during the next century: in 1995, a vast network of thousands of institutions enrolled fourteen million students, almost 57 percent of all 18- to 24-year-olds. Higher education grew thirty-two times faster than the country itself, and by virtually any measure of economic output and growth, eclipsed manufacturing and other sectors of the economy many times over. In the process, universities were transformed from the exclusive havens of clergy and the nation's urban upper crust to institutions serving the needs of growing middle, working, and immigrant classes.

Numbered Napkin Rings

In 1869, the question of how to organize a college was not a settled matter. It had been less than a half-century since Thomas Jefferson experimented with university structure and instruction when he founded the University of Virginia. A confusing array of church-related schools that imposed denominational requirements on students, teachers, and curriculum made the situation even more chaotic. But the Morrill Act would be a vehicle for channeling public funds to higher education.

When it created the land grant colleges, Congress also made stakeholders out the state and federal governments. From that point on, responsible management in higher education was a public concern. Before the Civil War, a typical university could be run by three administrators: a president, a treasurer, and a librarian. In 1860, the median number of administrators was four—a number that would prove to be woefully inadequate to run the new institutions—but the newcomers were so focused on trying to emulate the more respected and established institutions in the East that they found themselves completely unprepared for what happened next. Even the traditional role of a president was not understood well enough to be a useful guide for the new land grant colleges.

Purdue University in West Lafayette, Indiana, became one of the first beneficiaries of the Morrill Act when John Purdue made his gift to the citizens of Indiana and established a campus devoted to the agricultural and mechanical arts. Purdue's trustees set out to find a suitable leader for their thirty-nine students—someone who, in addition to academic skills, was up to the task of managing Purdue's six buildings and other assets. Their first choice was a sitting president, William S. Clark, president of Massachusetts Agricultural College. When he turned them down, they turned to an eminent local scholar, Richard Owen, the son of the utopian founder of New Harmony, Indiana. Owen had a medical degree and was already on the faculty at Indiana University where he taught science, the military arts, and foreign languages. His breadth of knowledge and prior experience was exactly what Purdue's trustees were looking for. The university was in need of definition, and Richard Owen's legacy was to have been the creation of curriculum and academic departments and the hiring of faculty in preparation for the rapid growth that a midwestern school specializing in the practical arts would surely experience.

Instead, Owen's first priority as president was to devise a scheme for assigning numbers to students that could be sewn into their clothing and other items such as towels and table napkins and used to organize all aspects of their lives on the new campus. He was particularly concerned that students take their correct places at dining tables and went to the trouble of designing numbered napkin rings for that purpose. He went on to nail down the details of faculty housing and dinner menus. His detailed plans were contained in a lengthy and widely distributed document. It was such an embarrassment that it was recalled, but not before local and national publications got their hands on it and held it up to ridicule. In 1874, less than two years after his appointment as Purdue's first president, and before assuming the duties of his office, Richard Owen stepped aside.

Public institutions grew quickly, and their boards of trustees were forced to take more forceful measures to organize their universities. Fortunately, most of them found more focused leadership. By 1900, the total number of college students had nearly quadrupled. There are few records from 1869 to 1929 that indicate the relative growth of public and private colleges, but enrollment statistics[1] show that enrollment in Yale College tripled in those years. Many other private universities evidently did see the same surge: by 1929, there were approximately equal numbers of students enrolled in public and private institutions.

Purdue's experience with Richard Owen must have been rare, because the land grant universities were soon overrun with administrators—nonprofessors who were responsible for financial and clerical matters—who all seemed to know what to do. Steep enrollment increases meant that there were new demands for services that professors did not like to provide, a fortunate turn of events, because they were in most cases not very good at it. Growth in size meant growth in the *administration*, new professionals who would be responsible for admissions, record keeping, and financial management. By 1929, the median number of administrators at an American university had grown from the Civil War level of four to more than thirty. Like the licensing managers who formed AUTM decades later, university administrators set up professional societies to share information and promote their own roles. With a few exceptions, administrators had little impact on the shape of their institutions, which by and large continued with the methods of governance that had been promoted by Johns Hopkins and a few other colleges nearly a hundred years before. Even legislatures took a backseat, but there were moderating forces.

One consequence of the growth in administration meant the emergence of *deans*, administrators who owed their allegiance to the faculty, curriculum, students, and institution in equal measure. A dean could be a moderating influence. As a faculty-centered university created an atmosphere of increasing scholarship and specialization, deans could "maintain human values" and resist "a full swing to intellectualism of their faculty."[2] But by far the most influential forces were the philanthropic foundations of the famous industrialists of the early twentieth century.

Philanthropy and Influence

John D. Rockefeller amassed a fund of more than $180 million to support colleges, medical schools, and in the liberal tradition of northeastern industrialists, schools for southern black students. Rockefeller was interested that his funds be put to good use and established the General Education Board to coordinate his gifts and grants. The General Education Board helped institutionalize sound administrative practices, making awards to eliminate duplication and introducing modern accounting and personnel practices, including pensions for university professors.

Andrew Carnegie's foundation and corporations added another $182 million and also established some basic standards—like requiring all department heads to have earned PhDs—for institutions to be eligible to receive a Carnegie gift.

It must have been incomprehensible to Rockefeller and Carnegie, who were responsible for so many modern industrial practices, that higher education, under the stewardship of state and federal legislatures, had failed to anticipate even the most basic consequences of growth:

> The states have not generally shown themselves to be competent to deal with higher education on a nonpartisan, impersonal and comprehensive basis. . . . Rival religious bodies have invaded fields fully occupied already; misguided individuals have founded a new college instead of strengthening an old one.[3]

Foundations were alarmed that students were admitted using the flimsiest excuses for standards, that educational experiences in one institution had no obvious relationship to experiences in others, and that there was not even agreement as to what constituted an academic unit of achievement.

University presidents were fiercely protective of their rights—and the rights of their faculty—to make such decisions without consultation. Some, like Ethelbert D. Arfield of Lafayette College, were not shy about declaring their independence from externally imposed standards:

> Lafayette College does not intend to be told by any board whom to admit and whom not to admit. If we wish to admit the son of a benefactor, or of a Trustee, or of a member of the Faculty and such will benefit the institution we are not going to be prevented from taking it.[4]

The forces for shaping American higher education came not from within academia—a loosely federated collection of cultures and societies focused on narrow goals—but from an outcry to bring order from chaos. That the outcry would come from the holders of the purse strings, who also knew something about the power of standardization to smooth over the impact of warring factions, presaged much of what followed in the story of twentieth-century colleges and universities:

> The truth of the matter was that national growth and collegiate and university growth, both public and private demanded something more than the chaos that had been traditional in American higher education. The foundations, using money

as a lever, became one of many agencies for bringing order into American high education, for standardizing, for organizing the academic community along chosen, rational lines.[5]

In the eyes of administrators, the cry for "order from chaos" had to be answered. Increasing enrollments meant increasing numbers of students in classrooms, and because labor costs were outpacing budgets, the question of how to scale classroom delivery of courses in the face of explosive growth could not be avoided much longer. Specialization was the enemy of growth, because specialization meant one professor in front of a smaller class. The problem that administrators faced was how to get more productivity from a university faculty without increasing labor or operating expenses.

But the problems went well beyond the classroom. Everywhere they turned, foundations found tangles of special rules and agreements that made it impossible to control either costs or quality. The foundations were run by industrialists—men who had faced problems like these in their plants and factories—and they insisted on modern business methods to shape the academic workplace. They demanded standardization, beginning with admissions.

Credits and Accreditation

At the end of the nineteenth century, there was no agreement on what constituted readiness for university study. Every applicant had to be considered on his own merits because there was no way to say what college preparation was. Harvard's Charles Eliot led the formation of the College Entrance Exam Board. Academic conferences to decide on uniform preparation in standard subjects like English were common. Agreement on a national secondary school curriculum was needed, and in 1892, the National Education Association appointed a Committee of Ten to oversee the development of such a curriculum. The ultimate in standards was an agreement about what should constitute a unit of admission credit—still called the *Carnegie credit unit*—for graduating high school students. But secondary school quality varied greatly, and mere completion of a standard high school curriculum said little about the quality of the student. It did not even guarantee adherence to the standard. New tools would be needed to measure the preparation of an individual student. Those tools were already being used in industry.

Factory plant managers had already discovered that manufacturing specifications were meaningless without the ability to test compliance. Academic planners reasoned that the same should be true for higher education. Every secondary school student with college aspirations was channeled to one or more of the standard college entrance examinations. The examinations themselves became more sophisticated in content and variety.

Shortly after the end of World War II, the percentage of high school graduates enrolled in universities jumped to 10 percent of all 18- to 24-year-olds, and the independent agencies that had been set up thirty years before found themselves swamped with ten times the number of applicants than they had been designed to handle. The workload was so staggering that even automation did not help. The American Council on Education, which had been founded in 1918, was one of the first to adopt punch-card data processing methods, but there were other problems with testing that automation alone could not solve. The College Entrance Exam Board and the Carnegie Foundation still used a patchwork of tests that were costly to administer. The tests were also problematic for students who—not knowing which results were acceptable to which institutions—were sometimes required to take multiple batteries of tests.

By the time the postwar growth spurt had begun, three of the largest testing services created a nonprofit corporation called Educational Testing Services (ETS) to develop and administer the standardized tests. The existing testing services did not necessarily disappear, however. Even today, ETS contracts about a quarter of its work to the College Board—the modern-day remnant of John D. Rockefeller's College Entrance Exam Board—that administers the ubiquitous SAT examination.

Admission requirements were not the only aspect of academics in need of standardization. In the 1800s, regional associations of universities were able to maintain lists of accredited institutions that were thought by their peers to offer sufficient academic quality to warrant the granting of degrees. The rise of land grant colleges, the rise of elective programs of study—and the collapse of a compulsory core college curriculum—meant new disciplines and a diversity of institutions. Some of the new schools were little more than diploma mills for worthless medical and business degrees or seminaries controlled by denominations that for one reason or another did not believe that their interests were being served by larger, more established institutions.

Specialization made it harder to answer the question "What is a college?" By 1935, there were forty-eight specialized associations, each concerned with program quality. Some were activist and intervened to make sure that states responsibly administered the state universities, but others were purely bureaucratic—stopgaps imposed by funding agencies to give themselves cover.

A large increase in students also meant a large increase in federal funding for returning servicemen. The Social Security and Veteran's Administrations used no standards at all; ultimately, federal agencies were created to coordinate state efforts. Layers of legislation like the 1952 Veteran's Readjustment Assistance Act gave authority to nongovernmental accrediting agencies for determining the quality of education and training of institutions of higher education. Those agencies for the most part adopted the same quality control disciplines that had been introduced to the factory floor a generation earlier.

By 1979, the U.S. Department of Education had officially recognized seven separate goals for accreditation, in addition to certifying that an institution has met standards and making sure that prospective students could identify acceptable institutions. Accrediting agencies were also permitted to help determine when credits were transferrable from one school to another, for example. Sometimes, as was the case with Eugene Talmadge's crusade to rid the University of Georgia of politically unacceptable behavior, agencies used the power of accreditation to protect academic programs against outside pressure. The portfolio of services offered by accrediting agencies and boards grew as they acquired staff and broad popular support, but the new services took them farther afield from their original purpose, diverting resources from operating educational programs to the bureaucracy of accrediting them.

Not content just with administering standards, for example, accrediting agencies became concerned with raising goals, helping weaker programs to improve, and involving faculty and staff in "institutional planning and evaluation." The irony that it was in the interests of relieving professors of unnecessary administrative tasks that academic administrative services were invented in the first place is not lost on critics of accrediting practices.

There are faculty members whose professional preferences steer them toward curriculum committees, accrediting boards, and standard-setting organizations, but even this strikes a discordant note on some campuses. Most academic departments welcome peer reviews. Review and constructive criticism are built into the open nature of academic life, and most institutions conduct self-evaluations with the help of *committees of visitors*, peers invited from similar academic departments to give their candid views on matters ranging from the quality of the faculty to the adequacy of institutional resources. These are not the committees that accrediting agencies send to conduct reviews.

Accrediting review teams are selected by the accrediting agencies and—in an attempt to create an unbiased team—they may contain representatives from wildly different institutions. A common suspicion at Élite institutions is that professors who serve on accreditation panels are often from less prestigious departments than the ones that they are evaluating, an idea that often casts doubt on critical recommendations that can be dismissed as "sticking it to the big guys." Even the on-campus organizations established to manage accreditation and reviews can be staffed by faculty members who are prone to display their authority, often at the expense of other campus leaders. The second most common complaint about accreditation is that accreditation teams are unqualified to judge program effectiveness. The most common complaint is the arrogance of the campus office managing accreditation.

What to Measure

A question that is much asked but seldom answered is exactly what in a multiversity should be measured. One common belief is that the modern university, like other modern enterprises, needs only to be instrumented and the resulting measurements gathered for analysis. It should be a straightforward task—no different from astronomical measurement or public opinion monitoring, the argument goes—but for distracting discussions of values and the inherent aversion of professors to being held accountable:

Improvement and change have no meaning without measurement. Much university conversation in the public sector involves complex, uplifting, and even entertaining controversy about the values and academic directions of the institution. Much public conversation turns on elaborate discussions of accountability and governance. Most of this is charming, well intentioned, but ultimately ineffective because it does not start with the measurable things. Universities, like all enterprises, cannot manage improvement unless they can measure the improvement. Academic measurement is the simplest of concepts and the most difficult of enterprises. University people have an aversion to self-measurement. Experts in the measurement of every other quantity in the universe from attitudes to behavior, from physical to cosmological quantities, academics resist the aggregate measurement of their own work.[6]

In this view, it is only the resistance of the institution that prevents management by modern quantitative tools. There are other views, however, that question exactly which aspects of academic performance are subject to measurement at all. Critics point to research as a function of the university that sounds like it should be easy to measure, but in practice resists even the most sophisticated quantitative tools.

The research enterprise is critically important in a modern multiversity, but study after study has concluded that research productivity, when measured, is like a puppy chasing its own tail—it measures only the factors used to define productivity. Take patent impact, for example. This seems at first blush to be a well-defined indicator of both research quality and output. However, data shows that the factor that correlates best with patent quality is research volume. That is, the quality of research output apparently depends more or less completely on research expenditures.[7] The same is true for graduate programs. It is possible to measure laboratory space, ratios of graduate students to professors, and research funding, but whether there is any correlation to graduate program quality—above and beyond subjective reputational rankings—has never been established.

The methods used for assessing undergraduate program quality are in even more disarray. In part IV of this book, I will talk about the gap between the "factory" models of output quality and the indicators of actual quality that have value to students, but the data are sparse and not very encouraging. Program quality assessment is based on something called *outcomes-based assessment* or *OBA*. OBA is a method for relating stated learning outcomes for a course to quantities that can be tested and measured. Accreditation panels require volumes of OBA data to be recorded. Faculty members are supposed to examine these outcomes and—in a process that looks like industrial quality improvement—provide mechanisms for incrementally improving their offerings so that stated outcomes can be achieved.

There are critics who say that OBA and other factory models of assessing quality are fundamentally flawed and that the handicraft nature of the educational enterprise dooms all but the most primitive attempts to quantify it. There are others who say that there are more direct, less intrusive measures of program effectiveness that are not nearly so convoluted. The British Higher Education Statistics Agency (HESA), for example, tracks both short-term and long-term employment for graduates of its accredited colleges and universities. HESA stunned British taxpayers last year when it announced that almost a quarter of the accredited university graduates from 2005 to 2008 had failed to find full- or part-time employment.[8] Furthermore, the correlation between reputational rankings and employability was nearly perfect.

Not in dispute is the growth of regulatory paperwork in American colleges. Added to the nongovernmental requirements for accreditation are the federal regulations under which most institutions labor. There are federal mandates that cover personnel, students, laboratories, and the environment. Some, like the A-21 Cost Circular enacted in the 1980s to restrict the growth of unchecked "overhead costs" on government contracts,[9] require monthly reporting by university faculty members of time spent on various activities, a fiction that is maintained by many institutions only by allowing professors to enter default accounting percentages in lieu of actual time reporting. Others, like the Federal Education Rights and Privacy Act,[10] or FERPA, put university administrators in the position of policing professors' records and outlawing the time-honored teachers' grade book.

Universities that receive federal funding are required to operate institutional review boards (IRB) or risk steep penalties. Originally established to protect human subjects from the most heinous medical and psychological abuses, IRBs are now an expensive part of the landscape for most colleges and universities. Their role has expanded to include virtually every kind of data that might be gathered from human subjects, including benign questionnaire and survey responses. Professors and graduate students often find their work delayed by months while a panel of reviewers—who may know little about the subject matter—pore over descriptions of research methodologies to determine the appropriateness of administering a classroom survey.

What Should We Manufacture?

There are currently seven regional accrediting agencies. In addition to those seven, church-operated schools report to one of four faith-based agencies, and professional schools must undergo accreditation by up to two career-related offices. Finally, academic degrees are covered by forty-six programmatic agencies. A given university may find itself under the control of sixty or more separate accrediting organizations and a dozen government agencies. Public institutions undergo review by state boards of trustees, and many professional societies that sponsor curricula require periodic peer review. A recent report of the National Commission on the Cost of Higher Education estimated that an institution like Stanford spends more than twenty million dollars per year—almost eight cents of every tuition dollar—on accrediting and compliance that offer little value to students. It recommended rethinking the entire accreditation process:

The cost of accreditation has also increased in recent years. There has been significant growth in the number of accrediting bodies, particularly specialized ones. Currently, accrediting activities are undertaken by approximately 60 specialized agencies overseeing more than 100 different types of academic programs. Institutions report that the self-study procedures involved with these accrediting efforts overlap and duplicate one another and absorb large amounts of faculty and administrator time. . . . The Commission believes a great deal of improvement is possible in developing both accrediting standards and evaluation review processes that focus directly on student learning. It believes accreditation should encourage a greater focus at both the program and institutional level on productivity and efficiency.[11]

Not all of the world's universities carry this kind of baggage, and when there are abundant choices in higher education, nimble institutions are more competitive.

Every aspect of academic life in America has been penetrated by the language and thought of the leaders who were the most influential people at the time that universities were trying to define themselves and find their footing. They happened also to be the leaders of an industrial expansion that would last for most of the twentieth century. It is no wonder that their concept of what a successful enterprise should be like was the one that prevailed. Under their influence, the modern American university was crafted to look like a factory:

On one assembly line the academicians, the scholars were at work; from time to time they left their assembly line long enough to oil and grease the student assembly line. . . . Above them . . . were the managers—the white-collared chief executive officers and their assistants. . . . The absentee stockholders sometimes called alumni, the board of directors . . . the untapped capital resources known as benefactors . . . the regulatory agencies and commissions in charge of standards.[12]

By the beginning of World War I, what it meant to be an organized academic institution had been more or less decided. The problem was that the implications of what it meant to be a modern academic institution—organized or not—were not yet apparent. It would be another thirty years before the real shape of American higher education became discernible. Enrollments at public universities in the second half of the century would grow at stunning rates (see figure 8.1), while traditional private universities, whose models of governance and funding were adopted by public

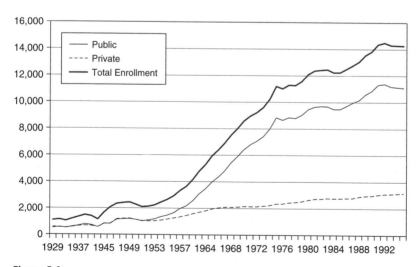

Figure 8.1
Enrollment growth 1929–1995.

universities, would grow hardly at all. For-Profit institutions had not yet made their appearance. Europe, India, and China had not yet appeared as serious challengers to the coming dominance of American universities.

By 1950, the factories had been built. The plant managers had been hired. The investors, assembly line workers, and regulatory bodies were all in place. A discipline of quality control was being instilled in the workforce. But neither the items that were to be manufactured nor those who would buy them had been decided.

9 Disruption

The president of a major research university once showed me an email message that he had just received from an alumnus:

I don't care about academics at all. And I don't want you to spend any of my money on it. The *only* thing I care about is winning football games. And if you can't get that right, I am not giving you another penny.

It was not an unusual letter, he told me, and it depressed him. Despite the doubts of some, most presidents think that intercollegiate athletics is a positive force for the university—a front porch that only expands the potential donor base and does not compete with academic fundraising—according to many interviewed for a 2009 study by the Knight Commission. Revisiting a 2008 report of the NCAA president observing that the cost of athletics programs was growing at an unsustainable rate—and citing a faculty critic who wondered, "What's the justification for a public university directing 60 percent of its capital expenditures over an entire decade toward a nonacademic auxiliary unit whose annual budget is only 8 percent of the entire university?"—the Knight Commission reported:

It is clear that the question for many presidents . . . is not whether the current model is sustainable but, given the forces at work, how long it can be sustained.[1]

A winning athletic program is just one institutional ambition, but the idea of *winning* dominates goal setting in the Middle. When it comes to setting goals, having a winning research program is right up there with athletics, but for more complex reasons. Faculty career aspirations drive investment—often despite institutional strategy. Professors who are not at research institutions collaborate with former classmates and other colleagues at more highly ranked universities. Alumni—perhaps motivated by patent licensing and economic development success stories—lobby senior administrators for more aggressive research programs. Presidents want a bold story to tell donors. By a sizeable majority, however, universities in the Middle enter the research game for financial reasons.

Institutions that are ranked lower in the Carnegie hierarchy plan to chase those with more prestigious research profiles by more aggressively pursuing federal research funds. They argue not only that the volume of research attracts more talented professors, but that research dollars are a much-needed supplement to a shrinking base of unrestricted revenues. In fact, the opposite is true. Research rarely pays for itself in the Middle, and universities subsidize growth in research by diverting funds from educational programs.

Athletics, research, and dozens of other institutional ambitions to climb the hierarchy are seldom central to education; and pursuing programs that are peripheral to the educational mission is a major reason that costs are rising in the Middle. As tuitions rise, institutions in the Middle find that some of their best students—their bread and butter—are now recruiting targets for Élite universities, while others—those who are simply priced out of the market—broaden their search for alternative choices.

There is also disruption from below. *Value students* compare the benefits of For-Profit institutions—often priced higher than their traditional counterparts—and choose the flexibility, services, and experience of online programs. In the past, these were nontraditional students, not part of the 18- to 24-year-old pool that dominate the fifteen million currently enrolled. Today, value students are drawn from the same pool of applicants that enroll in the Middle. In order to compete for these students, an institution in the Middle needs two things: an equally compelling value proposition and a way to deliver it at reasonable cost. Both require reinvention. Many traditional universities in the Middle find themselves not only unable to articulate their value, but also unable to reinvent themselves. It is not clear how much disruption the two thousand universities in the Middle can tolerate, but for many, resources are already stressed beyond the breaking point.

Aspirations

The most striking thing about inaugural addresses of university presidents is that they are devoid of aspirations. Political leaders use their inaugurals to outline not only the great goals that the electorate ratified—and now expect them to achieve—but also how they will depart from the ways of their predecessors. Newly installed corporate leaders announce product plans or a strategy to achieve market supremacy. An archbishop signals to his flock what will be expected of them.

Apple CEO Steve Jobs waited a year to give his inaugural speech. But when he did—the keynote address at the 1998 MacWorld Conference—he left little doubt that the meandering course that Apple had set in recent years was not going to be tolerated in the future. It was less than six months after the company had been rescued from a death spiral. After recounting the chaos of past Apple product strategy, Jobs announced, "If we had four great products, that's all we'd need."

New York Mayor Fiorello Laguardia was sworn in on New Year's Day, 1934. He did not give a traditional inaugural address, but mindful that faith in the New York City government was important to the county, he did give a national radio address, proclaiming:

New York City was restored to the people this morning at one minute after midnight. It is my duty from now on to guard and protect and guide the complete, peaceful, and undisturbed enjoyment of that possession.

It is the norm for a leader of any sizable enterprise to use the occasion of an inauguration to set the stage for what is to come. It is not the norm in academic life. The soaring inaugural addresses of Daniel Gilman and Charles Eliot are overshadowed by the crushing silence of most newly elevated university presidents, who seem unwilling to articulate either personal or institutional aspirations. The speeches of university presidents resemble not so much inaugurals as sermons intended to help the audience along a pathway whose origin and destinations were both set long ago. They are generic. For the most part, they could be swapped among presidents and no one in the audience would be any the wiser. These are speeches of stewardship, not aspiration.

University of Illinois professor Eldon Johnson analyzed all of the inaugural speeches of state university presidents given prior to 1860:

Examination of the addresses has yielded findings which can best be presented in relationship to five intellectual themes . . . (1) the reflection of self-conscious nationalism in new educational institutions to match the new republic, (2) the emphasis on character building, morality, and discipline in student relationships, (3) educational concern for, if not involvement in, the "big issues" out in society, (4) the secularization of the state university and with the emergence of strong progressive devotion to science, (5) the changing relation between higher education and church and state.[2]

These are addresses that proclaim the superiority of the American ideal and connect the "Christian ideals" of training the mind with the discipline to be imposed on students, faculty, and presidents who stray too far from it. Despite rhetoric about the "well-being of society,"

there was little interest in external affairs of the time and an appalling indifference to the great issues later defined by history.[3]

They set a high moral tone, but among all the inaugural speeches before 1860, there is not a single direct reference to slavery or the role that universities and enlightened citizens might play in abolishing it. On the great social issues of the day, modern presidents have not been so reticent. Dwight Eisenhower, for example, used his 1948 Columbia inaugural to foreshadow the danger that "arises from too great a concentration of power in the hands of any individual or group," but on the nature of his forthcoming presidency, he would only commit "to devote my energies to the support of Columbia's able and distinguished faculty, in the service of America, in the service of all humanity." In her 2007 inaugural speech, Harvard's Drew Gilpen Faust took on the "host of popular writings from the 1980s [that] charged universities with teaching too little, costing too much, coddling professors and neglecting students," by noting:

Universities like Harvard and its peers, those represented by so many of you here today, are beloved by alumni who donate billions of dollars each year, are sought after by students who struggle to win admission, and in fact, are deeply revered by the American public.

She went on to promise accountability for Harvard's future—a future shared by Élite institutions and perhaps so well understood that further elaboration would not be useful.

But what about the institutions in the Middle? In the Middle, presidential speeches emulate Columbia and Harvard. They routinely promise to "cultivate in our students profound professional expertise," "encourag[ing] leadership across the university," and "be inclusive not exclusive in service to a diverse student body."

Northwestern's Morton Shapiro explained the rationale for his inaugural speech:

I don't view inauguration speeches as the place to lay out grand strategic plans, especially since I've been part of this community for all of six weeks. I've mainly been listening rather than talking, and I'll continue to do so for some time before I feel qualified to present my thoughts about the Northwestern of the future.

Yet nearly every president quickly takes action. Sometimes actions are forced on presidents by external events—an economic downturn that crushes the budget, a tragedy that demands administrative response, a gift that changes the course of the institution. More often, however, modern presidential actions are guided by carefully crafted strategic plans that have been developed throughout many months in taskforces, retreats, and town hall meetings. A typical university strategic plan emphasizes strong, action-oriented concepts like winning, achieving research excellence, fundraising, service, improving reputation, and student achievement.

There is no doubt that newly named presidents know that these are the directions toward which their energies will be directed. Leaders of Élite universities take on agenda-setting, aspirational projects. Presidents in the Middle with high aspirations, but—with meager resources to match them—chart courses to take them from the Middle to the top by emulating the Élites. Their presidents spend much of their time with alumni, students, peers, and friends of the institution. But for the most part, presidents spend their time with their faculty—the same faculty whose careers are bound to the inconsistent nature of the multiversity.

The Price Tag for Ambition

Michael Crow's 2002 inauguration as the sixteenth president of Arizona State University was unusual precisely because he was specific about his plans for the university, a sweeping vision that he called the New Gold Standard for a New American University. Much like Steve Jobs's 1998 speech, Crow committed ASU to clear aspirations: to focus on the social outcome of research, to be an academic enterprise, "a force, not only a place." It was an ambitious inaugural address that sought to redefine what it means to be a public institution in the twenty-first century.

The price tag for academic ambition, however, is high. As reported in *The Chronicle of Higher Education*,[4] the University of Kansas, in expanding its faculty, staff, and facilities during the last twenty years, has nearly doubled its state budget to $150.6 million. The downside of this impressive growth is that it represents an overall 50 percent decline in the proportion of total operating costs covered by the state.

Today, like most top public universities, the flagship campus in Kansas relies on the state of Kansas for about 20 percent of its operating costs. The gap has been filled by research funding and private donations, but the largest component of new funding in Kansas has come from increases in tuition and fees. Since it was granted autonomy to set its own tuition and control its own spending, the University of Kansas has raised its student costs at three times the rate of inflation.

Do these increases translate into value for students? It sounds like it, because according to the *Chronicle*, much of this new funding has been directed to enhance learning experiences: new faculty, counselors and success centers, and programs such as writing centers and special programs for learning disabled students.

But some of these funds are also used for marketing—Kansas, for example, sends a quarterly newsletter to parents. The Kansas Student Success Office is staffed by 850 academic and nonacademic professionals and is managed by a vice provost. Research buildings and equipment; multimedia-enabled classrooms and language labs; programs to increase the effectiveness of classroom teachers; and infrastructure such as computers, networking, and power have also received a significant infusion of new investment.

New faculty and staff increase costs beyond salaries and wages. Laboratories and expensive equipment can add a million dollars or more to the cost of attracting a senior professor in the sciences, and the continuing costs of maintaining an experimental research program in science and engineering easily doubles the annual expenditures for personnel costs. Like many other industries, health care consumes an increasing share of the Kansas personnel costs, rising 290 percent over the last twenty years.

Like others in the Middle, Kansas also expanded its research programs. I have already described in chapters 6 and 7 some of the ways in which funds are diverted in research universities, but lofty ambitions can raise overall costs in much more subtle ways. In a research university, professors staff new programs, centers, and laboratories, which means that many faculty spend fewer hours in the classroom. This is an effective increase in the cost of faculty, a cost that is funded by institutional resources and passed along as increased costs per student, but it is not the determining factor in overall costs. Costs associated with faculty have been shrinking as a proportion of institutional costs for at least a decade. Rising costs and cash-starved state budgets have put particular pressure on public institutions because they must continually sell their value to increasingly impatient taxpayers.

Arizona State University, like all public universities, relies on the state for partial support of its programmatic mission. Today, state funding accounts for only 20 percent of the university's total budget, making it comparable to other top-ranked research universities. It has been an accelerating transformation for ASU—part of what ASU president Michael Crow calls a *reconceptualization*—from a regional university to a research institution with national standing and global reach. Just at the point when there were signs that its agenda was succeeding, the university was forced to confront the impact of a budget crisis of historic proportions.

In a public and bitter 2009 budget clash with members of the Arizona legislature, ASU threatened to scale back on its ambitions rather than divert funds or raise tuition.[5] Arizona spends approximately $12,500 per student, a number already well below the national average of $14,058. It is a cost that is divided approximately equally between state subsidies and student tuition ($5,923). That makes today's state support on a per-student basis almost exactly what it was in 1980, before the university undertook its ambitious plan. The state subsidy is also below international averages. The average amount of money paid from public funds in the thirty member nations of the Organization for Economic Cooperation and Development is a little more than $8,100 per student. Michael Crow's commitment to increased access to ASU and promoting an improved quality of life across the state does not seem to be falling disproportionately on the shoulders of Arizona taxpayers.

ASU regarded tuition increases as a last resort, but according to the Delta Project, tuition increases outpaced all other revenue sources for both public and private universities. The largest increases were in public research universities, and most of these funds did not end up in classrooms. In fact, the Delta Project estimates that among all expense categories at all institutions except for community and two-year colleges, instruction ranked nearly dead last[6] in benefitting from tuition increases. Instead, tuition increases made up for lost revenue.

Tuition increases have prompted a public focus on university costs. One national survey measured public attitudes about costs and reported that 54 percent of the respondents believe that "Colleges could spend less and still maintain a high quality of education."[7] According to a report of the National Center for Public Policy and Higher Education, the cost of higher education at the nation's colleges and universities has risen four times faster than the overall cost of living.[8]

University presidents argue that students have received overall improvements in success factors in return, like completion rates. But as these factors have improved, colleges and universities have become increasingly less affordable to families: forty-three states failed to receive passing affordability grades according to a recent report card issued by the National Center for Public Policy and Higher Education.[9] Figure 9.1 is a graphic depiction of this failure. Over the last quarter-century, college tuition has grown 375 percent, nearly one and a half times the next most volatile component of costs that consumers bear: health care.

This is an "Are you teaching this summer?" moment, a disconnect of enormous proportions in which universities and the public at large have very different viewpoints. The National Center for Public Policy and Higher Education interviewed twenty-eight university presidents about costs, access, and quality at their institutions. By and large, universities argue for increasing the public's share of the financial burden of operating their institutions:

Most of our respondents called for a major rethinking and reprioritization of the role of higher education, which would translate into significant public reinvestment in higher education. Although most are not optimistic that this will actually happen, many strongly believe that governments should define higher education as a public good (which should be supported by the community), rather than as a private good

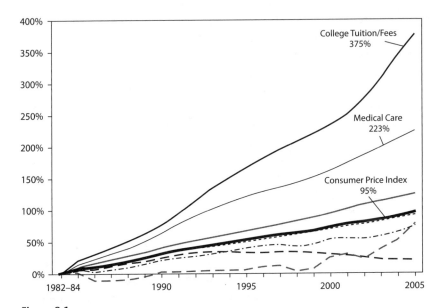

Figure 9.1
Tuition costs 1982–2006.
Permission to reprint granted by National Center for Public Policy and Higher Education.

(which should be supported by individuals). And they feel that such a definition should lead to greater funding for higher education.[10]

Surveys of public attitudes, on the other hand, show little patience for this view:

We find no sympathy for the argument that colleges and universities are starved for financial resources. If higher education leaders want to make the argument for a significant reinvestment in higher education, they may find that their words fall on deaf ears given the public's current state of mind.[11]

Mission Creep

At least one university president can put his finger on a root cause of the decreasing affordability of a college degree. Universities are trying to increase their value:

I think it is true that schools want to grow out of their mission. I think that it's a natural for any organization to want to move up the pecking order—and there are definitely pecking orders in higher education. Just look at community colleges.

Community colleges are doing a whole lot more these days than they used to, such as economic development. I don't know whether you call it mission creep or whatever, but it is definitely becoming rampant.[12]

What happens when value delivered to a marketplace comes at a cost that is increasingly unaffordable to customers? Harvard Business School's Clayton Christensen has studied this question extensively:

In their efforts to provide better products than their competitors and earn higher prices and margins, suppliers often "overshoot" their market: They give customers more than they need or ultimately are willing to pay for. And, more importantly, it means that disruptive technologies that may underperform today relative to what users in the market demand, may be fully performance-competitive in that same market tomorrow.[13]

This is the *innovator's dilemma*: in order for a business performing well at the high end of its market—making sustained progress by listening to its customers and investing in the features, products, and services that the market apparently demands—to anticipate a disruptive technology that will in the long run hollow out the leader's value, the leader must stop—or at least reduce—investing in the sustaining improvements that have made it successful and begin investing in an inadequate approach that has little market acceptance today. The dilemma is that it requires management to do something that is, in essence, irrational. The list of products that have disrupted existing markets is long and ranges from digital photography— which disrupted silver halide photographic film photography—to electric minimills that crippled the U.S. steel industry.

The same dilemma faces university presidents. The Knight Commission noted as much by underscoring the decreasing affordability of intercollegiate athletics:

A president of a university with a particularly successful equity program warned, "We'll get to the point where we literally can't do it. And we're one of the rich schools. TV contracts won't continue to grow. The money will cut itself off. We're going the way of NASCAR, which priced itself out of its market by building too many training facilities and the like."[14]

It is not only cathedrals to house supercomputers, expensive technology transfer offices, and cost-shifting that threaten to overshoot the higher education market in the United States. It is growth in the number and kind of institutional priorities, and it is the kind of mission creep that seems irresistible to multiversities. Here is just a small sample of the ways that American colleges and universities have found to expand their missions:

1 Simulated stock markets   In an effort to capture students during the explosive growth of financial markets that ended abruptly in 2008, many business schools built multimillion-dollar "simulated trading floors" complete with workstations for traders and high-definition screens for real-time trading of financial derivatives. Operational costs for these facilities can easily exceed a half million dollars per year, even as the Wall Street positions for graduates of such programs disappear.

2 Nanotechnology research centers   Inspired by the success of microelectronics fabrication facilities in the 1990s, a number of engineering schools have built newer, more expensive plants, some costing in excess of $100 million. The reasoning behind such an investment is that companies will readily contract with universities for small fabrication contracts that use state-of-the-art equipment. The rebound in individual and corporate giving after 2000 that would have funded these laboratories never materialized and many now sit empty, a debt burden to the university that generates no revenue.

3 Distance learning facilities   In an effort to capture nontraditional students, corporate training markets, and international programs, universities invested in high-tech distance learning facilities—many with $10 million price tags—complete with high-speed network connections, large screen conferencing facilities, and professional studios. As the market for these facilities was slow to develop and operating costs exceeded projections, many have ceased operation.

4 Learning centers   Reasoning that an improvement in classroom experience would add value to a degree program, a number of institutions embarked on the construction of expensive learning centers, with specialized lecture halls, colocated advising, counseling, and other student services. But learning centers are often staffed by nonprofessorial staff and administrators, and they often come at the expense of investments in new curricula and laboratories. Worse—however impressive they might appear to parents and donors—there is little evidence that a generic learning facility adds anything of value to a student's education.

5 Hotel and conference centers   Many universities have become operators of commercial meeting spaces, often subcontracting to hotel chains and corporate event managers. Campus hotels and conference centers are a favorite destination for commercial training courses and meetings, whose organizers find it easier to market their events if there is even a subtle hint of a university endorsement. Because external groups pay retail prices, university groups, who pay heavily discounted wholesale prices for the same space, often take a back seat. The net effect is that on-campus facilities, designed to make it easy for faculty and staff to host on-campus meetings, are frequently priced out of the range of affordability for departmental and student activities. When

on-campus facilities are unavailable, internal customers find themselves paying the same high, retail rates that they would have paid had the university facilities never been built.

6 Industry research centers   Originally sponsored by the federal government as a way of improving industry-university collaboration, industrial research centers now offer heavily discounted R&D services to member companies, who—in addition to getting access to inexpensive student assistants—often are allowed to tie up research deliverables with exclusive licensing arrangements. Research quality varies wildly. Many research papers are so specific to near-term problems that they are not publishable in peer-reviewed journals.

7 Federally Funded Research and Development Centers (FFRDC)   Although they are almost always staffed by full-time nonuniversity professionals, the federal government's twenty FFRDCs that are operated by universities are an important revenue stream. Some, like the University of California's Los Alamos National Laboratory in Los Alamos, New Mexico, are so remote from campus operations that local activists use contract renewals as an opportunity to protest the operation of facilities that are essentially research arms of federal agencies.

8 Performing art centers   Always a result of gifts from alumni, state-of-the-art theaters and performance venues are frequently campus showcases. They host plays and concerts in much the same way that city and community theaters do.

9 Foreign campuses   When officials from Saudi Arabia approached academic leaders in the United States and Europe about partnering to build a new university along the Red Sea, many were skeptical. But a chance to share in a $10 billion endowment—professors from cooperating institutions were selected to receive sizeable research grants—was an irresistible inducement for many universities, including Stanford. In promotional materials for Saudi Arabia's King Abdullah University of Science and Technology (KAUST), Stanford's role is carefully defined: "Stanford's main role will be to assist in the selection of an initial cohort of 10 faculty members in the fields of applied mathematics and computer science and to help create a curriculum in these disciplines. KAUST, however, will be responsible for the actual faculty recruitment."* The rationale for involvement, beyond the obvious financial one, is to extend the reach of the university in a global way: "I think KAUST is a visionary project by moderate people in Saudi Arabia. By helping these people, we have a chance to make a big impact in this country, and since Saudi Arabia has become the most important Arab country—a role that Egypt had had in the past—we can also have a major impact on the region."

* Stanford News Service 2008.

There are hundreds of ways in which American colleges and universities expand their missions with interesting projects that—although they are peripheral to core programs—satisfy demands of faculty, alumni, students, and donors for more innovation, a more global outlook, and more relevance to society and the nation. In virtually every case, programs like these are the result of rational strategies,[15] but those strategies are built on assumptions that lead many institutions astray. University presidents in the Middle, for example, find themselves in a never-ending race to compete with more prestigious institutions in a desperate climb up the reputational hierarchy. Here is how one president describes the dilemma:

Evidence of mission creep seems to be everywhere, but when I sit and I look at a full range of institutions—from community colleges through research universities—I see them talk about what they're trying to do and what they're trying to accomplish. They don't sit there and say to you, "We're trying to compete with Harvard." They sit there and say, "We're trying to serve our constituency."[16]

These programs may give students and alumni more than they need; because there is always a shared cost that is spread unequally across the university, they may ultimately cost more than students are willing to pay for. When students stop paying tuition, the bubble can quickly collapse.

What about the disruptors, the institutions that focus exclusively on education, that rise or sink on the success of their value propositions? Many of these institutions, like the proprietary universities, are far down the pecking order. As recently as 2003, observers of the important trends in higher education were generally dismissive of the ability of For-Profit institutions to significantly threaten traditional, mainstream universities:

Schools such as Stanford and Williams, whose endowments allow them to subsidize their students heavily, have nothing to fear from the likes of the University of Phoenix, which must make money from tuition in order to remain in business.[17]

The cash reserves on hand for the Apollo Group now rival endowment earnings for many Ivy League institutions. Private, mainstream universities that rely on skyrocketing tuitions for 80 or 90 percent of their operating funds now look precarious as gifts and subsidies that would have been cushions in normal times dry up. Most importantly, many students like the disruptors. Enrollment at proprietary universities continues to grow at an annual rate of 10 percent or more. For disruptors, growth is good.[18] What is good for the disruptors is not necessarily good for mainstream institutions.

How Much Disruption?

There is no single tipping point beyond which the great universities in the Middle become financially unstable, although the financial crisis that began in the fall of 2008 has already pushed some smaller private universities dramatically close to instability.[19] Other institutions have been more creative.

Arizona State University president Michael Crow must have heard the bridge begin to creak when he wrote an extraordinary open letter on January 21, 2009, describing how budget cuts proposed by the Arizona legislature would "reverse the progress ASU has made and set the institution back a decade or more."[20] In the end, federal stimulus funding helped to prevent the realization of Crow's worst case scenario, but not without some tough decisions. The university eliminated 1,400 faculty and staff positions and furloughed 12,000 employees. They eliminated some academic units and merged others. Despite Crow's public commitment to keep the academic core of the institution intact and preserve the quality of undergraduate education, a March 17, 2009, *New York Times* article characterized Arizona State's dilemma as follows:

This year, Mr. Crow's plans have crashed into new budget realities, raising questions about how many public research universities the nation needs and whether universities like Arizona State, in their drive to become prominent research institutions, have lost focus on their public mission to provide solid undergraduate education for state residents.[21]

The view up close is very different. Crow believes that the *New York Times* article mischaracterizes the university's direction and said so in a March 29, 2009, letter in which he disagreed with the article's premise:

While it is generally taken for granted that excellence and access are mutually exclusive, the New American University model we are advancing is focused squarely on Arizona students and seeks to prove that it is possible to combine the highest levels of academic excellence, inclusiveness to a broad demographic, and maximum societal impact.

When I asked Michael Crow what affect the budget challenges had on his plans, he focused not on the university's research mission but on his efforts to realize the vision of access and impact for the citizens of Arizona. "We used the budget situation to accelerate our transformation. We collapsed seven colleges into other units, eliminated more than two dozen departments by merging them into others, and reduced a number of graduate programs. We raised our tuition but expanded our financial aid, and that gives us huge control over how we devote that money to our access agenda," Crow said. ASU may have staved off the most dramatic, immediate effects of a 21 percent reduction in state support, but Crow told me that the underlying problems remain: "We were propped up temporarily with federal stimulus money, and we will eventually have to replace that with tuition money, but the impact of the crisis intensifies our focus on this agenda."

Arizona State is just one of many state universities in the United States that have weathered budget storms during the past fifty years. You would expect that the systems that states have set up to administer higher education would be an important factor in helping institutions through troubled times, but increasingly, universities have found themselves at odds with the larger university systems of which they are mere component institutions. Surprisingly enough, the goals of university systems and their universities are not necessarily aligned. In some cases, university systems work on a totally different value system.

A large university system, like the State University of New York (SUNY) system, enrolls hundreds of thousands of students on campuses ranging from small community colleges to the large research campuses. SUNY head Nancy Zimpher, like most system chancellors, is rewarded for controlling costs, expanding access, and improving outcomes for the entire range of institutions. Those are goals that do not always resonate in the Middle, where institutions see themselves as fierce competitors for shrinking resources. The 465,000 students of SUNY have been led by three chancellors since 2005, and the lack of continuity shows. Like other system chancellors, Zimpher struggles with a "we all succeed together" policy that is trusted by neither administrators nor faculty members. It is not just smaller budgets that bother the individual universities: it is the sense that the university system may prosper at their expense. It is an especially severe problem in New York, where SUNY bureaucracy extends to even relatively minor fiscal decisions that are left to the discretion of leaders in states with more autonomous universities.

The University System of Georgia (USG) enrolls 283,000 students in thirty-six campuses. Its flagship campuses, Georgia Tech in Atlanta and the University of Georgia (UGA) in Athens, are routinely ranked among the leaders in both public and private universities, but it has been a quick ride for both campuses to their current positions. The strategy they have used to achieve their rise through the rankings has made them vulnerable to disruption as the USG leadership tries to balance the needs of the larger institutions with the demands of lesser-known campuses in far-flung regions of the state. Unlike SUNY, Georgia's system has had continuous leadership. USG chancellor Erroll B. Davis has been in his position for several years, and the system has had continuity in leadership ranks for almost two decades. But Davis also represents a break from the past. He is an African American, for one thing. That is an important step for a system that was plagued with racial segregation a half-century ago. Even more significantly, Davis had limited academic experience before accepting his current job. He has an industrial background, which makes it easier for him to talk about system-wide success for USG's strategic goals of access, affordability, increased capacity, and excellence in undergraduate instruction. The question that SUNY's Zimpher faces head on is seldom voiced at USG: what if success for USG comes at the expense of Tech and UGA?

The alarm bells sounded at the research campuses as soon as Davis started talking in public about his commitment to all of the colleges and universities in the system and his skepticism about the ability of a faculty-centered culture to adapt to the processes he wanted to import from the business world. In an op-ed article for the *Chronicle of Higher Education*, Davis compared the problem of institutionalizing system-wide transformation to administering change processes in a company: "In the academic environment, processes are seen as something bureaucracies do to you and not for you. The culture reinforces a strong sense of self as opposed to the team—a strong sense of individual goals versus a sense of the greater good or common goal."[22]

It is easy to see why an appeal to the greater good has little appeal to an institution like Georgia Tech. Georgia Tech is highly selective, with a specialized mission, although the distinctions between Georgia Tech and UGA are becoming increasingly blurred as UGA adds engineering programs and Tech adds liberal arts, education, and humanities programs. In a typical year, Georgia Tech accepts less than 30 percent of its 20,000 applicants, a number that is significant because it keeps the college's quality indices high. Access is important to USG, so Georgia Tech's low acceptance rate needs to be balanced elsewhere in the system. In-state applicants who are not accepted at Georgia Tech but who are eligible for a HOPE scholarship can find engineering programs at four other USG campuses, thus spreading—in the name of access—scarce funding for the expensive engineering programs over a larger number institutions. When resources are expanding, that does not create an insurmountable problem. But when—as occurred during the 2008–2010 recession—successive years of double-digit budget cuts force the system to choose among strategic goals, tuitions rise to help protect programs. In the spring of 2010, Davis proposed a 77 percent increase in tuition for USG's research institutions, but the public outcry eventually forced the state legislature to pass a more modest increase.

One effect of increasing selectivity is that it narrows the range of students who enroll. Students whose high SAT scores make them attractive to Georgia Tech also make them eligible for acceptance at an Élite institution. There is no data to indicate how much the applicant pool at Georgia Tech overlaps the Élites, although it is safe to assume that as the fourth-ranked engineering program in the country, located in an attractive city with a pleasant climate, many top students would include Georgia Tech in, say, their top ten choices, along with Stanford, MIT, and Berkeley. Georgia Tech's tuition—even for out-of-state students—is among the lowest in the country, which gives it an advantage among competing programs. A 77 percent tuition increase would have changed the minds of some top high school students, taking a big bite out of Georgia Tech's bread and butter, its best entering freshmen.

This is a threat to aspiring state universities in the Middle. They are vulnerable to system-wide tuition fluctuations because their low tuition allows them to compete with the Élites. They are also vulnerable to system-wide attempts to increase access and capacity because it spreads budget dollars across more campuses and programs. However, compared to other disruptions, the impact of system-wide decisions might turn out to be minor. Colleges and universities in the Middle are completely exposed to the threat of proprietary universities.

Disruption from Below

How about disruption at the other end of the spectrum? Although the University of Phoenix estimates a 15 percent market overlap with nonprofits, it is very unlikely that there is significant overlap with Georgia Tech's applicants. When I was dean at Georgia Tech, the Indian software and consulting giant Wipro proposed a cobranded undergraduate computer science program aimed at DeVry, Phoenix, and similar students with an aim to provide an enhanced workforce for Wipro's new U.S. data centers. The potential demand for such a program was less than 10 percent of our applicant pool, so we turned down the proposal, but as costs rise for engineering programs, there will be an increasingly significant overlap between the applicant pools at the For-Profits and the smaller USG campuses, diluting the applicant pool at Georgia Tech as well. If Tech were to lose 15 percent of its best applicants to Élites and For-Profits, it would have to make offers to the next tier of entering freshmen with lower SAT scores, lower grades, or both.

It otherwise risks an overall reduction in the number of entering freshmen. This, in turn, imperils the funds it uses to pay freshman instructors and teaching assistants. It is a process that could cascade through the entire university system, putting pressure on all institutions to lower admission standards, reduce the size of programs, or find ways to increase the number of highly qualified applicants. At the same time, the For-Profits are putting increasing pressure on the lower end of the quality scale, so all USG institutions have to pay more attention to price-sensitive students. In every alternative, all universities in the system would have to change their underlying business models to remain competitive.

Every institution in the Middle has to face disruption from above and below. Adding new programs and services increases costs. Cost increases make the most attractive students vulnerable, either to a more compelling value proposition from an Élite or a lower-cost alternative. Cutting costs without fundamental change is not the answer, either. For-Profit institutions, online universities, and creative users of new technology have already deconstructed their offerings and put them back together in imaginative ways that increase value to their students. Mainstream higher education in the United States falls further behind as it struggles with real organizational and financial issues but remains locked into an increasingly uncompetitive set of assumptions—assumptions that are questioned by alarmingly few of their leaders. In the view of many, "higher education is out of touch with changing realities and suffers from many of the same structural flaws that have harmed the healthcare system."[23]

III A Better Means of Expressing Their Goals

10 The Value of a University

When a university has been doing *useless* things for a long time it appears at first degrading to them to be *useful*.
—John Henry Newman, *The Idea of a University*, 1899

There is an ancient pattern that governs academic institutions. Modern colleges and universities are essentially unchanged since medieval times. Contemporary academic regalia replicate the formal social attire of professional guilds and civic societies of thirteenth-century Europe. The administrative structure of departments, deans, and rectors has been handed down intact from the masters at the University of Paris who were divided into faculties on the basis of disciplines. Medieval universities conferred degrees with contemporary-sounding names, like Bachelor, Master, and Doctor. The idea of a curriculum—and even the name "liberal arts"—comes directly from the required courses of study at the first universities in Italy, France, and Spain. Oxford and Bologna had many of the same "town and gown" conflicts that Duke and Purdue have today.

The only aspect of day-to-day academic life that seems to have changed substantially is the plight of the university student:

For him there is no rejoicing in the days of his youth, and no hope even of a competence in the future. His lodgings are wretched and neglected; his dress is miserable, and his appearance slovenly. His food consists of peas, beans, and cabbage, and His bed is a hard mattress stretched on the floor, and sleep brings him only a meagre respite from the toils of the day.[1]

Many of the conflicting ideas shaping higher education today were also the important forces when universities were born. For example, whether a university is run for the benefit of its students or its faculty has always been a source of bitter contention. The risks that a university faces when its curriculum is frozen—and of marginal practical value—were known to the sixteenth-century institutions whose economic models failed to survive the

Renaissance. Even the impact of abundant choices on the course of higher education was known. Its imprint can be found in the fate of medieval universities.

A Few, Charismatic Teachers

Rooted in medieval Europe, modern universities owe their existence to an interesting cast of characters and events, both political and religious. At the start of the twelfth century, there was a renewed interest in learning. Aristotle's lost writings had been rediscovered, and they raised profound questions about the relationship between faith and reason—questions that scholars had ignored for centuries. Charismatic teachers like Thomas Aquinas, Saint Anselm, and Peter Abelard became popular by showing their followers how to use logical, systematic tools to reopen debates that had been considered settled. Intellectual life in southern Europe was in swirling, turbulent ferment at the exact moment that universities were founded.

The French monk Peter Abelard is today known mainly for his disastrous love affair with Heloise—leading eventually to his castration and her forced servitude in the convent of Argenteuil—but his real contribution to the West was the establishment of schools organized around his teachings and methods. He was famous for using rational argument to best the leading scholars of the day, but it was no doubt his arrogance, stature, and striking looks that also drew thousands of students from across the civilized world to his lectures. His master work was a text called "Sic et non"[2]—literally, "Yes and no"—that cleverly challenged theological orthodoxy by using the words of Church fathers "to formulate certain questions which were suggested by the seeming contradictions in the statements." The goal was ostensibly to help students acquire dialectic skills, but the effect of "Sic et non" was to annoy orthodox scholars. Abelard was aware of his effect on ecclesiastical leaders,[3] and cultivated the broad appeal of this ability to irritate authority. It was a trait that resulted in his serial condemnation. He was persecuted literally to his last breath, but his insistence of freedom to criticize—without obligation to accept unquestioningly the word of authority—left a lasting impression on the communities of teachers that would become the first universities.

Abelard in Paris was not the only one with influence.[4] Students were attracted to schools where the scholars had great names. An Italian jurist named Inerius studied the entire body of civil law in Bologna at the same time that a Benedictine monk—also in Bologna—named Gratian was teaching canon law, so twelfth-century law students were naturally attracted to

Bologna. Students of philosophy went to Paris. Padua and its anatomical theater attracted medical students from around the world. When French-English relations soured during Henry's reign, English students in Paris returned home to make Oxford an important center of learning in philosophy. Students were attracted to Vicenza in Italy, Salamanca in Spain, and Toulouse in France.

The first universities were loose associations of scholars like these. Sometimes the teachers and pupils together numbered only a few hundred, but within a few decades Bologna, Paris, and Padua grew to communities of several thousand scholars. The Vatican and local civil authorities registered them as Studia Generale and dispensed special privileges to the *masters*, as the teachers were called.

Kings and popes could declare masters at a Studium Generale to be docents (*jus ubique docendi*), which gave them the right to teach at other Studia. This of course encouraged much smaller and insignificant schools to also claim Studia status. Unchecked, this kind of competition would have led to chaos, so to qualify as a Studium, an institution needed to show three things. First of all, a true Studium was not to be operated only for the citizens of its own town; it had to draw international students in significant numbers. Secondly, a Studium had to have a legitimate claim on excellence by having a significant number of masters to teach students. Finally, a Studium had to offer a recognized curriculum; it was required teach the seven liberal arts and one more advanced field like theology, law, or medicine. Getting agreement in medieval Europe on this kind of regulation was not as difficult as it would seem. Religious and civil authorities gave dispensations to Studia, so they were motivated to agree on a way to register them. Papal registration did lead to some anomalies, however. Cambridge was a Studium, but Oxford was not. Padua did not accept a Papal grant until 1346. It had asserted its right to operate as a Studium years before, and it accepted the grant only as a recognition, not as a conferral, of its privilege.

Within decades, the first famous degree-granting Studia Generale of Europe became well known as theatrical backdrops for the performances of secular scholars as well as the many Benedictines, Dominicans, and Franciscans who attracted talented and ambitious students in large numbers. The popularity and prestige of the medieval professors rested on their control of the university and the powerful positions attained by their students, but it also was sustained by their ability to entertain and enthrall. Masters were encouraged to lecture across Europe and to share documents and learning. The Studia became focal points of political tension as ambitious scholars clashed with burghers and clerics. Perhaps inspired by the maverick priest Abelard, disruption was key to the success of early western universities.

The self-governing, self-regulating model evident even today helped maintain the culture of excellence and inquiry through the centuries, despite Church intrusions into academic matters. Free inquiry could lead to heresy, a crime that meant catastrophe for the perpetrator, and the ever-present threat of intervention by the Church had a moderating effect on free inquiry. Orthodoxy of the sort that forced Galileo to recant his astronomical discoveries slowed the pace of innovation outside the arts, but it did not stop it completely.

What had been loose associations of pupils and masters—bound by academic, not national, culture and a common need to protect their interests from religious and civil interference—became more formal entities. They became *universitates*—literally, corporations. A *universitas* was the academic version of a guild in the world of commerce.

Conservative Homes of Outmoded Knowledge

Part of the motivation for more organization was a desire to create a framework for operating the university. Bologna was mindful of its place among the Studia and enacted statutes that detailed the responsibilities that its faculty members had to both students and colleagues:

For the utility and benefit of scholars and students, it is hereby declared that disputations should be held by the doctors and professors in the manner specified below; namely, that the junior faculty should begin with the first lecture once each week, in the morning if it is a holiday or in the afternoon if it is not; and the following week another teacher will lecture upon another question. . . . He who has argued a question of theory must afterwards argue a question of practice. And every doctor or professor must be personally present at each of the disputations straight though until the end, and must participate in the discussion or be punished by a fine.[5]

The universities in Bologna and Paris moved along separate paths. They were two completely different kinds of associations. The University of Bologna was a guild of students, in which students legislated for themselves. Paris was a masters' guild, complete with rules for dividing into the faculties that were to become the center of academic life and with hierarchies organized around them. Every other European university followed one of these paths. The southern universities in Italy, Spain, Portugal, and parts of France were for the most part student universities. Northern universities were run by the masters.

Every aspect of academic life in masters universities was thoroughly documented, and it is because of those documents that we know much about both their structure and day-to-day life. This documentation survived the centuries, and it would have been readily available hundreds of years later to the founders of colonial universities in America who adopted the structure and rules of the masters as their own.

The rules at student universities were informal, so daily life in them is not as well documented. We do know that students attended universities to acquire professional skills. They were all training to be doctors, lawyers, or civil servants. They were the offspring of poor and working-class families, because the children of wealthy families had no interest in pursuing a profession. For the privileged classes, there was no value in a university degree. Most of the students were already members of a profession, and many were members of the clergy.

The guilds at student universities were associations of foreign students, divided into Nations, and "they early recognised the necessity of union if full use was to be made of the offensive and defensive weapons they possessed."[6] Indeed, students frequently found themselves at odds with both the masters' guilds and the local authorities. The masters, who took great pride that they—in contrast to the students—practiced a profession, resented the freedom and authority that student universities gave to students—mere apprentices—to make academic choices for themselves. Students did little to help their own cause. Local officials had to contend with rowdy students fueled by alcohol, prostitution, and poverty.

On the other hand, the students were not without "offensive weapons" of their own: they used purse strings to check both faculty and civil authority. Masters did not draw salaries from the university. They were financially dependent on the students and would remain that way until the masters' guilds were organized enough to restrict the flow of teachers into the profession. Civil authorities also depended on the students. A city's prestige— and a great deal of its income—rested on the reputation of its university, so city officials lived in constant fear that the students—who had no real local roots—would just pick up and leave.

By contrast, masters' universities were faculty-centered. They focused on internal matters more germane to building the teaching profession, which rapidly became more organized. A professor's main allegiance was with the faculty or academic department where he held an appointment and with the deans who oversaw the faculties. This inward focus led masters universities after Abelard to become quite conservative. Paris banned the teaching of the "new Aristotle" for some time and focused to an alarming degree on questions like how fast a master should deliver his lecture: "Were they to dictate lectures or to speak so fast that their pupils could not commit their words to writing?"[7]

The most visible influence of masters guilds were the barriers they erected to control the admission of students. All instruction took place in Latin, so students had to demonstrate fluency by passing an examination before entering the university. Masters in Paris also added French requirements, asserting that it would not be possible to function without fluency in French.

They also set up a pecking order in the curriculum. At the top of the liberal arts was the *Trivium*—grammar, rhetoric, and logic—and the more quantitative disciplines of the *Quadrivium*—arithmetic, geometry, astronomy, and music—were viewed as relatively unimportant, except for such specialized purposes as reckoning ecclesiastical dates.

The spread of universities in northern Europe followed the model of the masters' guild. The first northern university was founded at Prague in 1347 and was followed by Vienna and then later by many German universities. All were masters' universities. The number of European universities doubled during the next century, but a shift in thinking about the value of a university was taking place.

No longer merely places to train for a profession, universities became part of a wave of European humanism, created by civil leaders who believed that society would be better off with a more educated population. The skills that were imparted were not only the professional skills of medicine and law. The principal skill that a master university taught was scholarship, a skill that soon became remote from practice. What universities taught became more codified as scholars agreed on the rules of scholarship, and as each new generation of masters became more invested in the rules, change became less acceptable. As their subject matter became more predictable and the curricula became more conservative, German and English universities became highly organized institutions for undergraduate instruction. It was the kind of conservatism that seemed to demand protection by civil authorities, so statutes were enacted that dictated both the core curriculum and examinations. Some began to call universities "conservative homes of outmoded knowledge."[8]

Under the influence of masters, German universities took on tasks that had only distant connections with their academic missions. While Italian universities continued their tradition of scholarly research, German universities filled a gap in civil society. They managed the European Reformation, for instance. In the absence of other authorities, a long list of German scholars managed Luther's *Theses* and the Reformation for the next hundred years.

The older Studia, now dominated by masters, had become the established civic universities of Europe. Above all, the master universities became arbiters of what it meant to be educated. Inevitably, this meant that faculties imposed their will on the students in the form of rigid courses of study—a core of knowledge that everyone who passed through their gates had to possess. Free-flowing dialog between undisciplined, demanding students and charismatic masters was replaced with austere, unpleasant classrooms, aloof professors, and the compulsion of a classical core curriculum.

Being That There Are So Many Grammar Books

By the early seventeenth century, European universities—particularly masters' universities—had hit a dead end. In the eyes of their critics, they were moribund, victims of events, driven to irrelevance by the Renaissance. Masters shouldered most of the blame. Above all else, masters were scholars, and they trained university students not so much to *practice* a profession as to be scholars who *studied* the profession. Intellectual conservatism had taken a firm hold on the Studia. And because Renaissance universities had no serious competitors, the desires of the masters always won out. They had no reason to change.

There was little that universities could do about the tolls exacted by war and disease—forces that affected all social institutions, including the universities—but they were slow to recognize that students had also changed. Gone was the mature—if rowdy—law student of Bologna, the poor son of a poor family, whose purpose was to acquire training as a jurist. He was replaced by the son of a more wealthy European family—a younger boy, who was not easily impressed by the fame of the local masters. Wealthier tuition-paying parents were looking for amenities that the comparatively austere Studia could not provide. They were looking for much more serious preparation for the uncertainties of life than could be offered by a bloated and sometimes irrelevant core curriculum. The Studia were slow to recognize that they had competition.

Students in the seventeenth century had alternatives. There were, suddenly, abundant choices available to them. In 1599, a small group of Jesuit priests working at Collegio Romano, a small, new college that had been founded a few years before by Saint Ignatius of Loyola, published a plan for educating priests. The Jesuits probably had modest goals for Ratio Studorium, as the plan was called. They clearly did not anticipate that enrollment in Collegio Romano would explode, but it did. The number to students grew so rapidly that within a year of its founding, it moved to a larger campus. Ratio Studorium became a blueprint for an international network of universities to rival civic universities, as the state-sponsored schools were called. Within a year, new universities were also established in Parma and Mantua, a 20 percent increase in the number of Italian universities.

Part of the Jesuit inspiration seems to have been a realization—around the middle of the sixteenth century—that there was little in the civic university experience that could not be duplicated and improved upon with better teaching. Textbooks were widely available, and it worried the Jesuits greatly that they had to find a way to be valuable beyond the rote memorization of what a distant scholar had written. This 1558 exchange between the Jesuit priest John Paul Nicholas and the bishop of Perugia shows how they struggled with the idea that the value of a university education was not in the—now interchangeable—texts:

Monsignor, being that there are so many grammar books as good as that of Sasso, it does not seem necessary to me to change, especially if Sasso's is no different than the others. . . . Monsignor, until now it has been said in town that we do not have a method for teaching; this is false, because we have much experience, but if we use Sasso's book, they will say what our students have learned, they have learned from Sasso, not from us.[9]

This is an eerily accurate foreshadowing of the open courseware movement that originated at MIT at the end of the 1990s. Open courseware advocates reason, as did Father Nicholas, that because there is little to distinguish the content of courses—including texts, notes, and other materials—content should be freely distributed to anyone who wants it. This, of course, places an increased burden on universities to distinguish themselves by the quality of the experience they offer to students.

The Jesuits were as flexible as the masters were inflexible. They offered boarding and activities like horsemanship and dance to attract wealthy students. Mantua offered a course of study in chemistry, a subject that was taught nowhere else in Italy. Parma was half-civic and half-Jesuit. Collegio Romano had neither a medical school nor a law school, which were required components of civic universities. The Jesuits were, however, inflexible on one point: their universities promised a preparation for professional life.

There was a similar movement in the Protestant world. In 1559, Jean Calvin and Theodore Beza founded the Geneva Academy. Calvin's new university was able to attract famous teachers in such large numbers that

Protestant students, particularly English students whose reformist beliefs locked them out of Jesuit schools, flocked to study in Geneva.

The masters' guilds reacted by circling the wagons. They became even more conservative and protective of their profession, but that did not stop the new, more liberal institutions from attracting the most prized students in large numbers.

This was the first of many migrations of students away from traditional institutions as newer and more pragmatic alternatives appeared. The displaced universities—older and more established—suddenly found themselves defenders of a principle, becoming even less willing to bend to the needs of students. Ultimately, by the end of the Renaissance, rigid and marginalized European universities were undermined by dozens of more liberal alternatives. It was a pattern that would be repeated centuries later in America, as a handful of American colonial colleges grew first to dozens and then to hundreds of public and private, secular and sectarian institutions. The pattern would reappear again at the start of the twentieth century, when established public universities were assailed—and forever changed—by the appearance of hundreds of alternatives, their value undermined from the top by the ascendency of private universities and from the bottom by ubiquitous state institutions. Now, at the start of the twenty-first century, we are poised for the next repetition, the result of the sudden availability of tens of thousands of new alternatives: an abundance of choices.

The American University

Some in higher education have seen the parallels with the past and tried to swing the pendulum back to students. There is a trend at many universities today toward a student-centered campus, but it is less a movement than a grab bag of marketing ideas. A typical student-centered university proclaims:

A student-centered university community is entirely committed to ensuring that students have opportunities to succeed in their academic, co-curricular, extra-curricular, social, moral, and civic endeavors while they are enrolled as our students and throughout the remainder of their lives. All members of a student-centered university community assist students in achieving their individual academic and personal goals while meeting the goals described in the university's mission statement. The student-centered institution inspires students to develop the attitudes and skills that are essential to a rewarding life of learning, leadership, and service.[10]

In the earliest universities, the tension between masters and students created two separate kinds of institutions. The impact on the course of higher education was profound, but there is no corresponding struggle in modern American universities. Modern-day student-centrism says virtually nothing about education. Despite the name, student-centered universities are quite traditional faculty-centered institutions. The same curriculum is taught in faculty-centered and student-centered universities. Governance is indistinguishable. Leadership is unchanged. But that does not mean that American universities are not on an evolutionary path.

American universities are a backdrop for a different kind of battle whose outcome is still uncertain. Much as Arizona State's Michael Crow searches today for a model of the New American University, every generation of academic leaders has struggled with defining a value proposition for American higher education that was compelling for its time and place.

With the founding of Harvard in 1636, the path for American universities was set. The first colonial colleges were founded by graduates of foundering European universities. Harvard was founded by Protestants who had attended Oxford and Cambridge. The English schools clung to the model of residential colleges long after the rest of Europe had abandoned it, so Harvard was established as a residential university. By statute, the contents of core courses of study and examinations in England were prescribed, and because its founders were Oxford and Cambridge graduates, Harvard also taught a classical core curriculum. Oxford and Cambridge were both masters' universities, so Harvard operated under the control of a master. Histories make no mention of famous scholars present at Harvard in its first years, so its primary hold in the Americas was its Puritan foundation, a foundation that would dominate the university until 1708. But since Harvard was a model for the colonial universities that followed, institutions of higher education in America thought of themselves as "smaller and poorer cousins of English universities."

This was apparent to Thomas Jefferson—an admirer of the Geneva Academy—whose University of Virginia in the early nineteenth century set up a system of electives to counter "superficiality and compulsion, the two evils which finally undermined the classical course of study."[11] It was not a successful experiment. Virginia itself abandoned the most radical of Jefferson's proposals and returned to a core curriculum within a few years.

It would be decades before the experiment—propelled by an affluent and restless population of students who were not at all convinced that they needed to study what their parents had once been compelled to study—was tried again. The experiments would be influential, but they would never be conclusive. Even after the introduction of majors and specialization abolished the most objectionable aspects of compulsion, the new American universities continued to struggle with what to teach and how to teach it. American students, on the other hand, were not as patient.

Maybe it was something in the American spirit that caused a resurgence of student-centered forces in the new universities, but like the thirteenth-century students who formed guilds, American students were drawn to extracurricular pursuits that were more in keeping with American culture. Students were no longer convinced that their preparation for life needed to be confined to classrooms. They were drawn to athletics, clubs, and fraternal societies in ways that European students were not. Like the old masters, nineteenth-century academic leaders had a dim view of this trend. They thought that organized activity outside the classroom was overtly subversive to the classical university model. At the very least, it "inspired vigorous young men to seek some better means of expressing their goals, their values, and their interests than the authorities were willing or able to provide."[12]

Before long, the university experience included entry into a self-governing social network that rivaled the established authority of the university. The campus was a place to experience higher education, although there was often not a clear connection between the experience and education itself. Students were demanding a "better means of expressing their goals," and universities were once again forced to confront the idea of specialization. They needed to redefine the connection between what students wanted to learn and what was being taught. It would no longer be possible to ignore the call for a system of electives and majors.

11 Of Majors and Memes

It is not always a pretty image, but college professors spend a lot of time thinking about how to chop knowledge up into pieces. Most of the time, the result is a new course or two, a change in exam schedules, or, rarely, a new major degree program. Most Americans know what a *college major* is, although most people would not be able to tell you the difference between a major in psychology and one in cognitive science. By the same token, most Americans understand that there is a difference between an Associate of Arts degree from the local junior college and a Doctor of Philosophy degree from Oxford University. Fewer know about the Columbia Curriculum or the Bologna Process, and fewer still have any idea what the holder of the Agregação or the Diplômed'Études Approfondies is qualified to do. It is apparent chaos, but to most people, the chaos does not matter, because they believe that there is a connection between these artificial labels and something that has value to students.

As long as there is an implicit agreement between the universities that package knowledge and students whose life goals require that knowledge, the jumble of degrees, diplomas, and majors is irrelevant. The value of a university is tied to this agreement, but as I have tried to show in other chapters, the reservoir of public trust in the agreement is not boundless. History shows that when the compact is broken, universities are faced with redefining their value, sometimes in profoundly disruptive ways. What is unique about the disruptions facing universities today is the scale of the problem: tens of thousands of new universities, billions of new students, and trillions of dollars in a global economy that all depend on higher education.

Understanding how universities might survive these kinds of disruptions requires a short detour into a modern idea: the peculiar economics of the Internet.

Most Majors Are Not Popular

The U.S. Department of Education keeps track of the degrees awarded by accredited institutions of higher learning, and the resulting data can be plotted on a bar chart, or histogram, that represents the popularity of the various major fields of study. Figure 11.1 shows the frequency distribution of degrees awarded by American colleges and universities for the academic year ending spring 2006.

Business is the most popular major. It is chosen by approximately 15 percent of all undergraduates. Business is followed in popularity by the social sciences and education, each of which is chosen by roughly half as many students. English and computer science, popular majors on most campuses, are 64 percent less frequent than psychology, which ranks fourth behind education. Not counting ties, or near ties, the most popular majors are

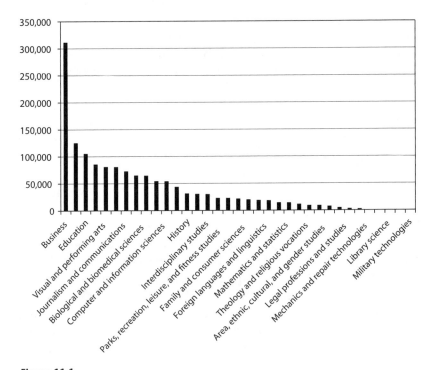

Figure 11.1
The most popular majors.
Source: U.S. Department of Education National Center for Education Statistics, 2004–2006.

roughly twice as popular as the next most popular. Interestingly enough, there does not seem to be much difference in the popularity of library science and a field of study called precision production. Engineering is very popular, but that is largely because the data does not break out the separate engineering disciplines like electrical, mechanical, textile, systems, and civil engineering. Some engineering disciplines graduate only a few dozen students annually, which would make them roughly equivalent to the least popular majors. Even so, engineers account for only 2.8 percent of all the graduates. On the other hand, there are many majors that are not individually popular but that constitute the majority of all college graduates. Of the roughly 2.3 million degrees granted in 2006, the majority were granted in majors like mathematics and philosophy that were not the most popular, but that together account for more majors than business.

A statistician might ignore the irregularities in the 2006 government data and draw a smooth popularity curve for college majors that looks more like the diagram in figure 11.2, making it clear that although there are a few very popular majors on the left, most people choose majors on the righthand side of the curve. Statisticians call that part of the curve the *long tail*. Even a quick glance at figure 11.2 shows how the long tail got its name.

American universities are organized around the idea of popularity. It is easy to find entire buildings devoted to fields that attract many students, like education, psychology, and journalism, but ethnic studies programs often share office and classroom space with geography and anthropology departments—all of which are relatively unpopular—on the edge of campus. On an American campus, it better to be popular; more students means more professors and more offices, laboratories, and support staff. Popularity means more resources, but it is not a hard and fast rule. There are also unpopular majors that seem to be well heeled.

Mathematics departments, for example, are often among the largest departments on a college campus. Despite a general lack of sponsored research

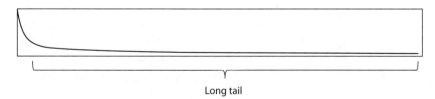

Long tail

Figure 11.2
The long tail.

funding in the mathematical sciences, there always seem to be ample supplies of graduate students to supervise freshman calculus recitation sections. The only reason relatively unpopular fields like mathematics get their own buildings is that virtually everyone on campus is required to take a math course. This has the effect of artificially enhancing the popularity of mathematics courses. There are no Department of Education data for the way that student credit hours are distributed. But at most universities, the statistical distribution does not look anything like figure 11.2, because general education requirements keep enrollments in some courses much higher than they would be if students were allowed to make unfettered choices. If all students were required to take the same, common set of courses, then there would be no long tail. In a university where all students take the same, common set of courses, all fields get approximately equal shares of the university's resources.

As soon as students are allowed to make choices, some courses become more popular than others. Some departments win the battle for budget dollars; others have to settle for less space, fewer classrooms, and fewer professors to teach the smaller number of courses that students choose. Absent required courses, the farther out a major is in the long tail, the more financially difficult it is for a university to offer it. At some point, it is not economically feasible to offer majors in the least popular fields. Universities, like many other businesses, struggled with the economics of popularity and unpopularity—the economics of niche markets—until the invention of the Internet.

Hubs and Spokes and the Internet

The Internet is full of rankings that look like figure 11.1. The web pages indexed by the Google search engine are listed in order of popularity. The popularity of a web page is in turn determined by something called its *page rank*. The page rank is measured by how many other pages refer to a given web page—pages that are mentioned by many other pages are considered more important and receive a higher page rank. When Google delivers its search results, the pages are listed so that the ones at top have the highest page rank. Experiments confirm that the page with the top rank is roughly twice as popular as the next page listed. The same is true for membership in Yahoo! groups (the most popular groups are approximately twice as popular as the next most popular group), as well as many other phenomena that have nothing to do with the Internet, such as the population of human settlements, the value of oil reserves, the historical return on stock prices, and the distribution of word frequencies in the English language.

Let's imagine a map of the World Wide Web that represents the popularity of web pages. To draw the map, start at any web page. We can use a dot to stand for web pages. For every link on the page, draw a line to the dot for the corresponding page, and continue this process until there are no more lines or dots possible. This is, in fact, how Google and other search engines work. They *crawl* along the connected dots and lines of the map of web pages to try and figure out which pages are the most popular. It is a never-ending process because there are many hundreds of millions of web pages to be crawled in this way, and there are always new web pages and links that appear. A map of even a tiny portion of the Web, like the one shown in figure 11.3, is enormously complex.[1]

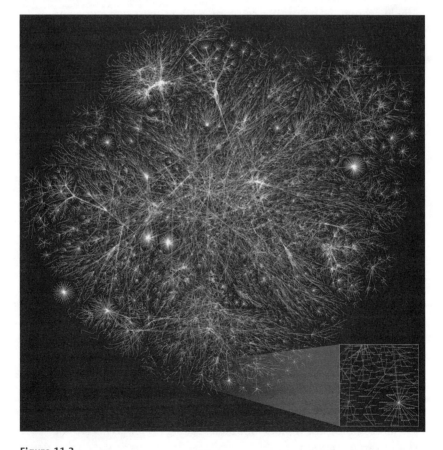

Figure 11.3
A map of the Internet.
Image courtesy Matt Britt; permission granted under Creative Commons Attribution 2.5 Generic license, 2006.

Although it looks like a spidery lace, a map of the Web is actually a network. If you zoom in to the nodes of the map in figure 11.3, you'll notice that it is a vast network of hubs and spokes. Hubs represent very popular sites like Amazon.com, and spokes depict the many connections that link to the popular sites from other—often less popular—sites far out on the long tail. Hubs and spokes are just another way of looking at phenomena in which there are a few highly ranked entries and many smaller ones. Although the higher-ranked items tend to receive much more traffic than the others, most of the population are not highly ranked. They lie on the long tail of the distribution.

Here is the key thing to remember about hubs and spokes and long tails (and college majors): as far as scientists can tell, as long as people make unfettered economic choices like selecting a Web site to visit, choosing a city to live in, or deciding on a college major, there will be winners and losers. The winners are hubs, and everything else is a spoke somewhere on the long tail of a popularity diagram. The more choices there are, the denser the spokes are around the hubs. It is not fair, but in the economics of the Internet, the rich always get richer and the long tail always gets longer.

Mass Specialization

Markets also tend to follow popularity laws, and that single fact has caused much disruption in the age of the Internet. To efficiently serve a market, a company or industry must acquire an economy of scale—it must generate business beyond infrastructure investments needed to service the market. That is why, before Walmart, supermarkets were rare in rural areas. There were simply not enough customers to justify the expense of building a large store; keeping it lit, air-conditioned, and staffed; and arranging to have large quantities of groceries shipped in on a daily or weekly basis.

That is also why, before cable networks, inexpensive satellite receivers, podcasts, and YouTube, there were only a few broadcast television networks. The costs of starting a traditional broadcast television network were so large that the national market could support only a few. Cable and satellite distribution alone made it feasible to launch national channels devoted to cooking, pets, music videos, and dozens of professional sports teams. Video distribution sites like YouTube have enabled hundreds of entrepreneurial content providers to establish web-based "channels."

A successful business model for broadcasting no longer has to include a massive capital investment. In fact, because the incremental cost of delivering content to additional viewers is essentially zero, new entrants in the broadcast content industry have a striking advantage over NBC, ABC, and

CBS—networks that still operate using business models that are successful only when they rank first or second in audience size. In the extreme, long tail distribution enables one-to-one marketing, or what analysts sometimes call *mass specialization*, in which a seller enters into a marketplace tailored to an individual.[2]

If each merchant in the long tail had to invest in all of the vertical capabilities (catalogs, mailing lists, classified ads, order processing and fulfillment, payment processing, customer service) needed to attract and serve its market niche, the merchant would have to charge much higher prices just to make up for the underlying costs of running the business. Higher prices might mean fewer customers, which in turn means less money to pay for all of those catalogs and customer service agents. The Internet makes it possible for merchants in the long tail to share these costs. It works only because merchants in the long tail of e-commerce have a *platform* that they can plug into—a standardized collection of technologies that are shared among many merchants.

Why the digression on long tails? Mass specialization is one of the driving disruptive forces behind the crisis in higher education; in order to understand the fate of colleges and universities, we would do well to use the language of long tails, one-to-one marketing, and technology platforms. One of the reasons Thomas Jefferson's idea of abolishing the compulsory core curriculum at the University of Virginia failed is that colonial universities were not yet platforms.

Colonial universities were vertically structured to provide instruction for entering classes that were committed to marching through a predefined curriculum in lockstep. Every variation meant more faculty members, more buildings, and more clerks and administrators to keep track of it all. Every variation created the hubs and spokes associated with unfettered choices. When it came to the business of running a colonial university, the fewer variations from the classical curriculum, the better. The invention of major fields of study made it impossible to avoid dealing with variation. Students had to be treated as individuals, and that shifted forever the business of operating a university to a long tail model.

Why Are There So Many Philosophy Majors?

My story of how American universities were born started on the Italian peninsula, so it seems fitting to return there to talk about where they are heading, beginning with their students. Student motivations have always determined the success or failure of Western universities. For the last hundred years, higher education has been the gateway to careers, advancement, and wealth. Students are motivated by jobs, and some majors (like business administration and architecture) aim to prepare students for future careers, which helps explain their popularity. But why are there so many philosophy majors in Italian universities?

What Value Is There in That?

In the early 1990s, I accepted a visiting professorship at the University of Padua in northern Italy. Medieval Padua was the backdrop for *The Taming of the Shrew* and *The Merchant of Venice*. *Romeo and Juliet* is set in nearby Verona. It is a city of canals, porticoes, piazzas, frescoes, and a famous cathedral named for Anthony, Italy's patron saint. Padua also played an important role in my recounting of the birth of universities during the Middle Ages. Padua is home to the second-oldest university in Europe.

The University of Padua has been as thoroughly romanticized by Italians as any American campus. Dante Alighieri, Giacomo Casanova, Nicolaus Copernicus, Michel L'Hopital, and William Harvey all studied there. Its medieval anatomical theater has been drawing visitors for centuries. I once lectured in the Hall of Ancient Documents next to the same podium that Galileo used. University buildings dot nearly every winding, narrow street.

University traditions are both serious and frivolous, but they are as ingrained as any American traditions. Graduating students—some of them in their underwear—are doused with shaving cream and adorned with laurel wreaths as their classmates chant an ancient, vulgar ditty and their parents look on with embarrassed pride. The university is thoroughly integrated into the life of the region, but—as the rector reminded me—it takes a lot to get them excited. It is not a place that changes readily.

I was asked to launch a postgraduate program in computer software that would cater to Italy's growing information technology companies. I had started such programs in the United States, and I knew that if I was going to succeed, I would need help from Italian software companies. Even though Padua's engineering school was among the finest in Europe, the university kept matters of commerce at arm's length. Fortunately, the local industry innovation council jumped in to help, and within six months we began to enroll students in the program. The next step was to recruit industry sponsors who were willing to participate by sponsoring students, committing open positions to graduates, and providing cash stipends for both students and faculty. Italian software engineering programs are well regarded internationally, so I approached local companies armed with what I thought would be an irresistible pitch: let us identify some technology problems and assign students to work on them. I was completely unprepared for the response.

By an overwhelming majority, the executives I talked to were perplexed by the offer. "What value is there in that?" said one vice president of engineering. A CEO asked me, "What does a professor have to do with my business?" I checked with a colleague at a nearby university, who some years before had set up a successful research consortium with some local high-tech companies. He told me not to get my hopes up. The consortium was run outside the university, in part because of the perception that universities had nothing to contribute to industrial innovation. We eventually convinced some of these companies to participate, and for several years there was an active market for graduates of the software engineering master's program.

The business leaders I talked to clearly believed that what took place inside Italy's respected universities was unrelated to their problems. American universities tend to have a cozy relationship with local companies. Faculty members consult, students intern, and university development offices count on the generosity of local business leaders for gifts and grants. American businesses seemed to find value in supporting academic programs, and I wondered what made Italy different.

Performance Art

Part of the answer has to do with the fact that European university courses are performance art. They are stages for the professors. This point was driven home several months later when I landed a consulting job for a company called ANSALDO, a public-private think tank working for the government-owned railroad. Part of my task was to assemble a seminar on cutting-edge technology.

I wanted to use local experts, so I asked a colleague from nearby University of Naples to help out. He agreed to give an internal talk to ANSALDO engineers. It was a one-hour presentation, and it was very entertaining. He rushed back and forth on the stage, his hands waving around to help us visualize the technology, his voice rising to a bellow and falling to a soft whisper. At the moment his talk was approaching its dramatic peak, he said, "And as you will remember from last Tuesday's lecture. . . ." I looked around to see who else had noticed. Everyone else seemed to be enjoying it. No confused looks or hands shooting up to ask what in the world he was talking about. Maybe I had mistranslated. And then it hit me—this was the matinée performance of a production that was in the middle of a twenty-year run. It was a very good lecture—better than I had seen in American classrooms and one that would have been well-received in any engineering department in the United States, but it was a performance rather than a discussion. My Neapolitan colleague was as divorced from ANSALDO as ANSALDO was from the classroom.

Culture and the Educated Person

The ANSALDO episode unexpectedly also helped answer another question I had about Italian universities: why are there so many philosophy majors?

Philosophy is not a degree that has much appeal for either students or employers in the United States. It is intellectually demanding, and because most students regard philosophy as a required course to be taken early in their careers, there is not even a large peer group to help attract new students. Out of the top thirty degrees offered in the United States in 2006, philosophy ranked twenty-fifth. The average graduating class of philosophy majors in the United States has fewer than four students. It is far out on the long tail of American majors, but philosophy and other courses of study that are not very popular in the United States hold great appeal for Italian students.

Why that is so has a great deal to do with who goes to college in Italy, and why. In Italy, as in most of Europe, public university education is free. University professors are civil servants, and the class sizes at even modestly large institutions are enormous. Italian students are on the average younger than their American counterparts. Eighty percent of all first-year students enroll within a year of graduating from secondary school. Young adults tend live at home longer than their American counterparts, so they do not tend to travel far from home to attend university. That trend is most pronounced in southern Italy and the Italian islands, where 97 percent of the students enroll near home.

Because there are no particular barriers to enrolling in university, you would expect to find students from across all social strata and family circumstances. But in fact university students tend to come from families in which one or more parents have also attended a university. In Italy, that means the probability of attending university is tied to social class, and students tend to come from advantaged families. Thirty percent of Italians have university degrees, but 60 percent of entering students have university-educated parents. This is a striking disparity because the birth rate in Italy has been less than the replacement rate for many years.

A substantial majority of first-year students are women, and as there are no cultural barriers to limit career choices for women, majors should be tied to job opportunities and intrinsic interest in the discipline. They are not. In reality, students seem to regard majors as irrelevant to future career choices.

Irrelevance of Majors

By an overwhelming 78 percent majority, Italian students choose their majors based on cultural factors. Only 9 percent say that their choices were determined by career opportunities. Forty percent choose to major in science, technology, engineering, and mathematics—a combination of fields that in the United States is called STEM. Most American STEM majors choose engineering, a major that tracks closely with future careers, but in Italy, engineering accounts for only 11 percent of the STEM total. On the other hand, Italian students are more than twice as likely to choose literature or philosophy as a major—majors that are not career-oriented—than their American counterparts.

The reason seems to be that Italian students are for the most part indifferent about the relevance of their majors to future career choices: only 44 percent of the men and 55 percent of the women say that their major matters. Twelve percent of them want to pursue teaching careers, a much larger number than choose education as a major. Nearly 14 percent intend go into health-related fields and social services. Close to half of all Italian students want to attend graduate school.[3]

Disconnected Classrooms

Italian students attach less importance to classroom learning. Final grades for courses are given long after the course ends and are mainly determined by separate, standardized examinations. Examinations that don't go well can be repeated. My experience in the Italian classroom matches what you might expect in such a system—it is difficult to motivate students because there is no clear line that connects classroom performance with a later goal. I realized this early in my tenure at Padua and tried to introduce some new ideas to help.

I introduced two concepts that are common in American classrooms, but were clearly alien concepts to my students: class projects and midterm exams. Most students were cheerful—if not terribly serious—about undertaking projects, but they were absolutely terrified by the idea of an in-class exam. One young lady in the front row blanched visibly as I described the importance of a mid-term exam in determining the final grade for the course. When I was finished, she raised her hand and, near tears, asked timidly, "What if we don't do well?"

Preparing for Careers

By contrast, career-related majors dominate in American universities. Four majors—business, education, engineering and computer science, and the health professions—alone accounted for almost half of the degrees granted in 2006. Virtually all of the graduates who receive business degrees enter business, and they tend to stay there. Ten years after receiving their degrees,[4] most of the American graduates who chose majors that led to service occupations actually remained in those occupations. Sixty percent of all engineering graduates actually take engineering jobs after they graduate, and after ten years, almost all of them are still employed in the engineering profession. If they leave engineering, it tends to be because they have moved on to managerial positions in the same industry. Half of all computer science majors remain employed in computer science, and many more find positions in other parts of the information technology industry. In general, career-oriented majors find positions in a cluster of relevant industries and remain in those industries long after leaving the university.

Perhaps because it is viewed as an upward economic pathway—and perhaps as a result of the Morrill Act—public higher education in the United States is concentrated on careers and is more broadly accessible to more members of society than in most of the world. A 60 percent majority of the parents of students at public institutions do not have university degrees, and almost a third of them have no more than a high school education. The majority of the research scientists in the United States come from families in which the parents do not have college educations.

True to the intent of the Land Grant movement, university education in the United States has become the gateway to the economic middle class. It is not a luxury afforded to families with social stature and wealth. If a university education is tied to preparing young people for careers, then major fields of study are by and large used to acquire job-related skills. Students choose majors to match their career ambitions.

Preparing college students for careers seems so natural today that it is hard believe that American higher education started out in a very different direction. The path to the current system was not an easy one. There was resistance to allowing students the kind of choice it takes to make the American system of majors work, and even today there are those who are opposed to allowing students to choose according to their talents, interests, and aspirations.

No Serious Purpose

It would be a mistake to imagine that the nation's colleges were throughout history filled with eager students, ready to consume all the knowledge needed to launch them on their chosen paths. In fact, there have been huge collective shifts in the psychology of college students since the first colonial universities were established. In the years after the Civil War—as the nation began to rebuild its wealth—university officials began to report growing numbers of "unmotivated students." Much as today's Italian students see little direct economic benefit from the classroom experience, college students in the late nineteenth century attached less importance to college education than their parents did.

Historian Frederick Rudolph speculated that the booming postwar economy meant that there were plentiful jobs awaiting college graduates,[5] so the career orientation of the classroom experience faded into the background. American families had money to spend on their adult children, and 19-year-old males were perfectly happy to take a few mostly enjoyable years off before entering a workforce that was increasingly aimed at growing businesses and did not require any particular skills that could not be picked up in fraternities, athletics, and social networks outside the classroom. This is a pattern repeated during other economic boom times: the 1920s, the Internet boom of the late 1990s, and the peak in public markets just before the economic collapse of 2008. Even at land grant colleges, where the ties between university preparation and future careers seemed to be part of the fabric of university life, college administrators complained that students could not answer the question, "Why are you here?" University of Wisconsin president Charles van Hise once complained that his students in the early 1900s had "no serious purpose."[6]

Life outside the classroom seemed much more interesting and relevant. Many students planned to pursue careers in commerce, where teamwork and other social skills were of prime importance. Students began to suspect that—despite the best efforts of their professors to motivate them with prizes, awards, and "honors" housing—the real preparation for life was on the playing field or in student organizations. Colleges were left with a hollow value proposition. "Study here," they seem to say, "although real learning takes place outside our classrooms and out of earshot of our professors."

There was another way to motivate students. It had been envisioned by Thomas Jefferson almost a century before. In a rejection of a classical European curriculum, with its axiom that all educated men and women should know the same thing, Thomas Jefferson's plan for the University of Virginia called for a college with schools for languages, mathematics, philosophy, history, anatomy, medicine, and law, in which all degrees would be granted. There were to be no university degrees, no a priori limits to the size of a school, and no gradations among students. Jefferson's belief in individual democratic principles and his dislike of central authority was at work in Virginia's system of electives: "Every student shall be free to attend the schools of his choice and no other than he chooses."[7] But universities had not yet figured out what a platform was, so Virginia's system came at a cost that was too high.

It was an expensive way to run a university, and the University of Virginia was forced to operate with resources that did not match the vision of its founder. Schools for practical subjects like engineering could not be funded, and within ten years, the university was offering a master's degree that represented the more or less classically determined curriculum. However, Virginia's experiment, and especially the moral justification for it, had a profound influence on the course of higher education.

Harvard's Disappearing Requirements

The elevation of Charles Eliot—a mathematician and scientist who had early in his career been dismissed from Harvard—to the presidency of Harvard in 1869 was intended to signal a new era for that university. Harvard had already embraced the Johns Hopkins model of a modern graduate school, and Eliot's presidency was supposed to be a sign of Harvard's greater ambitions. Eliot was also aware that many Harvard students were unmotivated. He was convinced that the lack of motivation in post–Civil War students was due to a prescriptive, compulsory classical curriculum, and that Jefferson's system of electives was the way to bring Harvard's classrooms back into focus. Even so, Eliot's inaugural address must have come as a shock to the trustees who had championed his candidacy:

In education, the individual traits of different minds have not been sufficiently attended to . . . the young man of nineteen or twenty ought to know what he likes best and is most fit for.[8]

In a few seconds, Charles Eliot overthrew centuries of European tradition and embraced the elective system of Thomas Jefferson. Eliot moved students to the center of university life, not with an argument about what would best prepare a student for a career, but rather by arguing that students who select what interests them will pursue their studies with a passion that compulsion cannot match—a difficult proposition to oppose in a country whose Declaration of Independence was based on individual empowerment.

Between 1872 and 1894, Harvard removed all subject requirements except two: modern language and rhetoric. Eliot understood clearly the financial implications in terms of increased demands for faculty, staff, and facilities. By 1894, Harvard's faculty had grown by a factor of ten, from sixty to six hundred. Eliot had a plan for how to pay for all this specialization: Harvard's endowment grew from $2 million in 1872 to more than $20 million in 1894.

Not all institutions could keep up with Harvard. Rutgers and others retained a curriculum based on the classical model. Yale chose a middle path, adopting a system of areas of concentration. Land grant universities followed with departments that demanded in-depth scholarship, effectively establishing the system of majors.

What Do Our Students Need to Know?

Every change in a curriculum means that professors have to reorganize the knowledge that is currently thought to be the underpinning of a university education, and nothing roils a university faculty like the question "What do our students need to know?" Sometimes that answer is evidently "a lot."

Perhaps as a reaction to Eliot's transformation, or perhaps out of genuine desire for a liberal arts graduate whose broad skills—acquired in the course of classical study—would carry him through a lifetime of learning even during uncertain economic times, strong forces have opposed academic specialization and choice. These forces argue that there is a body of knowledge that needs to be preserved and shared and that the price for calling oneself an educated person is to be steeped in it.

Columbia University's Core Curriculum was the most influential of these forces. The Core Curriculum had its beginnings with a Columbia professor named John Erskine, who designed Columbia College's undergraduate "Introduction to Masterworks of Western Literature." By 1919, Erskine's vision had become Columbia's main curriculum, a curriculum that also required courses in Western civilization, art, music, modern languages, and science. Often criticized for its focus on western culture, it has been called Anglocentric, and during the 1960s it came under fierce assault from feminists, non-Western groups, and politically radical organizations.

The argument goes on. No less an expert than Harry Lewis, the former dean of Harvard College, in a scathing indictment of Harvard's "abandonment of its soul,"[9] railed against what he perceives as the excesses of the system of electives pioneered at his institution a century before:

Within academe it is hard to inspire support for a core for a simple reason. We have not come to agreement—indeed we have had little discussion—about the purpose of higher education. In the absence of any big concept about what college is supposed to do for students, both students and faculty members prefer the freedom of choice that comes with the elective curriculum. We would each rather do our own thing than embrace our collective responsibility for the common good. But the argument that students have nothing in common is false, and the conclusion that a college education should have no core is wrong.[10]

Lewis's critics argue that he is wrong because what it means to be an educated person changes depending on where and when you are, but there are no serious critics who argue that "students have nothing in common." Lewis and others go further. Having successfully batted down the idea that students share no intellectual goals, they go on to impose a set of assumptions ("most will be citizens"[11]) about what it is that students have in common. The knowledge and skills that a student needs to acquire are not absolutes. Even uncontroversial skills, like how to work in a team, are tempered by whether the team is culturally homogeneous and where it located.

This point was hammered home to me in early 2005 by Joe Licata, who was then CEO of Siemens Enterprise Networks. I was briefing Licata on Georgia Tech's summer program in Barcelona. The program was successful, and students loved the idea of studying on the Mediterranean coast. Halfway through my remarks, he stopped me and said, "Let me get this straight. You transport your students to Spain and teach them exactly the same material they could have learned here in Atlanta? Don't you know that everything about doing business is different there? Do you teach them how teams function or how European corporations work? Do they know how to disagree without being insulting?" The CEO of the North American division of one of the largest multinational corporations in the world would know. Licata knew that we also had international programs in Korea, Singapore, and China. "The cultural differences in Asia are even more important to understand. We can hire a lot of people with language proficiency. We really need people with cultural proficiency."

Joe Licata was right, of course. Even the underlying assumptions were different. Whatever it is that students—from the Élite, from the For-Profits, from the Middle—have in common, it is unlikely that it will be captured in a fixed set of courses. But this argument is not only about Harvard's liberal arts curriculum, it is repeated in every faculty curriculum committee attempting to answer the question "What do our students need to know?"

The Noble Goals of the Core Curriculum

The course catalog for an engineering degree at one top-ranked engineering school requires 128 classroom hours, of which exactly three hours are "free electives," during which a student can pursue interests outside of a prescribed set of courses. That means of the thirty-eight courses an engineer needs to take, there is only one opportunity to explore a passion for music or museums, economics or ethnic studies. And that opportunity will not arise for three and a half years. To be fair, there are electives in the second and third years but a student has to satisfy history and humanities requirements. A social science *elective* at this institution is really a *required* social science course. Indulging passions, exploring new interests, making mistakes—all of the benefits of a university education—do not fit into the intellectual life of a budding engineer. And if an engineering student would like to sample a more advanced topic in an area like cryptography or robotics, there are no more free electives to accommodate the four additional courses that the computer science department says are prerequisite to the advanced courses.

The engineering professors, on the other hand, argue that classroom time needs to be devoted to the essential elements of engineering: there is a body of knowledge in which all graduates must be conversant if they are to call themselves engineers. Academics have a name for the courses that are required of all students: a *core curriculum*.

These engineers join Harry Lewis and John Erskine, who also had noble goals in mind, but there is substantial opinion that the urge to standardize a required body of knowledge in a core curriculum is not always noble. It is motivated at least as strongly by economics, organizational psychology, self-promotion, and other forces that shape faculty-centered universities. To the extent that these are also the driving forces behind inflexible, compulsory curricula, there is nothing noble about it.

Faculty Self-Interest and Required Courses

The Harvard Business School Case Study titled "The Required Course Subcommittee: A Sentence from Hell"[12] defines the problem in a way that is recognizable to every college professor because the dynamics are universal. It is a thinly disguised account of a continuing discussion at an Ivy League business school about replacing its inflexible, bloated core curriculum with something modern and flexible. The same principles apply to every department in every major research university. The problem starts with the inconsistency of academic life. The problem starts with tenure.

In chapters 2 and 3 of this book, I described the forces that shape tenure decisions at research universities: visibility and recognition in a research peer group, attracting students and collaborators in sufficient numbers to generate research income, and evidence of research that impacts the field. The forces that most influence the decisions of young faculty virtually ensure that a core curriculum represents faculty self-interest.

Core courses evolve to reflect the current research interests of professors, rather than the common interests of the students. At first blush, this seems counter-intuitive. After all, a well-meaning professor motivated by the best interests of the students would reason that teaching core courses increases the value of the curriculum in the students' eyes. Enthusiastic teaching of core courses should help the department's reputation, increasing a professor's value to the university, and therefore should reflect well on a candidate's record at tenure time. Because the core courses, almost by definition, should not cater to the research program of any particular professor, it seems obvious that—if only for economic reasons—a core curriculum should remain small and that the teaching duties should be shared among many professors.

"Required Course Subcommittee" dashes this hope, because teaching effectiveness in the core curriculum is simply not an important factor in tenure decisions at research universities. It seldom represents capital that can be spent elsewhere. A professor who focuses on teaching core courses and later decides to change jobs finds that it has no value to prospective employers. Core courses indeed need to be taught, but teaching outside one's research specialty—although it helps a current employer—does not help a professor secure a new position in case tenure is denied, and in Ivy League schools, tenure is frequently denied.

On the other hand, teaching advanced courses in one's research specialty is easy and enjoyable. It helps strengthen research credentials and is useful for identifying promising new graduate students. As a result, most departments bow to faculty pressure and slowly add content to the core to reflect the research interests of the professors. But a research-oriented course, once added to the core curriculum, is nearly impossible to remove. Dropping a course in a professor's specialty from the current core is an admission that the material is not central enough to be taught to all entering students, so it rarely happens. The result is a bloated core curriculum, like the thirty-eight-course engineering program that gives a student real elective choice in only 3 percent of the courses.

Changing to a system that does not try to march students in lockstep through a predetermined curriculum—that recognizes the individual traits of different minds—is difficult, but not impossible. Charles Eliot fundamentally changed the nature of higher education by simply throwing out the idea of core curriculum. He created a student-centered university in which faculty-self interest is balanced by student needs and interest. Harvard began an experiment with higher education in the long tail.

Memes and Patterns of Thought

If a compulsory core curriculum is at one end of a spectrum, then *patterns of thought* that motivate students are surely at the other end. The British evolutionary biologist Richard Dawkins popularized the concept of a *meme*[13] as a way of describing units of transmittable ideas, beliefs, or patterns. It is an idea that is particularly well-adapted to the Internet and the World Wide Web. There are examples everywhere of ideas, hoaxes, and behaviors that are born and propagated worldwide by Web sites and networks.

The producers of the 1990s film *The Blair Witch Project*,[14] for example, created a Web site to launch and propagate a legend for a series of supernatural events. The fictitious Maryland town drew thousands of believers who wanted to investigate for themselves a disappearance that never took place of characters who never existed.

"All your base are belong to us," a mistranslation of the phrase "All of your bases are under our control" in the opening scene of the video game Zero Wing,[15] was swept along by viral videos, online magazines like *Wired*, T-shirts, and signs placed along public roads. The phrase became an Internet phenomenon, leading to a small panic when the video Web site YouTube™ used the phrase "All your video are belong to us," as a notification that the site was down for maintenance.[16] Memes can be large or small, they can influence just a few people or entire populations, and they can be ephemeral or enduring. The plot of Neal Stephenson's science fiction novel *Snow Crash*[17] revolves around the viral transmission of memes throughout human civilization.

Dawkins's idea that there are cultural analogies to genetic units of transmission is controversial, and there is even contention about whether the study of memes is a valid field of scientific inquiry. Some critics even call it pseudoscientific dogma because of the implications on cultural evolution,[18] but there is little doubt that small changes in the way objects are perceived and imitative behaviors and small systems of belief are passed from person to person, and that the Internet has sped up the process enormously.

Students around the world are highly motivated by the desire to transmit or receive memes,[19] and they have become skilled at the use of technologies like instant messaging and social networking to accelerate the speed at which concepts spread through communities. Identifying and delivering important memes pushes to the long tail concepts like Joe Licata's *cultural proficiency*—concepts that are a way of looking at the world and are best transmitted outside of the classroom.

A Way of Looking at the World

Patterns of thought are not easy to incorporate into standard degree programs because they cut across the entire curriculum. Many American students in the late 1990s were notoriously dedicated to the idea that the point of engineering education was innovation that could lead to the creation of a new company and therefore to great wealth. Business schools began incorporating entrepreneurship into their standard undergraduate courses.[20] *Service learning* is at the other extreme.[21] Motivated by a desire for positive societal change, students in increasing numbers are seeking out opportunities to apply skills acquired in the classroom to problems that affect communities. Classroom success in both entrepreneurship and service learning has been mixed, largely because what is needed for success is a different way of looking at the world, not necessarily a specific set of skills. To entrepreneurs and social activists alike, the most critical experience occurs outside the classroom. To advocates of study abroad programs, the critical missing piece might be cultural proficiency. It is also acquired outside the classroom. There are dozens of meme-like patterns that are important to students, but that are unlikely to be transmitted in the classroom.

This is what led Charles Eliot to overthrow the compulsory classical curriculum: students whose motivations can be satisfied by extracurricular activities learn to devalue classrooms in favor of networks, associations, and experience that are more relevant to their career goals. In the twenty-first century, the successful universities will be the ones that have learned how to capture the passion of those students.

Architects, Not Engineers

Between majors and memes are concepts that have great demand, but are so specific to locales and situations that large-scale delivery is not feasible. In 2004, the government of South Korea asked American universities for help in designing a non-Korean solution to a problem that was distinctly Korean.

South Korea's emergence as a producer of automobiles and consumer electronics has been fueled in part by fierce economic competition with the Japanese. Although it is one of the world's largest economies, Korea is still a small country with close ties among government, commerce, and education. It is not uncommon to see federal initiatives that promote commercial goals by involving leading academic institutions.

Engineering and computer science graduates of Korean universities are well prepared in theoretical subjects. They are mathematically sophisticated, their teachers are demanding, and there is national pride in the achievements of South Korean students—particularly when compared with their American, Chinese, and Japanese peers. It was something of a surprise, therefore, when in 2004, the South Korean Ministry of Information and Communication declared that even the best software engineering programs in Korea were aiming at the wrong set of skills.[22]

It was a national priority to raise the level of design capability in companies like Samsung and LG. Although Korean technology competes with the best in the world, companies like Sony in Japan, Apple in the United States, and Lenovo in China were widely thought to have a competitive edge when it came to putting the technology pieces together in ways that were compelling to hundreds of millions of increasingly sophisticated consumers of cell phones, computers, and digital cameras.

Wooing this next generation of customers would take not only cutting-edge electronics but also a compelling user experience: a mix of reliability, ease of use, and beautiful design. Complicated user manuals, frequent operational glitches, or a clunky look and feel would not cut it. Companies like Sony and Nokia had become global brands by providing just such experiences for their customers, and their architects tended to be fluent in not only design, but also cognitive science, artificial intelligence, e-commerce, and computer-human interfaces. Successfully applying new design concepts to a global consumer market requires the ability to take ideas from each of these fields and synthesize them into new product features and capabilities.

Unfortunately, graduates of Korean universities were taught mainly technical skills. As I. P. Park from Samsung's corporate technology office explained it to me, "We are very good at producing programmers, but what Samsung needs are software architects who can synthesize. This is a pattern of thought that is not being taught in our colleges and universities."

The Korean government approached Georgia Tech and a number of other top-ranked engineering schools with a distinctly non-Korean proposal. As the Minister of Information Technology told me in late 2004, "We would like you to offer a new post-graduate degree program in software architecture, and we will select one of our best local universities to work with."

This was a very non-Korean approach to a problem that is uniquely Korean. Korean companies did not need more expert programmers; they needed more expert synthesizers—software architects. The Koreans were going to select a non-Korean partner to teach their professors how to teach their students how to think about software architecture. The Georgia Tech/Korea University Joint Master's in Embedded Software Architecture began enrolling students in the fall of 2005 with a plan to turn the entire program over to Korea University (KU) in 2009. KU would then be the launching pad for a new software engineering curriculum that would gradually replace the older, more technology-oriented program with one that was more suited to the needs of Korean industry.

The Korean experience marks a trend, not a fad. As more students join the global higher education market, the concept of a standard set of courses to meet "the common needs of all students" seems less relevant. Abundant choice means abundant variety, so universities that cling to principled but inflexible curricula are less likely to be able to survive the competitive onslaught that surely faces colleges and universities in the Middle.

No serious observer of higher education anticipates that curriculum design will evolve toward the chaotic pattern of fleeting thoughts and catchphrases that are captured in Internet memes, but there is much effort being devoted to capturing less transitory patterns of thought as a way of organizing the collegiate learning experience. In the next chapter, I describe a large-scale experiment that is based on just such an effort.

12 Threads

Once we've brain-drained all our technology into other countries, once things have evened out . . . once our edge in natural resources has been made irrelevant . . . once the Invisible Hand has taken all those historical inequities and smeared them out into a broad global layer of . . . prosperity—y'know what? There's only four things we do better than anyone else

music
movies
microcode (software)
high-speed pizza delivery

—Neal Stephenson[1]

Computer science has been a recognizable academic discipline for a scant forty years, but it is already a model of academic innovation. It remains today one of the most popular undergraduate majors. Published curricula and current practice identify core concepts and skills, many of which are highly prized by employers. But for a brief period beginning around 2001, it appeared possible that computer science might actually disappear as an academic field of study.

A Downward Spiral

Undergraduate enrollments and degree production in computer science have shown a dramatic up-and-down pattern throughout the past twenty-five years (see figure 12.1), but in early 2002, some department heads and deans started to wonder why applications had not recovered from the most recent dip. Beginning with the collapse of information technology companies in 2000, enrollments in undergraduate computer science degree programs began a precipitous decline.

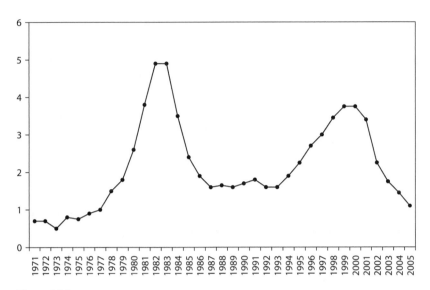

Figure 12.1
Enrollment changes in computer science (percent of total enrollment).
Source: Computing Research Association.

The number of undergraduate computer science degrees increased signif-icantly from 1981 to 1986 and decreased significantly from 1987 to 1997.[2] Enrollments peaked again during the dot-com boom of the late 1990s. They started falling again in 2001, but this time alarm bells went off in academic circles. There were fundamental reasons that students were bailing out of computer science as a career choice.

An August 2005 *New York Times* article reported that "the number of students choosing computer science as a major is 39 percent lower than in the fall of 2000, the last of the dot-com bubble years."[3] In the summer of 2004, a *CNET News* article provided the following snapshot of undergradu-ate computer science programs:

MIT's electrical engineering and computer science department-new undergraduate majors down to under 200, from 240 in the previous year; Carnegie Mellon's school of computer science—applications down to 2,000, from 3,200 in 2001; University of California at Berkeley—undergraduate computer science majors down to 226, from 260 in the spring of 2003; and Stanford University—undergraduate computer science majors down to 118 in the past year, from 171 in 2000–2001.[4]

Even more ominously, the number of women entering the field fell quickly into the single-digit range. Some linked the decline in under-graduate computing program enrollments to negative student and parent perceptions, especially given the prominent media reports of outsourcing, offshoring, and the fear of future job losses.[5] By 2005, more than half of the Fortune 500 companies surveyed reported outsourcing software work to India. Predictions were that a quarter of the jobs in the U.S. computer, software, and information technology industry would be sent offshore by 2010.[6] So although there was an urgency for preparing American students for the new, flat world described by Thomas Friedman,[7] students and parents seemed to be coming to the realization that a degree in computer science no longer offered the lure of guaranteed employment that it once seemed to offer.

To further complicate matters, students had abundant choices. Computing had become so linked with other disciplines—within engineering and science and beyond—that students interested in computing no longer had to major in computer science to pursue their interests. Humanities departments, business schools, and graphic design programs all offered their own versions of introductory computer science—courses that were more relevant to their problems and where students could get away from what some said were the "socially challenged" and "geeky" computer science majors. Significantly, these alternative courses attracted the same female students that computer science departments were trying desperately to recruit for their programs.

Ironically, the predicted demand for computing jobs in the United States remained robust, but only for graduates whose academic background included courses outside the traditional core programming courses. According to the *New York Times*, "for people who stay in computing, the job outlook is brightest for those skilled in the application of technology. While jobs in categories like programming have declined since 2000, according to the Labor Department, the need for information technology experts has not."[8]

Underlying Problems

Professional societies and the Computing Research Association (CRA)—the principle organizing body for academic and industrial research centers in computing and related fields—mounted task forces to counter what was by late 2002 perceived to be a mounting threat to the survival of computing as a discipline and to the future competitiveness of U.S. industry. In 2002, I became dean of Georgia Tech's College of Computing, and I acutely felt the need to identify the causes of the sudden drop in enrollments. Although I was being paid to fix the underlying problems, I had serious doubts that the problems were solvable.

Though many of my colleagues believed that there were no fundamental problems with computer science education—and that what we really needed were a better explanation of the value of a degree in computer science and more aggressive marketing of the field—I was suspicious. I had just returned to higher education from industry, where I had seen firsthand what happens to a product that a company thinks is great even as its customers say otherwise. I knew it was never a good idea to try to outsmart a marketplace in which customers have many choices.

I thought it equally likely that the computer science field itself had become inwardly focused and—like medieval masters' universities—bent on preserving a set of academic practices and traditions that had become increasingly irrelevant. If that were true, then the best course might be to imagine what value a computer science degree might have by looking beyond the production of the programmers and technicians who dominated the graduating classes of the country's computer science programs.

A Certain Kind of Mind

My years in industry had also given me a chance to see in person the effects of the current approach on careers: graduates of top computer science and computer engineering programs with great credentials and problem-solving ability whose careers were nevertheless adrift after five years. I saw engineers unable or unwilling to work on teams in which design and storytelling had to blend seamlessly with architecture. Worse yet, I saw narrow technology views and biases carried over into the workplace—students who had inherited a professor's penchant for referring to Microsoft as the Evil Empire or who would only program a certain brand of computer. It was very expensive to retrain these students, and many times they never added enough value to the company to justify training costs.

What had value to me and the companies I helped lead were computer science graduates who were extremely adaptable, adept at forging new and dynamic relationships, tackling novel challenges, and synthesizing the big picture. The most valuable new employees were more competent at utilizing creativity and tacit knowledge. I thought it very likely that the current way of teaching undergraduates in computer science was not well tuned to this goal or to the increasingly interconnected, global economy generally. It was equally likely that Daniel Pink's *A Whole New Mind* had it right, and that his vocabulary could be used to define the value of a university education:

The last few decades have belonged to a certain kind of person with a certain kind of mind—computer programmers who could crank code, lawyers who could craft contracts, MBAs who could crunch numbers. But the keys to the kingdom are changing hands. The future belongs to a very different kind of person with a very different kind of mind—creators and empathizers, pattern recognizers, and meaning makers. These people—artists, inventors, designers, storytellers, caregivers, consolers, big picture thinkers—will now reap society's richest rewards and share its greatest joys.[9]

Like other highly regarded computer science programs, Georgia Tech's degrees in computer science had become locked into a single view of computing, aimed at producing a single kind of graduate. We were not graduating students who would be the artists, inventors, and big picture thinkers who would be in the most demand. What the marketplace was demanding was a computer science graduate with a *different kind of mind,* and we had no idea how to attract and educate such a person.

The task forces mounted by CRA and others eventually came to the same conclusion: computer science had become ossified and inflexible. It was an eerie repetition of history. We had become the new masters' universities, unable to meet the needs of students or the requirements for individual competitiveness of the kind required by the new, global knowledge economy. We had become very good at producing a single kind of graduate.

Strangely enough, the day-to-day lives of computer science faculty members were unruffled by all of this. In fact, graduate enrollments were up. Top-ranked PhD programs saw applications rise as recent graduates discovered that jobs were hard to find and decided to spend a few more years in school. In a faculty-centered university, attracting more doctoral students is a sign of good things to come. The decline in undergraduate enrollments was an added bonus: it meant less time teaching introductory courses, and more time to spend on research. However, declining undergraduate enrollments meant declining budgets, so department heads and deans could not ignore the situation. They had to act, and they had to find creative ways to convince their faculty to act.

No More Core

Some leading universities began reviewing their computer science programs. One approach was to create a new computer science core curriculum, a strategy that was doomed from the outset. If students were not choosing computer science as a career, it was not because they hated the core curriculum. It was because they did not like what we were telling them about life after graduation. We were training undergraduates for unappealing and increasingly unstable careers. Although there had been investment in computing-related education innovation at the graduate level for many years[10], there had been no major innovations to undergraduate computer science curricula and programs for many years.

Another approach was to search for other disciplines to merge with, an approach that was called *CS+x*. The problem with this approach was that the other disciplines (the "*x*" fields) had already figured out that they did not need computer science to attract good students. They were happy, for example, to offer a creative writing course to computer science majors who wanted to specialize in the design of video games, but the game design studios had already discovered that their best prospects were graduates in the arts and humanities who also had an aptitude for technology.

There were many practical reasons to reject CS+x as a viable approach. There was evidence that naïvely combining two academic cultures led to superficiality in both and therefore to quality compromises, so CS+x posed the serious risk of leading to the pursuit of short-term "trendy ideas." Like most programs, the Tech curriculum was a warren of prerequisites, requirements, and multisemester course sequences. Matching computer science students to other curricula—particularly in fast-paced fields where specialty courses were changing all the time—would have been complex and expensive. Like most universities, we lacked a platform for CS+x, so I was sure that such a program was not sustainable.

Some departments experimented with new components of their computer science core curriculum: international studies, core courses to broaden students' experiences and expand their horizons, a reduction in requirements, an expanded range of capstone experiences, and interdisciplinary studies.[11] Although these were necessary changes, they did not solve the problem. What was happening around the country did not go far enough in fundamentally changing the way undergraduate computer science was taught; more importantly, none of these approaches would dramatically increase the market value of computing graduates.

Beginning in the fall of 2004, the faculty of Georgia Tech's College of Computing made a choice that the faculty members in "Required Course Subcommittee" were unable to make. They decided to try to redesign the entire undergraduate curriculum to better match the needs of the global information technology workforce, while at the same time maintaining the high quality standards of the university. The problem to be solved was how to do that in a traditional curriculum with its vertical, layered hierarchy of core courses and electives. The result was a radical departure from the vertically organized concept of a major in computer science. We called the curriculum *Threads.*

The idea of a *threaded curriculum* does away with a monolithic core and various pools of electives. By treating computer science as a discipline in an increasingly inclusive spectrum of concepts, skills, and memes, students would all of a sudden have the ability to select an interesting part of the spectrum.

Threads are nine sets of broad, horizontal skills, any two of which could be intertwined to make a degree in computer science. In total, there are thirty-six possible combinations of Threads. The number nine is not magic. Other institutions have defined other threads that they think are important. Some programs, like Stanford's, use just a few threads, and some, like MIT's engineering program, use many. Students learn a robust set of technical skills in all Threads, and much of the basic content in each Thread overlaps. Regardless of which two Threads a student chooses, the combination of Threads yields an accredited Bachelor of Science degree in computer science.

Combining Threads

Here is an example of how all of this works. One of the Threads is called Computing and Media. It prepares students to work at the intersection of computing and design by helping them understand the technical capabilities of systems that are used in the creative arts. It contains technology courses but it also contains courses in, for example, literature, so that a student understands the concept of a narrative arc. Another Thread is called Computing and Modeling. It prepares students with the technical knowledge and skills necessary for designing mathematical models from physics, chemistry, or even psychology.

Many Georgia Tech computer science graduates subsequently go on to work in the film and entertainment industry, where the Tech brand is known and respected. Though it was important to us that a graduate of the new Threads curriculum would continue to be as attractive to these potential employers as someone with a traditional Georgia Tech degree, it was also important that these Threads would produce a new kind of graduate. We were aiming to attract students who wanted to learn about animation, perhaps to work for a studio like Pixar or a video game company. Students in the Media and Modeling Threads would be creative storytellers with a feeling for the humanities and the arts, who would be attractive to studios in ways that CS+x graduates would never be. It was a risky approach, but

I was not asking my faculty members to bet everything on a hunch that it would all work out. We had good reasons for believing that Threads was going to be a successful experiment.

Even before Threads was implemented in 2006, we had begun enrolling undergraduates in a new degree program called Computational Media that incorporated the essential elements of these two Threads. It was an experimental prototype for Threads and was designed to tell us whether the new approach would be effective. The results were dramatic and immediate. While other computing programs were still in steep decline, the Computational Media program had enrolled sixty students in its first semester. By the end of the first year, enrollment topped one hundred students and doubled every year for the next three years. This program now rivals the traditional computer science degree at Georgia Tech in popularity. Significantly, well over half of all Computational Media students are women.

Curriculum Engineering

A real problem with a flexible curriculum is determining exactly what a student has achieved upon completion of a program. Accreditation in computer science has been a controversial idea since its inception in the 1980s, and many highly ranked programs at private institutions dismiss it as irrelevant to their missions. Georgia Tech is a public university, so a dean is not free to pick and choose how programs are accredited, but, even at its best, accreditation is only a threshold requirement, not an indicator of program quality. Despite my personal discomfort with the idea of accreditation and the agencies that administer it, accreditation was a fact of life at Georgia Tech that I could not fight. I decided to use accreditation to make a connection between the "old" degree program that had brand recognition and significant market challenges with the new Threaded curriculum that had great market acceptance but no established brand. Threads was designed from the beginning to yield only degrees that would be accredited by ABET, the agency for accrediting engineering and computing degrees in the United States.

More important was the impact that Threads would have on the brand value of a degree. Alumni were generally supportive of the changes— especially after the wave of favorable publicity put a spotlight on their alma mater—but some existing students were resentful of the changes, and frankly fearful that the degrees would be "watered-down" versions of a difficult curriculum in which they had achieved considerable success. Employers—especially those in emerging areas like biomedical information technology who perceived that Threads would increase the supply of graduates in health-related disciplines—were in the main supportive of the new programs.

There were some, however, who had come to rely on our program as an important source of master practitioners, graduates with high levels of skill and sophistication in programming and system design. The Georgia Tech brand was important to these companies. With the introduction of Threads, I found myself explaining to them that they were still going to be able to hire the same kind of graduate, but that the portfolio of skills would be broader and would appeal to other employers in other industries.

This was such a concern that we inserted a new element into the program to reflect student career aspirations and employer expectations. This new element had many of the memetic features that I talked about in the previous chapter of this book. It was aimed at providing skills and knowledge outside the classroom that would help students align their academic preparation with longer-term career goals.

We called this new element "roles." We intended roles to be memes that would propagate outside formal coursework. A role encapsulates a set of experiences and a network of colleagues and mentors that represent student talent and interests. For a student who wanted to be a master practitioner, we created a role called *master practitioner* and assured employers that great programmers could be found there. Master practitioners could be found participating in and supervising programming contests, grand challenge prize competitions, and robot tournaments. Likewise, there were roles for entrepreneurs: business plan competitions and incubators for student-led startups. Service learning students received foundation grants to implement projects with a positive impact on society. Research grants and formal appointments in research labs allowed students who wanted to continue their education in graduate programs to get a head start on their careers.

Threads and the Long Tail

Combined with the thirty-six possible threaded degrees, roles effectively allowed us to create ninety highly tailored undergraduate experiences, each with its own identity and reputation. Threads replaced a single, monolithic, and rather inflexible curriculum with ninety separate degree programs and in the process moved computer science majors at Georgia Tech well into the long tail of the distribution of disciplines. How were we going to explain exactly what a graduate of Threads knew about a particular topic? The answer for most degree programs is accreditation, but accrediting agencies purposely turn a blind eye to the reputations of the institutions they are certifying.

Our problem was different. We needed to find a way to assure employers that our reputation would remain intact. There is a complicated relationship between reputation and the American accreditation bureaucracy, a system that was an accidental by-product of philanthropic support for early universities. There were examples of countries that had not tamed this chaotic relationship, and we wanted to avoid falling into the same traps.

India's modern university movement struggles to overcome its recent history. The ghosts of ineffective and corrupt regulation still haunt higher education. Compared with the three thousand or so accredited universities in the United States, India accredits more than eighteen thousand institutions that altogether enroll eleven million students. Many of these schools are little more than storefront operations that offer programs of such low quality that graduates are not qualified for any position that requires competitive skill levels. According to some estimates, only 20 to 30 percent of their graduates are employable.[12] Only a small fraction of these are internationally ranked top schools. Accreditation is supposed to provide quality guarantees, but Indian employers so distrust the local system of accreditation that companies like Wipro cobrand undergraduate programs to expand the number of qualified graduates. The ties between accreditation and quality are tenuous, and without underlying networks to validate university brands, a chaotic marketplace like India's cannot possibly succeed. Threaded programs and even more extreme degrees of specialization could threaten the American higher education marketplace with similar chaos.

Our approach was pragmatic, but not very exciting. We relied on traditional accreditation so that we could begin enrolling students. This is, however, not a solution that scales well to hundreds of degrees and hundreds of thousands of specialized programs. We had to add establishing and managing reputations to the growing list of problems that arise when there are abundant choices in higher education.

IV Abelard to Apple

13 The Stardom of Leonard Susskind

Physicist Leonard Susskind is an unlikely rock star. At once gruff—he is the son of a New York plumber and once thought about entering the trade himself—and engaging, he speaks with a matter-of-fact economy about quantum mechanics, the most perplexing of physical theories. Susskind is one of the small band of inventors of string theory—an ambitious, complex, and controversial mathematical explanation of how certain subatomic particles are bound together—but it is his lectures on more basic subjects that draw the most attention these days.

In Stanford lecture halls, he roams the stage, sipping on coffee from a Styrofoam cup and occasionally choking on one of the large cookies he keeps on hand. He does not use Microsoft PowerPoint presentations, preferring instead to scribble equations and matrices on a large whiteboard. He confuses terms ("Is this a bra- or a -ket? I never can remember"). Students whose questions venture into metaphysical interpretations of the literal mathematics (the *mechanics* of quantum mechanics) are not encouraged. This is all despite his recent popular book on quantum theory that ventures into speculation on the nature of the universe.

Leonard Susskind is also one of a growing band of university professors who open their classrooms to the world, simply because there are thousands of students who are interested in what they have to say. Joining Susskind are economists from Oxford, art historians from the University of Montreal, and mathematicians from a dazzling array of universities. Sometimes they broadcast video of their lectures online, and most of them distribute their course materials for free. Some are committed bloggers who attract tens of thousands of visitors to topics ranging from the 2008 financial crisis to abstract mathematical theories that would otherwise be inaccessible to most people. At times, they even rival the most sensational celebrity gossip and political blogs in popularity. They do this not in exchange for tuition or textbook royalties, but because—like Peter Abelard—they are at the forefront of a revolution that will lead to a new kind of higher education.

Between Mr. Wizard and Fr. Abelard

Leonard Susskind's course on quantum entanglement is rigorous, but it is clearly intended for students with minimal preparation in physics and mathematics. He develops the notation and mathematics as he goes, and it appears to be effortless. The aim of the course is to explain a physical principle that even Einstein called "spooky." Nobel laureate physicist Richard Feynman publicly despaired of really understanding it. Quantum entanglement tries to explain how measurements of otherwise independent bodies (such as electrons) can be correlated even across vast distances—for all its weirdness, it is a serious tool in fields like microelectronics and medicine.

In 1951, Donald Herbert, an unknown actor armed with a general science degree from Wisconsin's Lacrosse State Teachers College, convinced WNBQ-TV, the local NBC outlet in Chicago, to air four episodes of a half-hour program aimed at young people that combined Herbert's interests in science, education, and acting. He called himself Mr. Wizard. The *Watch Mr. Wizard* show became a runaway hit, airing on more than a hundred stations around the world. Mr. Wizard was praised by NSF, backed by General Motors, and honored with awards from the Peabody Foundation. The show was widely credited with raising NBC's brand as a producer and broadcaster of educational programming, and it was a dramatic demonstration of the disruptive power of the new medium of television on education. At the height of Herbert's popularity, there were fifty thousand Mr. Wizard clubs across North America. Using clever props, young partners, and light, witty dialog, Don Herbert made hands-on science exciting and accessible to an entire generation of children. It would be easy to imagine a *Watch Mr. Wizard* show about quantum entanglement that brings into play the quantum physicists' colorful language of parallel universes and undead cats.

But Leonard Susskind is not Mr. Wizard. The Stanford course on quantum entanglement uses no props (beyond a pointing stick that Susskind hauls out on occasion to indicate the direction of a vector) and no animations. Susskind is deliberate, however. Each lecture builds on the layers of mathematical vocabulary—what physicists call the "machinery"—established in prior lectures to establish the increasingly abstract insights that can be achieved only by manipulating the machinery. It is not easy, and the audience asks questions that sometimes betray confusion and frustration. Some of the students clearly have advanced preparation in other fields, but

Susskind discourages easy "isn't this just like . . . ?" analogies that do not fit into his orderly progression of the material. Sometimes students are way out in front of him. When Susskind finds himself in a conceptual box, he has to find a way out. That might not happen until the next lecture, after he has had a few days to think about it. He is most patient with questions from students who are clearly struggling with the material. He often starts a lecture by returning to a particularly tricky explanation from the previous class to try it one more time. Leonard Susskind's course on quantum entanglement is a real, take-no-prisoners physics course, and it was for a brief period in late 2007 perhaps the most popular university course in the world.[1]

Physics-Colored Glasses

Walter Lewin *is* Mr. Wizard. He paces in front of projections of colorful photos in his MIT class on the birth and death of stars and talks about marshmallows with the energy of atomic bombs. Wild hair flying about, Lewin—who is in his seventies—swings on a pendulum for his freshman physics course and stalks stuffed monkeys in full safari regalia. The notes for his courses can be downloaded for free from a Web site called MIT World by anyone with an Internet connection. They are the same notes that MIT freshmen use for their introductory physics classes.

If Leonard Susskind is not Mr. Wizard, neither is he Peter Abelard. But he may play as important a role as universities transcend their traditional boundaries in search of their value in the twenty-first century. He joins Walter Lewin and others in the global classrooms enabled by Apple's iTunes and other technologies that draw thousands of students from around the world in much the same way that medieval scholars did.

iTunes U is a section of Apple's popular site for downloading music and video that has been reserved for educational materials. Nearly three hundred universities from around the world have placed materials on the iTunes U site, a number that grows by a dozen or more every month. The diversity of participating institutions is enormous. Tallahassee Community College has recorded its Anatomy and Physiology Lab, and along with dozens of other courses, uploaded them to iTunes U, but so did Yale's John Rogers, whose twenty-four lectures on Milton constitute course number ENGL 220 from the Yale undergraduate catalog.

iTunes U is not the only shopping mall for university courses. The University of Texas operates a Web site called World Lecture Hall[2] that aggregates courses from universities around the world. The Yahoo! Distance

Learning Directory is a gateway to 460 colleges and universities that offer free content. Academic Earth[3] collects video content from Élite universities and encourages its viewers to download, embed, and share the videos in any way they want.

Google's YouTube EDU combines thousand of lectures with the twenty-first century versions of *Mr. Wizard* broadcasts. Jim Kakalios, a physics professor from the University of Minnesota and author of *The Physics of Superheroes*[4], was a science consultant to Warner Brothers for its science fiction film *The Watchmen*. His video *Science of the Watchmen* poses the following question to viewers: "In *Watchmen*, Dr. Manhattan has amazing superpowers. Are any of these powers possible?" The answers are intriguing even for viewers who already know something about physics: "Well, there is no such thing as an intrinsic field, but if there were . . . perhaps he is diffracting his quantum mechanical wave function." A graphic novel—a type of comic book—is turned into an opportunity to teach the physics of waves to anyone who happens to be browsing the popular aggregator of videos.

On many of these Web sites, there is a link to a university that has a vaguely promising but unfamiliar name: The Open University. Following the link to the Open University (OU) leads to a web page that advises visitors: "Warning! Content may transform your life." OU looks like one of a hundred other online college Web sites, but it is not. OU is the royally chartered distance learning university in Great Britain.

The Open University was founded in 1969 and is today the largest university of any kind in the United Kingdom. It has one of the largest alumni networks, but it is OU's embrace of the Internet that has made it one of the most influential universities in the world. In 2006, OU turned off its traditional media broadcasts and now conducts all its courses on the Internet. OU is unabashedly British, and it draws its instructors and inspiration from its older cousins, Oxford and Cambridge, but like the new American universities of the nineteenth century, the ties to OU's historical roots are tenuous. OU is not simply a collection of courses. It is a university.

Oxford and Cambridge have been slow to adapt to the Internet. They offer online courses only in fields that cater to nontraditional students, and their offerings are sparse. In the spring of 2010, Cambridge offered only eleven online courses, all of them aimed at students interested in real estate training or executive coaching. Nearly four hundred years after Harvard imported the rigid, circumscribed curriculum and outmoded organization of Oxford and Cambridge, some American universities are starting to imitate OU, another British model for higher education, and the long-term effects might be more profound.

The Open University tracked its adoption rate during the first thirty-one weeks of operation on iTunes U. A total of 313,100 visitors downloaded 2,373,799 lectures from iTunes at an average rate of 100,000 downloads per week.). One new student was added to the university every forty-five seconds. One out of every six iTunes customers clicked through to the Open University Web site.

In many ways, the Open University resembles the first medieval universities. Most of OU's scholars are drawn from distant lands: 88 percent of Open University downloads are to computers located outside the United Kingdom. But these are surface characteristics. Online students rarely ever meet, so they do not band together in the same way that, for example, students in the Spanish guild did in fifteenth-century Bologna. Nor are students bound to the university by the attraction of a famous scholar like Leonard Susskind. There are technologies that would help, but OU does not use them. Students flock to Open University for different reasons.

Open University is a rare success story. Most traditional universities that band together with other institutions on iTunes U, World Lecture Hall, or the dozens of other Web sites that aggregate online courses never achieve the level of recognition that OU has achieved. For every Stanford University—whose "Computer Science 101" course has been downloaded a million times—there are ten small colleges in the Middle whose course materials are only accessed by their current students. Nevertheless, it makes perfect economic sense for universities to congregate at iTunes U, even though there may be much larger and more successful universities that will get most of the web traffic. Internet entrepreneurs have a name for this kind of cooperation among competitors. It is called *coopetition*.

In the hubs-and-spokes world of web commerce, it is better to be near a hub than out on the end of a spoke where there are few connections. It is the same for universities that want to attract students. The Open University is successful online because it has a forty-year-old brand in distance education, and iTunes U makes it easy to find OU courses. Stanford's computer science department is ranked number one in the world, so it is a natural destination for anyone who wants to sit in on an introductory course, and iTunes U is a convenient on-ramp. Both universities have brand-name recognition, and they would be hubs even if iTunes U did not exist. But most of the institutions that list themselves in online catalogs would not otherwise be close to a hub in the map of the Internet. Coopetition is the only way for them to survive online. Even so, many find that the costs of maintaining their online presence are not manageable, and they wink out of web existence.

The Open University is a traditional university that specializes in distance education to nontraditional students who are interested in traditional degree programs. It does not really enable higher education in the long tail, but because OU was created for nontraditional students, the economics of running the university have been tuned to match the costs of their distribution technologies. OU's costs are manageable because there is an existing demand for their programs, and the incremental cost of adding another student to an online classroom is essentially zero.

One of the reasons OU has been so successful is that the entire university was designed around the idea of a platform, so the costs of additional instruction can be spread across many students. When OU used television to broadcast its courses, the British government cross-subsidized the courses through its ownership of the channels. The move to the Web changed the business environment for OU, but web distribution has its own cross-subsidies to help out. The Web sites that market and provide access to universities like OU have some costs to absorb, but those costs tend to be offset by the profit-making components of web businesses—music and video sales in the case of Apple and advertising in the case of Google, for example.

Although iTunes U is a long tail technology, most of the institutions that it aggregates are—like OU and Stanford—traditional universities that offer traditional degrees and courses to nontraditional students. Their degree programs are not in the long tail. Institutions without an overwhelming brand advantage have no chance of success—even in this environment—because their degree programs have little value. Even coopetition cannot overcome that hurdle. More radical changes, like Threaded curricula, would help, but most universities in the Middle are years away from beginning to think about change on this scale.

One reason that it is so hard for universities in the Middle to contemplate the kind of massive change needed to prosper in the long tail is the fragility of their business models. It is not clear how much disruption they can tolerate. Establishing a business base for a Threaded or any other long tail curriculum requires a revolution in how a university is funded, and how its stakeholders value their educational experience. As the number of stakeholders gets larger, they will have a different view of their university experience.

Meanwhile, those universities with more attractive value propositions will continue to gain an even larger competitive advantage. Some of this disruption will slowly happen from below, as proprietary, for-profit universities gain market share. But disruption from above will be sudden, as nontraditional students discover the online hubs that have overwhelming value in the long tail.

As reported in the *New York Times*,[5] students in Walter Lewin's MIT introductory physics course are much more frequently going to be like sixty-two-year-old florist Steve Boigon, who wants to "look at life through physics-colored glasses." The idea of physics-colored glasses is so far out on the long tail that it is almost a meme. How many Boigons are out there? If there are only a hundred, the physics-colored glasses meme is already much more popular than some majors with textbooks and curricula and around which traditional universities erect buildings. It turns out that looking at life through physics-colored glasses is not very far out on the long tail at all.

MIT and Velvet Ropes

In early 2001, MIT president Charles Vest visited me in my offices at Hewlett-Packard to describe his plan for making virtually all of MIT's course materials freely available on the Internet. It was an interesting conversation, and I probably asked a few polite questions, but I was not thinking very much about higher education in those days, and so I missed completely the importance of what Vest described that afternoon in my Palo Alto office. Chuck Vest had given me a glimpse of how a revolution gets started.

It is one of the inconsistencies in the life of a university that it can with all sincerity proclaim itself a beacon of learning and open inquiry for the community—and make itself available to outsiders through lectures, seminars, and exhibits—and at the same time close its doors to those who want to attend its classes. As I discussed in chapter 5, there is no cost to most universities when a visitor plops down in a back row seat for a day or even a semester of "Introduction to Chemistry," but the practice of sitting in on a course without paying tuition—once common practice on college campuses—is today forbidden at most traditional institutions. The argument that colleges give for the velvet rope that allows only a favored few to enter is an economic one: where is the fairness in treating paying customers and nonpaying browsers the same? In those rare cases in which a professor has published a textbook, an interested outsider can always get a taste of a class by purchasing the book, but—however attractive the financial rewards might be to the professor who pockets twelve cents of every textbook dollar spent—it does not help the university's bottom line. Universities whose faculty members write a shelf-load of best-selling textbooks still have velvet ropes controlling access to their lecture halls, because they believe that the classroom experience defines their value.

An occasional observer might slip past the guards and find his or her way into a lecture or two, but the teaching materials for the course are out of legal reach. The course syllabus, schedule of exams, problems sets, and lecture notes are all kept under lock and key, accessible only to paying customers. Once the province of teaching assistants who would spend long hours cranking blue copies from mimeograph machines for distribution to students at a penny per page, the production of course materials is now a business. Major college campuses are surrounded by commercial copy centers that dispense copies of course materials—along with school supplies, courier shipping, and business card printing—at whatever rate the market will bear.

Even more notable is the shift to electronic distribution of course materials, a move that must have disrupted plans for companies that relied on the profitable volume of campus copying. Enterprising professors have been emailing notes to students or posting them on Web sites for years, but now entire universities have moved into the business of electronic distribution. Campus software called *course management systems* allows institutions to have the best of both worlds: cost-free distribution and access control. Universities can use course management systems to publish electronic versions of course materials, while retaining a measure of control over who can see next week's reading assignment or the answers to last week's quiz, and they can build into student fees the enormously expensive costs of purchasing and operating the software. A course management system is a very effective way of letting only the right people into the classroom, and—for those institutions that believe in the value locked behind the classroom door—the velvet rope of access control is the whole point of the university.

Vest was muted, almost tentative, the day he described for me MIT's plans to bring that belief crashing to the ground. In a move as bold as Charles Eliot's dismemberment of Harvard's required core:

MIT pledged to make available on the Web, free of charge to teachers and learners everywhere, the substantially complete teaching materials from virtually all of the approximately two thousand subjects we teach on our campus.[6]

He did not say so at the time—because web-based video distribution was still in its infancy, and iTunes U had not yet been created—but Vest's plans would grow to include video access to lectures from the likes of Walter Lewin.

The Vest plan was just as dramatic as Eliot's, but—unlike Harvard in the 1860s—MIT shook the foundations of higher education. In the space of a few months, MIT's OpenCourseWare project fundamentally changed the value equation for all colleges and universities by increasing the alternatives for all learners around the world—for free. Increasing the number of alternatives is a disruptive force in higher education.

Like the Bishop of Perugia in 1558, every university administrator in the world would now be faced with a modern-day version of the Jesuit priest Nicholas, who would point out that "if we use Sasso's book, they will say what our students have learned, they have learned from Sasso, not from us."[7] MIT ushered in the era of *open courseware*.

At first, even Vest had trouble with the concept. After all, MIT's initiative had its roots in a plan to mount a profitable distance education subsidiary, so the jump to free distribution of almost everything that both classroom teachers and their institutions held dear involved a substantial leap of faith:

OpenCourseWare looks counter-intuitive in a market-driven world. It goes against the grain of current material values, but it really is consistent with what I believe is the best about MIT . . . it expresses our belief in the way education can be advanced— by constantly widening access to information and by inspiring others to participate. . . . Simply put, OpenCourseWare is a natural marriage of American higher education and the capabilities of the World Wide Web.[8]

No matter how revolutionary, distribution of intellectual property by any means is governed by an international set of laws, regulations, and conventions. In the United States and Western Europe, printed and electronic content is created and published under international copyright laws. The penalties for violating U.S. copyright law can be considerable: up to $150,000 in civil court and federal criminal penalties on top of that.

Electronic distribution of music and video has made it even more complicated to follow the letter of the law, as music companies and movie studios rush to enforce copyright law as a defense against illegal piracy. Developing countries sometimes see electronic distribution as a way of freely acquiring content that they would otherwise have to pay for: a concept abhorred by copyright owners, who in turn set up complicated legal and technological protocols for sharing protected material. The serious business of OpenCourseWare would have been doomed to a thicket of conflicting laws and practices were it not for an unlikely marriage of lawyers, anarchists, and troublemakers.

The information technology industry has struggled for a generation over who should own the software that adds all the value to otherwise inert hardware that makes up a computer. Large software companies like Microsoft and Oracle claim that their products are the result of product development investments, funded in large part by their shareholders. They argue that the only fair way to treat those investments is to allow them to protect their intellectual property with patent, trade secret, and copyright laws that prohibit others from swooping in, copying products, and distributing them in a black market bazaar of vendors who do not recognize property rights. "No so fast," say others, who point out that the financial benefits reaped by software companies depend not only on their own inventions, but also on the inventions of hundreds of thousands of others. The vendors in the bazaar say that there are many thousands of programmers who contribute small amounts of technology to a kind of intellectual commons that is being sacked by the big commercial outfits, who incorporate free material from the commons in their proprietary products. Vendors in the bazaar think that they end up paying for material that they had helped create.

An activist community called the *open software movement* grew out of deep-seated resentment in the software world over this kind of inequity. In the 1980s, an MIT graduate student named Richard Stallman took up the banner of open software as a moral imperative, declaring war against proprietary software vendors and encouraging a generation of computer programmers called *hackers* to distribute only software that can be freely shared among all users, often in violation of copyright law. A certain outlaw culture grew up around Stallman's GNU licenses.[9] Stallman's brand of licensing allowed, among other things, something called *copyleft*, a claim that a programmer who referenced even a few lines of open software in an otherwise copyright-protected work contaminated the entire program, thus invalidating any future proprietary claim. Stallman's positions and methods were extreme, but by the early 1990s, the hacker mentality had a firm foothold in the software industry. The popular Linux operating system and much of the infrastructure underlying the Web today operates under a less radical—but equally abrasive to proprietary vendors—version of Stallman's radical licenses.

In 2001, three activists, Stanford law professor Larry Lessig, MIT engineering professor Hal Abelson, and an open software advocate named Eric Eldred founded a nonprofit organization called Creative Commons. All three were devoted to expanding rights of authors to create and share works along the lines advocated by the open software movement. A Creative Commons license allows authors to publish and distribute works that waive some rights while retaining others. Simple to read and easy to understand, Creative Commons licenses require only that authors select from a list of four conditions that specify how the work is to be treated in the future: attribution that allows unlimited copying, provided that the author is given credit; whether the work is commercial or noncommercial; whether derivative works are allowed; and a form of copyleft that requires redistribution under the original terms.

Abelson was also one of the creative forces behind MIT's OpenCourseWare. When it came time for Vest and others to select an alternative model for freely distributing materials that would at once promote and protect the MIT brand, it was not surprising that they chose Creative Commons as the licensing method "so that [materials] can be used, distributed, and modified for noncommercial purposes."[10]

Creative Commons distribution is today the standard for most web-based delivery of materials from traditional universities; many institutions have joined MIT in opening their entire course catalogs, resulting not only in millions of downloads, but also in substantial revision to traditional curricula in regions of the world that would be isolated from the newest advances without OpenCourseWare. In China, a country with a spotty record in respecting traditional Western intellectual property rights, Lucifer Chu's Fantasy Foundation is translating MIT's materials for learning communities. Chu's project is one of many in Asia and developing countries.

With the benefit of hindsight and looked at from the point of view of the long tail, Vest was too timid about the place of OpenCourseWare in a market-driven world. It has become a significant market force, but the company that demonstrated the real market power of the long tail was Google; in 2001, Google was still a small company.

Google's aim is to increase web usage—not necessarily only for Google pages but across the broadest spectrum of users and environments.[11] Google believes that the more web traffic there is, the more likely it is that web users will make use of their searches, maps, or shopping services, all activities that lead directly to revenue for Google. It is the economics of the Web at work. OpenCourseWare architect Hal Abelson understood well the economics of the Web: all things considered, it is better to be a hub. The underlying motivation for MIT had to have been clear to Vest when we first spoke about his plans: the more people are convinced that they are *connected* with MIT, the more connected MIT will be with the rest of the world.

Charles Vest is quick to point out that, without question, the value of an MIT education is personal interaction within a community of learners, between students and a human teacher—that is, an advisor and mentor who shapes the learner and guides the learning process:

Let me be clear: We are not providing an MIT education on the Web. We are providing our core materials that are the infrastructure that undergirds an MIT education. Real education requires interaction, the interaction that is part of American teaching.[12]

If Vest is right, then the value of long tail distribution course materials, even from an institution like MIT, depends on whether the technology also promotes the creation of real learning communities where none have existed before. As we will see, there is dramatic evidence that learning communities are the natural result of compelling content; but in some respects, technology has overshot even Chuck Vest's vision:

The model that was proposed over and over again for higher education was "find the best teacher of a given subject, record his or her lectures, and sell them in digital form." There is an appealing logic to this proposition, and I very much believe that there are important roles for this kind of teaching tool, but the image of students everywhere sitting in front of a box listening to the identical lecture is one that repels me.[13]

What Vest—and perhaps the entire OpenCourseWare movement—did not foresee is the role that technology would play in avoiding such a repellant future. Vest underestimated the growing sophistication of online course delivery, and no one anticipated the rapid rise of social networking.

14   Unkept Technological Promises

The walls of Galileo's classroom at the University of Padua are lined with ancient documents. University officials have preserved his podium. There are no whiteboards or blackboards, but the room has been outfitted with a portable screen and a projector that can be connected to a computer. The Hall of Ancient Documents at the University of Padua is in every way a modern classroom.

Technology has had remarkably little impact on classrooms, which for the past millennium have consisted of spaces for a teacher to stand, facing rows of seats for students. Chalkboards did not make a classroom appearance until 1801. Erasable writing surfaces not only enabled teachers to present information to an entire class, but also eased the burden of note taking for students, whose families sometimes found it difficult to afford paper and pencils. Black slate boards were inexpensive, easy to use, and they did not require much upkeep. Despite a constant flow of new gadgets, the blackboard was the last invention that had such obvious pedagogical value that it became a ubiquitous classroom fixture.

Every generation finds a new way to enhance—and in some cases, replace—classrooms with new devices and capabilities that empower teachers to instruct and pupils to learn. Educational technology specialists today experiment with wireless Internet connections, handheld computers, collaboration tools, and web-based courseware. Every few years, there is a celebration to mark the arrival of the classroom of the future—the educational equivalent of a Detroit concept car—to integrate the latest technology into schools and colleges. Aside from some technical improvements in the concept of a blackboard, classrooms remain virtually unchanged, because underneath it all, the goal of the classroom of the future has little to do with education.

In the 1990s, NASA's classroom of the future beamed video to specially equipped classrooms in an effort to increase awareness among elementary school students of NASA programs.[1] The Mayo Clinic's classroom of the future was part of an antiobesity initiative.[2] It had no desks, so students were required to move around. Office furniture suppliers and multimedia equipment manufactures fill their marketing showcases with new product demonstrations in their classrooms of the future. Still other projects equip traditional classrooms with sensors and computers so that the room itself becomes intelligent, recognizing, for example, that the act of picking up a whiteboard marker during a PowerPoint presentation can cause the lights to turn on and the projector to pause.[3] The research landscape is littered with hundreds of projects and products, bells and whistles that once held great promise for fundamental change in classroom education that never materialized.

There is a reason that so many projects—once touted as visionary— failed. The story of the unkept promises in educational technology is really a story of failed assumptions about what matters in education. At the heart of the story is a simple message: it is hard to replace a charismatic, engaged teacher and a responsive system of educational services with cold hardware.

Spontaneous Learning

There is wide a gulf between the experience of a live lecture and the passive act of viewing an iTunes video of the same lecture. Many think it is an unbridgeable gulf and dismiss the value of the video experience. Others take it as a challenge to improve the video experience so that it rivals a live lecture. Still others wonder whether human mentoring is needed at all, because there is ample evidence that real spontaneity, rivaling even the best classroom instruction, is a natural consequence of human learning.

Some spontaneous learning is simply the result of raw individual talent. There are so many examples of self-taught geniuses, mainly artists and engineers who achieve great things despite a lack of formal training, that it hardly seems remarkable. Occasionally, however, there are individuals who—like the mathematical genius hero of the Academy Award–winning film *Good Will Hunting*[4]—go beyond what can be explained by remarkable ability and are able, without teachers or instruction, to recreate a body of intellectual work to rival the best university education.

Mathematics produces more than its share of these self-taught geniuses. From 1897 to 1907, beginning at age 10 and working entirely from elementary algebra and trigonometry books, Srinivasa Ramanujan generated original mathematical research in such volume that he won a scholarship to a local Indian university. His talent was limited to mathematics, however.

He failed his other subjects, eventually leaving the university to work as a postal clerk.

By the time he was in his early twenties, Ramanujan had compiled a notebook of thousands of mathematical identities. Many of them were already known and some were false, but some were profound discoveries that would take mathematicians years to understand. Ramanujan sent his notes to Cambridge mathematician G. H. Hardy, the greatest mathematician of the day. Hardy, recognizing Ramanujan's genius, invited him to Trinity College in Cambridge, where Ramanujan spent the remainder of his short life, creating a body of mathematical work that is still pored over by contemporary mathematicians.

Nobody knows how individual learning like this takes place, but there is something known about the dynamics of groups that promotes spontaneous learning. Indian educator Sugata Mitra had the idea that young children could be taught to use computers without any training whatsoever using a principle he calls "minimally invasive education."[5] In 1999, he drew concentric circles on a map to identify the rural regions in India that were far enough from New Delhi so that English was an uncommon language and computer usage was rare, but close enough to have a stable infrastructure and general awareness of information technology. In a series of experiments that helped inspire the award-winning film *Slumdog Millionaire,*[6] Mitra placed primitive computer kiosks in some of these rural communities and videotaped the children who played with these "holes in the wall."

The Mitra experiments are remarkable because they document the power of spontaneous, self-organizing learning communities. The children quickly taught themselves to surf the Web and download games, overcoming obstacles such as language and primitive input devices, and it was not long before they started asking for "a faster processor and a better mouse." In other experiments, where the kiosks presented older children with concepts from an advanced biology course, it was not long before a group of learners began asking how to prepare DNA for laboratory experiments, an idea that was far beyond the scope of the kiosk material.

Minimally invasive education might lead to complete disruption of the role of the mentor, and it has been a recurring theme among distance learning advocates who want to take teachers out of the picture altogether, replacing human instruction with technology. Hundreds of researchers over many decades have tried to automate instruction, but their efforts have largely failed. However, to be completely fair, some of their experiments may have been hampered by primitive technology.

Georgia Tech's School of Information Science was an early adopter of technology to support its distance learning programs—mainly professional master's programs offered to industry and government clients. In the 1970s, buoyed by the sudden appearance of low-cost communications and media equipment, Tech was awarded a research grant to construct an Audiographic Learning Facility (ALF).[7] ALF was intended to bring down the costs of distance learning programs and ensure consistent quality in the classroom experience, using banks of dial-in systems and electromechanical writing devices to transmit lectures.

The audio portion of a lecture was captured on a standard magnetic recording tape. The instructor's writing was converted to analog signals and recorded on a separate audio track. A student who wanted to replay a lecture was supposed to use a standard telephone to dial into the right recording and connect the telephone to a local writing device using rubber cuffs that captured audible signals from the phone's earpiece and turned them into digital signals for voice playback and pen movements for the writing devices. Telephone line noise frequently caused the pens on the electromechanical devices to behave erratically, spraying ink on the unfortunate students who happened to be seated closest to the device.[8] Students were understandably upset by this, and the experiments were halted, but as technology matured, there were other experiments that had more positive outcomes.

When Frank Oppenheimer founded San Francisco's Exploratorium in 1969 as an immersive science museum and a destination for children who may not have responded to classroom science instruction, he had in mind a combination of playground and science laboratory where students could move from exhibit to exhibit, interacting with levers, gears, and wheels with no particular goal in mind. In this way, he reasoned, learners would spend time with the topics that were interesting to them, solving problems, learning concepts, and having fun in the process. He was explicit about the role of participation in learning about science.

Oppenheimer's catchphrase, "Nobody flunks museum,"[9] is even today sprinkled through conversations with the Exploratorium leadership. Based on this simple principle, the Exploratorium became one of the world's premier science museums, by allowing its visitors to recreate the act of scientific discovery. As web technology improved, the Exploratorium experimented with handheld computers to share, store, replay, and combine experiences with other students[10] For the next forty years, the Exploratorium attracted a range of projects in informal skill and knowledge acquisition. Today it maintains one of the largest independent science education programs in the country, but it is a long way from the cool exhibits of the Exploratorium to a bare college classroom. Universal access to computing technology held the promise of changing all that.

Ever since the Web made its first appearance in the early 1990s, computer scientists have dreamed of using its graphic capabilities to create virtual laboratories and its organizing power to allow people with similar interests and motivations to find each other and begin interacting. Early researchers even imagined an entire university constructed around this concept.

Stanford computer scientist Jeffrey D. Ullman was one of the first to try to construct a web-based curriculum. In the middle 1990s, Ullman was already making plans for a Web site he called "Computer Science 101.com." But Ullman's vision went well beyond a simple informational Web site. He wanted to use the power of artificial intelligence to anticipate the lumps in a student's curriculum—perhaps to augment a student's reasoning power with an ever-present, intelligent assistant. In 2000, he founded a company called Gradiance. Gradiance provided online services to accelerate learning processes for project- and laboratory-based courses. Ullman's software helped instructors create homework and lab exercises that would force students to conceptualize problems and related concepts.

From the student's point of view, Gradiance-enhanced learning appeared to be spontaneous: presented with a set of multiple choice questions and answers, students could navigate predefined concept maps in ways that would mimic complete-sentence responses to questions. The idea enjoyed a measure of success. Gradiance software was included in dozens of university textbooks, but like many technology promises in education, it was never widely adopted.

The goal of replacing human teachers with automata remains elusive, but that never kept technologists from using advanced computing technology to make the live classroom experience more efficient. The most spectacular attempt was called PLATO.

PLATO

PLATO was an effort to create true computer-based instruction. It began life as a research project in the early 1960s at the University of Illinois and grew in scope during the next twenty years. PLATO also grew more costly, and in late 1960, the underlying technology was acquired and commercialized by the now-defunct Control Data Corporation (CDC). CEO William Norris promised that half of CDC's revenue would come from educational services based on PLATO courseware hosted on the company's supercomputers.

PLATO was impressive in a number of dimensions. The computer technology was state of the art and continued to evolve during its lifetime. It incorporated the most advanced display technology and both text-to-voice and voice recognition, not only to ease the burden of mastering basic computer skills, but also to avoid the disastrous user experience that systems like ALF gave to both students and teachers. Backed by massive computing power, ALF's primitive telephone-based access was replaced by high-speed data access. As networking technology improved so did PLATO's availability and responsiveness.

Recognizing that courseware creation was fundamental to PLATO's success, CDC funded the development of extensive authoring systems. Several independent studies concluded that replacing classroom teachers with PLATO terminals had little impact—either positive or negative—on classroom learning. This should have been a warning signal to project planners, but it is a long-held principle among computer scientists that seamless replacement of a human skill by a computer program is a benchmark for success, so this was viewed as a spectacular technical achievement.

The total R&D investment in PLATO soon topped a billion dollars, a cost that CDC needed to recover. Central to CDC's plan for PLATO profitability was the price to be charged to institutions. The cost of accessing the computers needed to power PLATO quickly rose to $50 per hour per student. This was many times the cost of human instruction. Even worse, for both CDC and its customers, there were no economies of scale, because each student required both a terminal and network access to the CDC data center. By the time Norris stepped down as CDC's chief executive in 1986, the company was looking for an exit strategy from PLATO and the education market.

Elements of the PLATO technology were transported to emerging, smaller minicomputers, workstations, and ultimately to personal computers. Projects at Xerox's Palo Alto Research Center (PARC) that were inspired by PLATO used even more advanced information technology. The results influenced products like the Xerox Star system, one of the earliest personal workstations to use high-resolution displays, mice, and the desktop user interface. Although PLATO was conceived in the days before email and the Web, developers invented an array of "community" tools to connect courseware designers, human instructors, and students.[11]

In the wake of PLATO, dozens of projects made more determined attempts to marry technology with traditional classrooms. Gregory Abowd's Classroom 2000 was an ambitious application of ubiquitous computing—the seamless integration of information technology into human environments[12]—to the classroom. Abowd's work was inspired by visionary PARC scientist Mark Weiser. Weiser imagined a world in which computers would fade into the environment, enhancing an array of human experiences. To Abowd, the classroom—which had until that point been immune to the appeal of new technology—seemed like the ideal laboratory for the new field of ubiquitous computing. Abowd does not agree that classrooms were resistant to change: "I don't think the classroom had been immune to technology. There was lots of technology, but much of it was in the aid of the presenter of the material and not for the students who were struggling to keep pace with the increased flow of information afforded by the technology in the hands of the presenter," he told me.

Mark Weiser's tragic death from cancer only fueled subsequent innovation in ubiquitous computing in the United States, as his many followers continued to build on the work done at PARC. Although he had an interest in education, Abowd is today known as one of the founders of ubiquitous computing research. Classroom 2000 focused on how to capture and recover the classroom experience, ideas that Abowd has applied to health care and other fields as well. The Classroom 2000 project shuttered its doors reluctantly in 2002, and Abowd is wistful about its unfulfilled promise. As he said to me a decade later, "It was a living laboratory filled with innovative gadgets that unfortunately remains more a dream than a reality."

This is a theme running through all learning technology research. Educational technology research begins with innovative capabilities. Without exception, the initiatives that have held center stage have been those that promote a new capability for which education is only one of many plausible applications. The principle professional association of information technology experts in higher education is EDUCAUSE, an organization whose mission is to "advance higher education by promoting the intelligent use of information technology."[100]

The belief that technology will spur new business approaches runs deep in the information technology community. In 2003, Nicolas Carr published an article in Harvard Business Review entitled "IT Doesn't Matter,"[13] which created a stir in business circles by pointing out that the fascination of the business world with infrastructure advances in information technology was understandable, but misplaced. Carr's careful analysis of infrastructure innovation showed a consistent pattern. Technological innovation is always greeted with a great clamor to find equally innovative uses for it, but as technology curves inexorably push the cost of the new technology down and as there are abundant choices for how to acquire the same capabilities at even lower cost, the attention of business leaders shifts back to the core of their own businesses. The new technology is no longer a differentiator, and it adds little incremental value. It is there, but it doesn't matter.

Information technology professionals hated Carr's arguments, which have been validated so many times in practice that few serious corporate leaders question the conclusions. Higher education is caught in a pre-Carr world in which organizations like EDUCAUSE can argue unchallenged that technology matters. It does not.

A 2005 *EDUCAUSE Review* article by William Plymale catalogs a half-dozen technologies aimed at providing automated support for the traditional learning process by concentrating on

possible positive effects that pervasive computing may have on productivity within our lives (at school, work, and home) [that] could be significant:

• Improved capabilities for communications, coordination, collaboration, and knowledge exchange
• Removal of time and space constraints for accessing information
• Enhanced decision-making abilities based on receiving and processing up-to-date organizational and environmental data
• Expanded user awareness of the environment through resource and service discovery.[14]

But, like so many other projections, this one does not attempt to predict what the actual effect would be on educational practice. EDUCAUSE proclaims on its Web site, "It is not about the information. Or the technology. It's what we do with the technology that counts."[15] However, if what a university is trying to do with the technology has little value, then it will never be worth the expense of adopting it. It makes no sense to automate a factory when specialized artisans are what are called for.

Resting on Failed Assumptions

Like many of the ideas I have presented so far, PLATO is a metaphor. As far as educational technology goes, there is nothing wrong with PLATO, but the entire project represents a set of failed assumptions: propositions that were widely accepted as valid for higher education, but in reality have virtually nothing to do with twenty-first century universities. PLATO and many of the educational technologies that followed it were conceived with a single guiding vision: just as computerization improves productivity and quality on the factory floor, so will computerization have a similar impact on educational institutions.

Disrupting Class, by Clayton Christensen, Michael Horn, and Curtis Johnson, makes the case that the analogy between factory automation and the classroom is not accidental.[16] Since the 1800s, the dominant model for organizing schools has been the factory. This is not simply a twentieth-century attempt to mimic the successes of the Industrial Revolution. As enrollments grew, universities needed to find economies of scale. It is a way of looking at the world: efficiency equals standardization.

As I pointed out in chapter 8, the academic factory was a result of two independent forces: the demands of the men who led the foundations that funded university growth at the start of the twentieth century and the massive increase in enrollments that forced institutions to seek greater efficiency. The way to cope with the increasing numbers of students that resulted from universal access—the argument goes—is to group students so that the same material can be taught in the same way to many students at once. Grouping students by age into classes seemed like the right way to identify people with approximately equal maturity and ability to learn material. Throughout the years, other groupings emerged within classes. As more students chose postsecondary education, it seemed wise to distinguish between college-bound students and those who were destined for careers in business or the manual arts, for example. Additional customization was costly, uncommon, and usually the result of government mandates.

Special needs instruction in public schools is a good example of such a mandate. By the 1970s, 10 percent of all public school students were involved in special needs programs. However, special needs programs in that same period accounted for almost a third of all spending in some school districts. Because overall school budgets were more or less fixed, additional pressure was applied to the instructional funds for the remaining 90 percent of the students, requiring higher levels of productivity, more efficiency, and therefore even more standardization.

Special needs students were at one end of a spectrum, and eventually, federal initiatives encouraged some school districts to offer a curriculum for students whose abilities and goals placed them at the opposite end of the spectrum. Advanced Placement courses, and later, International Baccalaureate degrees offered college credit-bearing courses to high-performing students. But there were no real educational innovations. The effect of the mandates was simply to create schools within schools. Each of them offered the same group-oriented vision of education: an instructor talking to a classroom of pupils, evaluating their responses, and students, passive except for recitations and examinations.

The impact of growth on colleges and universities was similarly profound. It had been noted in Jefferson's time that replacing the classical core curriculum with a system of electives would be costly: more professors, more classes, more customization. The system of majors must have seemed like an ideal compromise to nineteenth-century planners. Majors allow some level of student-centered specialization, but relieved economic pressures by moving batches of students through one of several predefined curricula. Academic departments, schools, and rigidly enforced degree programs all serve the same purpose. They help determine a fixed course of study for degrees. The business model for higher education depends on it, because economies of scale are achieved by teaching the same material in the same way to all majors in a discipline, which means that in an efficient university, the classroom is king.

But, as I argued in part III of this book, it is hard to implement a long tail approach to higher education by only focusing on the classroom and not on what is taught. PLATO addressed computerized automation of the classroom. Even if its grandest visions had been achieved, PLATO by itself would have only automated a process that figures less and less prominently into what students expect from universities.

The Efficiency of a Factory Floor

It is difficult to overstate the degree to which these assumptions have skewed the strategy and practice of education in American universities. Practices geared to the factory floor not only influenced the "batching" of students for instructional efficiency, but also to a large extent determined what it means to be a successful university. Institutions pursue improved reputational rankings by becoming increasingly selective about which students they admit. They pursue accreditation goals by removing as much variance as possible from learning outcomes. They plan for quality by raising the amount of money spent per student while simultaneously decreasing the productivity of their faculty.

A successful university has to concentrate on classroom efficiency. It is the only variable that is under its control. But a university that concentrates its resources on classroom efficiencies cannot also be mindful of the needs of students—in fact, the whole notion of classroom efficiency sacrifices what the student needs. A student who is having trouble with classroom material that others are breezing though requires special help outside of class. But one-on-one services like that are not efficient. It turns out that what is good and efficient for classrooms is usually also good and efficient for professors, so classroom-centered institutions are, to an overwhelming degree, also faculty-centered. Take, for example, the lengths to which modern American universities go to remove all sources of variance from some prescribed learning outcome.

Advocates of outcomes-based assessment (OBA) dominate accreditation institutions for academic university degree programs. OBA is an attempt to drive the outcome of the learning process to specific, quantifiable goals in much the same way that statistical control theory is used to reduce the variance of manufacturing processes and thus ensure quality in manufactured parts and products.[17] Because the idea behind OBA had its start in the desire by industrialists to monitor the effectiveness of educational institutions, the relationship to manufacturing is perhaps not surprising.

Here is how it works in a factory. A manufacturing process (let's say it's for bearings) can be expected to produce bearings with mechanical characteristics that vary from the ideal by some amount. By sampling bearings that leave the assembly line, a quality-control engineer can develop a quality diagram for the plant that counts the bearings that vary from the ideal, as well as the frequency above and below the ideal, as shown in figure 14.1.

Defects mean variation from the ideal, so reducing defects in the tail of this distribution also reduces the number of bearings that are outside this tolerance band. If the number of bearings—the outcomes of the manufacturing process—in the tails of the distribution is reduced to zero, the plant then consistently produces bearings with zero defects.

The language of OBA is statistical quality control. During accreditation reviews, university administrators are required to produce the documentation, the sample from which statistical inferences can be drawn, and the

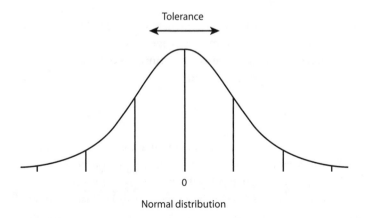

Figure 14.1
Variation from ideal in manufacturing.

process feedbacks so that statistical quality control can be applied to higher education. These are the methods of the factory floor. The only thing missing is numerical precision. Not surprisingly, as OBA has grown in popularity, it has also enraged university faculty such as humanities professor Laurie Fendrich:

Outcomes-assessment practices in higher education are grotesque, unintentional parodies of both social science and "accountability." No matter how much they purport to be about "standards" or student "needs," they are in fact scams run by bloodless bureaucrats who, steeped in jargon like "mapping learning goals" and "closing the loop," do not understand the holistic nature of a good college education. For all the highfalutin pronouncements accompanying the current May Day parade of outcomes assessment, in the end they boil down to a wholesale abandonment of the very idea of higher education.[18]

Fendrich is most concerned that OBA is bad for education in the arts and the humanities, but she allows that it might make sense for other fields—science and engineering, for example—a point of view that is dissected by Donald Woolston, an expert in engineering education at the University of Wisconsin: "Manufacturers control what is manufactured in a way that educators cannot (and should not expect to) control what is learned."[19]

For Woolston, the matter goes far beyond simple tweaking of a badly applied analogy:

Ultimately the kind of human behavior we are interested in shaping in engineering education is not measurable in a sufficiently precise and reproducible way to allow manufacturing analogies to apply.

If the classroom-centered model is motivated by operational efficiencies, why continue to concentrate on an analogy that provokes such extreme responses, rather than other, more promising technological building blocks of twenty-first-century university education?

Automation and Mass Production

The answer seems to be that there is no agreement about what it means to be a promising technology in higher education. Prying technology investments from cash-strapped universities is difficult enough, but investments that do not appear to be aligned with the current business objectives are nearly impossible to fund with institutional resources, and there are few federal programs that will fund investigations into disruptive technologies. It is not surprising, then, that most investment dollars are used to prop up the current ways of doing business—not an altogether inappropriate strategy in light of other effects of the factory model.

The factory model focuses on reporting and review. Layers of reporting requirements get deeper every year, and new layers of bureaucracy are needed to audit compliance as information systems strain under the weight of new federal, state, and institutional regulations. At some institutions, multimillion dollar budgets are needed for internal audit functions alone, and because many compliance requirements are tied to institutional statistics, even more millions are needed to support data gathering and analysis. One regulation alone—the Federal Education Rights Privacy Act (FERPA)—accounts for such a large portion of campus administrative overhead that many question whether the money is well spent. FERPA places strict rules on how student data are handled and exposes universities to stiff penalties and withholding of federal funds for violations. Universities are so concerned about the impact of FERPA violations that many take positive action to locate and destroy records containing information that is clearly not sensitive. Some universities interpret FERPA so cautiously that all documents—even routine press releases from athletic departments and letters to parents—are scrutinized for information that might violate FERPA rules. Others selectively enforce FERPA rules to decrease transparency, which is clearly not what the legislation envisioned.

Outside of the research labs and basic business systems, *course management systems*—the complex software that is supposed to tie elements of the educational experience together in a single environment—consume the largest portion of campus information technology (IT) budgets. A course management system, or CMS, manages not only the content and delivery of courses but also key interactions and resulting data that can then be fed back into a well-managed assessment and evaluation program.

If this sounds a little vague, then you get the idea. CMS boundaries are conspicuously fuzzy. During my tenure as a dean, I saw the university investment in CMS rise from a few tens of thousands of dollars per year for a homely but more or less helpful collection of Web sites and databases spread over a dozen academic units to several million dollars centralized in a software organization chartered with identifying and implementing new, more sophisticated features.

A CMS is an academic cousin of the software systems that that are used to manage large manufacturing operations. As integrated manufacturing plants grew in size, the tasks associated with receiving and processing orders, tracking supply chain parts and services, managing inventories, and performing the associated financial accounting—all of the "back-office" operations that are used to run a complex business—cried out for automation. Even relatively simple installations of these systems cost tens of millions of dollars, and because each company's internal processes are unique, consultants and specially trained integration contractors are often needed to perform adaptation and tuning. Software like this is so costly and so hard to change that during the last thirty years corporate operations have been redesigned to conform to the restrictions imposed by the software, rather than the other way around. A university that operates like a factory needs such software.

One dominant CMS is a system called Sakai, open source software that is supposed to tie registration, payment, compliance, course content, grading, and record keeping into a unified set of coherent processes. Sakai is not the only CMS on many campuses, either. A factory can enforce rigid rules to limit the proliferation of different software systems, but universities are imperfect replicas of factories. Enforcing software standards is not easy, so midlevel administrators and instructors who are unhappy with Sakai might operate a dozen or more other CMS installations, each with the same goal, but separately consuming additional millions of dollars.

Let me be clear: I am steeped in information technology—I am a true believer. So I am not questioning the value of information technology in creating more efficient institutional operations. The pencil-and-paper heritage of record keeping and processing in higher education often leads to duplication of data and resources and is a significant factor in driving up operational costs. But like Nicolas Carr, I am skeptical of ever more costly investment in IT that doesn't matter, and from the point of view of students, a CMS does not matter.

The software that controls manufacturing operations in large enterprises by itself adds no value, but when supported by internal processes, it can be the differentiator between success or failure in the marketplace. Manufacturing automation, for example, has meant increased value to buyers of personal computers or automobiles who can place a custom order on a Web site that uses software to reach far into networks of suppliers and shippers. Days later, a customized personal computer arrives on a consumer's doorstep.

One would think that college IT departments would have learned these lessons from their commercial counterparts and would make IT investments that not only relieve the regulatory and budgetary burdens in institute operations, but also provide some additional value to students. By and large those investments are nonexistent.

Rather than enable the open sharing of courseware or facilitate large-scale collaboration among students, a CMS erects barriers to collaboration. It promotes efficiency, but extracts a price because it controls access. It manages student identities, but only if students give up the identities they had before they enrolled. A CMS makes reporting easier, but the reports it produces are used to control the factory floor. A CMS like Sakai automates common tasks like recording test scores and calculating final grades. But Sakai also makes it difficult for teachers to create individualized grading procedures, offering instead a single, standard grading scheme. Critics charge that, above all, a CMS is needlessly, wastefully expensive. Even Sakai with its open source pedigree is based on technology that has to be maintained by a small army of specialized programmers. Meanwhile, there is a chaotic, sometimes frenetic, world outside the university where openness, sharing, and innovation—all of it carried out on a shoestring budget—threaten to rush past traditional universities.

15 A Substitute for Deep Reflection

If a small, public, liberal arts college in rural Virginia seems like an unlikely twenty-first-century technology battleground, then Jim Groom is an even more unlikely battlefield commander. Groom, who in 2006 gave an identity to his cheery brand of academic anarchy by calling it *Edupunk*, works at the University of Mary Washington, on a campus tucked into a rolling hillside near Fredericksburg, Virginia. Looking a little like one of the punk rock musicians whose penchant for reinvention of musical form inspired the name, Groom wants to "blow up college as we know it." His boss knows about Groom's subversive ways and is happy to encourage that sort of behavior.

The University of Mary Washington—or UMW, as the locals refer to it—is named after George Washington's mother, Mary Ball Washington, but it was called the State Normal and Industrial School for Women when it was established in 1908. It became the women's college for the University of Virginia in 1944, and in the early 1970s it gained a measure of independence as a separate coeducational institution. It is a liberal arts college in the Middle whose programs run decidedly toward the creative arts and humanities.

True to its roots as a college for women, many UMW buildings are named after prominent women in American history, including Thomas Jefferson's daughter, Martha Jefferson Randolph, and women's rights figure Frances Willard. It seems like a natural—almost serene—place for Groom to have ended up after completing his graduate work in American literature at Queens College and the City University of New York (CUNY).

Never mind the irony of its location on the site of the Battle of Fredericksburg, or its brief association with the University of Virginia, where Thomas Jefferson first articulated the vision of a uniquely American institution of higher learning. There is nothing serene about a conversation with Jim Groom. He holds onto sentences with conviction and relinquishes control only when you make it clear that the conversation is moving on.

Groom and his colleagues are committed to universities that are the opposite of factories, and they are willing to break some glass to do it. "The whole idea is a reaction to the over-engineered, badly designed, and intellectually constraining technology that has been foisted onto the American higher education system as a substitute for deep reflection about what the universities should be evolving into," Groom told me.

Edupunks

Like their rock brethren, Edupunk purists don't mind alienating the establishment. Edupunk, according to Groom, "is about the utter irresponsibility and lethargy of educational institutions and the means by which they are financially cannibalizing their own mission." Groom blogs extensively about his views. Those views are both widely disseminated and widely discussed in a growing community of educators who believe American higher education is seriously off track.

Some of Groom's online colleagues have adopted their own Sid Vicious personae online. One of Groom's colleagues maintains a blog that shows off the letters E-D-U-P-U-N-K-S crudely tattooed on his knuckles like some inner-city gangster. Amid all this turmoil, you would think that administrators at the University of Mary Washington would be at least a little uncomfortable with the unsavory associations. Apparently not. According to Groom, who reports to UMW's provost, "the university has said nothing about Edupunk. They neither promote it nor tamp it down."

Fiery rhetoric aside, Edupunk has mainstream goals. As Groom explains it, one of his motivations is to brand UMW: "We are a teaching university— not a research university. We want to be known for innovation, and we are innovating with technology." The question facing Jim Groom and his team of educational technology (or "ed-tech") specialists at UMW is how to do that within limited budgets. He sometimes turns to organizations like EduCause, but only to make contact with like-minded revolutionaries. In Groom's view, Edupunks are ahead of the trends. EduCause is the cheerleader for the status quo. And the status quo is not sustainable for many colleges and universities in the Middle.

A favorite target for Edupunk is CMS. "These are big, closed access control systems," says Groom. A popular CMS called Blackboard was adopted several years ago by UMW, but it does not connect with the important social networks on the campus. Edupunks like Groom look at Blackboard as a way of controlling who has access to university resources that takes scarce investment dollars away from more open technologies that provide value to students, faculty, and alumni. Openness is an important part of the Edupunk agenda, and its adherents draw much of their inspiration from the open software movement, which is not surprising, as much of the software that powers the Internet is distributed under open source licenses.

I asked Groom how he felt about Sakai, thinking that because it is based on open source software, it might be an approach to CMS that the Edupunks could live with. He was not impressed. "In the first place, it's Java," he said. Java is a notoriously difficult language for writing software. "It takes an expert team to add any features at all. Why not use PHP?" PHP is the language of amateurs, and it used by hundreds of thousands of bloggers and Web site operators around the world. "That would make it more democratic," he added, "and it's still closed. I can't feed any of my public blogs into Sakai. It's a terrible move. You might just as well use Blackboard. It's not much better, but at least there's a company that supports it." For Edupunks, open source licenses are not enough. A system has to be democratic—it has to accept everyone. A system cannot dictate the terms. The system itself has to be open.

It is a small step from *open software* to *open systems*, an approach to information sharing that enables anyone to plug into a simple, easily understood interface: no hassle, no restrictive standards, and—best of all—no guard at the door to check credentials and turn away those who do not satisfy the admission criteria.

The open system concept—the ability for a community to manage the distribution and growth of systems without a centralized authority—is a touchstone for Edupunks. It is a very democratic, Jeffersonian concept. Open systems are intended to fit hand in glove with other ideas borrowed from the open source community, like OpenCourseWare. To the Edupunks, OpenCourseWare was a demonstration that closely held content was not key to a university's value. UMW embraced openness immediately. It is a core value and is woven through all of its technology. The Ed-tech group at UMW spends much of its time refining what Jim Groom calls "a Web 2.0 platform so that all of these other systems can talk to each other. We don't care what you bring to us. It should all work together."

Despite their subversive demeanors, the movement is home to technology realists. They are attracted to the simplified technologies like Web 2.0 that make it easy to connect Web sites together with information pathways and cool applications that do not require an expert team of Java programmers. PHP—the name itself is an insider's joke—is the scripting language that can be used to tell a Web site "first do this, then do that, then display the result." PHP may be democratic, but it is also simple to use, and that makes it powerful. There is also a large warehouse of preprogrammed applications that web developers can simply paste onto a web page. Some are as simple as using a *syndication service* to gather the output of a hundred blogs into a single column of a professor's home page. Others require some additional—and more complicated—glue so that login credentials can be passed from one Web site to another.

Web 2.0 programming is not a small industry. Microsoft and Google are behind it. So are the three hundred member companies of the World Wide Web Consortium, who together define the standards for all web technology. Given a choice between a hulking, closed system that is the province of a few dozen university IT departments and a technological tidal wave like Web 2.0, Edupunks are not so subversive after all. Being democratic might be a side effect of adopting open systems, but the motivation is pure business: having hundreds of IT companies on your side is better than siding with a single vendor whose product is closed, proprietary, and expensive.

Jim Groom is a true believer, but he is also a true entrepreneur. He has a core belief that openness adds value to the student experience, and that the decentralization of resources and management is a pathway to the kind of flexible environment that new approaches to college teaching will demand. When pressed, he can make the case in dollars and cents: the cost of the decentralized administrative approach was thirty dollars per month per student when Groom and his team of ed-tech specialists began experimenting with open courses. Today, when virtually all UMW students, faculty members, and administrators are connected to each other by Web 2.0 technology, the cost of the entire operation is $6,000 per year. That is probably why Groom's initiatives have survived a change in university administration and a severe downturn in the economy.

The cause has been picked up by some mainstream organizations. In 2009, the United Nations Global Alliance for Information and Communication Technology and Development founded a free, online university that uses the open standards social networking. Not all of Groom's colleagues warm so easily to the Edupunk image, but they are all subversives.

Brigham Young professor David Wiley wears a necktie and keeps his hair cut, but he predicts that unless they find a way to embrace openness, "universities will be irrelevant by 2020."[1] He announces on his Web site that he is a practicing Mormon in a Mormon institution. There is a sense of missionary zeal in his goal of "increasing access to educational opportunity for everyone around the world." The issue for Wiley is not technology: it is cost. Open content allows students anywhere in the world to syndicate a curriculum by picking and choosing from among the best universities in the world. He even started a company, Flatworld Knowledge, to promote open source textbooks.

Edupunks socialize with mainstream educational technologists from EduCause at national meetings, but Groom says, "We don't really attend any of the sessions. EduCause is a good excuse for all of us to get together to share our experiences." The radical fringe of open content talks incessantly about technology and cost, and they are aggressive in their predictions that universities that don't move quickly are going to be left behind. When asked about value, they nod vigorously and start to tell stories about what their movement means to students.

Or maybe it's just that Jim Groom is an unrelenting cheerleader for the University of Mary Washington: "I want to have an impact on our reputation. I want us to be known as a kickass place."

They Arrive with Digital Identities

Most university Web sites are professionally produced marketing tools with easily identifiable access to campus maps, academic programs, and press releases. A click of a mouse takes a visitor to web pages containing the fall football schedule. It is easy to find the alumni association's reminders to make a gift today. Sometimes a smiling president welcomes visitors with a short message. Clean, readable text wraps around color photographs of historical buildings, campus events, and notable people. There are images everywhere of smiling students, engaged professors, and sometimes classrooms. There might even be a box into which search terms can be typed, so that a visitor can more easily navigate what would otherwise be a maze of information.

There is no way to confuse a university's Web site with the university itself—even online universities tend to keep their doors closed to outsiders who just want to browse. There is information about making donations, the comings and goings of the president, and the hottest research projects, but there are no lectures. A student cannot get help with a problem on the university home page. Alumni and applicants alike are strangers to the university. There are no class rosters, because the FERPA violations would bankrupt the institution, and it is not possible to talk with a professor.

The home page for the University of Mary Washington is also a slickly produced affair, and visitors can easily navigate to important information and resources. It is like every other university Web site except for one feature prominently tucked into a list, just to the right of a picture of the main administration building: a button that reads "UMW Blogs." A visitor who clicks that button is taken immediately to the university itself. At the University of Mary Washington, learning takes place in the digital spaces engineered by Jim Groom and his band of Edupunks. At UMW, learning takes place in blogs.

"Blog" is Web 2.0 shorthand for "web log," an idea that is less than a decade old and that—along with other social networking concepts—has transformed the Internet. Blogs are online creative spaces that allow anyone with a Web browser to publish—to "post," in the language of blogging— anything for the rest of the world to read and to comment upon. In the world of blogs, the comments to a blog post are sometimes as entertaining as the original post.

A blog is not a broadcast. It is an invitation to comment, to agree or dis- agree with a post, to helpfully add to a conversation, or to disrupt it with an angry rant. Blogs are democratic, so the only thing that determines whether a blog is successful is its audience. Freed from the need to find a publishing outlet, some bloggers succeed by catering to a narrow band of like-minded political allies—a trend that has changed the face of national politics; oth- ers peddle news, gossip, and personal diaries.

Several years ago, newspapers—alarmed that blogging was a free, two- way dialog between journalists and readers—started attaching their own brands to blogs, creating a mass market online audience for some bloggers. Blog popularity is measured by the volume of traffic that visits it, that is, the number of times it is viewed—a number called a *page view*. The most popular blogs receive hundreds of thousands of page views on a good day. The least popular blogs get no traffic at all.

The companies that provide the platforms, tools, and servers for blog- gers—blog sites—keep track of their blogs' traffic. WordPress[2] is one of the most popular blog sites. It is home to millions of individual blogs, but to make it into the WordPress top one hundred list—the top 0.01 percent—a blog has to attract only a few thousand page views per day. Blog popularity follows the Internet's hub-and-spoke economics: there are a few very popu- lar blogs with much traffic, but most of the traffic visits blogs that are not the most popular. Blogging is a very long tail way of publishing, so a blog that attracts only a few hundred visitors is a runaway hit.

The UMW blogs are the polar opposites of PLATO. There is no fancy hardware to buy, and most students already know how to blog. UMW class- rooms are just as inefficient and chaotic as other universities, and there are no plans for distance learning programs. In many ways, it has not embraced the Internet. The university is not listed on iTunes U, and UMW profes- sors are reluctant to make their lectures available on the Web. UMW does not have a technology that is in search of an application, nor does it try to dictate what technology to use or how to use it. In Thomas Jefferson's back yard, it has found a democratic way of tapping into the deep desire of students, professors, and visitors to create, share, and grow. UMW has a way of connecting people together.

There are more than 2,500 public blogs at UMW—blogs that are accessible from outside the university. The educational technology department does not know how many private blogs there are because they do not even try to track the number. Every campus organization, class, professor, and most of the students have a public blog. Jim Groom thinks of all of UMW's blogs as learning spaces, and there is considerable evidence that most of UMW's students see blogs as just another space to do work.

Groom suspects that many students actually maintain several blogs because there are so many different kinds of work that an individual student does. The university offers many different options for interactive authoring tools and sharable media, but does not dictate which of the many possible blogging platforms the students must use. In fact, there is only one rule for blogging at UMW: you must use an open system so that others can easily locate and connect to your blog.

Except for a noticeable tendency toward the creative arts and literature, UMW's public blogs look much like other blogs. There are blogs for poetry and short stories, and the comments are a sort of continuing review and analysis of the work. Because many blogs are public, it is not uncommon for an outsider to stumble into a UMW blog, find that there are interesting people to talk to, and jump uninvited into the middle of a conversation. Professors sometimes make their class blogs public, which draws a certain amount of outside traffic as well. But mostly the UMW blogs are used by students to create and to share what they have created with their classmates. The UMW blogs and their online social networks give students digital identities that are at times hard to distinguish from their physical identities, but their digital identities did not start with their enrollment in UMW. The university is just another step along a path. Students arrive at UMW with digital identities.

Not surprisingly, the university attracts students who have been steeped in digital culture since childhood—*digital natives*, who have online histories that they would prefer not to abandon. Figuring out how to make use of digital identities is an important conceptual leap—ignored by mainstream educational technologists—that the open systems advocates make. There is no doubt that Americans under the age of 20 make little distinction between digital identities and identity in the physical world.

Jeff Cole, director of the Center for the Digital Future at the University of Southern California's Annenberg School of Communications, has been studying these trends since the inception of the Internet. He wants to know how shifting patterns of work and leisure have changed our life and culture because of the Internet. "It's a shame," Jeff told me, "that no one thought to do this when television was invented. Americans used to spend six to eight hours a day watching TV. Where did that time come from? What did they stop doing? How did it change life? Since I was here at the start of the Internet revolution, I wanted to document how the Internet has changed us."

For well more than a decade, Cole has collected data on Internet usage and its impact on culture that tell us how we have changed. As Internet usage has spread globally, his study has expanded to include Europe, Asia, and Africa, and he can say with certainty that digital natives do not think there is anything special about their digital lives. "Teens are not impressed with all this new technology," Cole told me. "It is simply the way it is. To them it is just there and not difficult to use." Many of them have been blurring the lines between real and digital relationships for a long time. "For almost a generation they have changed the reach of their relationships, and the ways they establish and maintain networks and friendships represents transformational change they will carry for the rest of their lives."

UMW students have Facebook pages. They share photos on Flickr, and they have hundreds of books archived at Amazon.com. The writers among them have many thousands of words that they have already published online. Avatars distinguish their classmate selves from their student selves. They belong to fluid networks of friends and adversaries that do not seem to have hard and fast membership rules. Although parents and traditionalists may worry that social networks drain time away from face-to-face relationships, "nothing could be further from the truth," according to Jeff Cole.

In fact, Cole's results show just the opposite: "While it is true that teens spend very little time other than sleeping or in school when they are not in front of a screen and are constantly interacting on social networks and revealing personal information, none of that has diminished interest in face-to-face communication. They use digital communication to interact with friends at times they cannot be with them: early morning, late night, or when they are away. Tracking for the past ten years, we see teens who are highly connected actually spend a little more time face-to-face than those who are not."

Asking UMW students to give up their digital identities—simply to conform to the limitations of campus technology—would be unthinkable to the university's Edupunks. In fact, it would intrude on their real-world identities because, as Jeff Cole points out, "One of the primary uses of social networking is the ease it creates in establishing meeting times and places."

It is too early to say for certain, but the ed-tech specialists at UMW also suspect that alumni do not want to leave their UMW identities behind when they graduate. At UMW, a course can be a continuing conversation. Networks of close friends do not want to drop their UMW associations when they graduate, only to find out later on that they cannot easily reconnect with each other. An artist's digital portfolio contains work that defines him or her creatively. Leaving it behind would mean starting life after graduation with a new artistic identity, and that would be unacceptable. Students arrive with digital identities that grow along with them during their time at the university. That is the identity they want to carry into the world after graduation. "They arrive with digital identities," says Jim Groom of the students who arrive on campus. "We wouldn't ask them to give up their identities."

That makes UMW unique. At some institutions, students and professors alike are actually robbed of their online identities—the online equivalent of shaving the head of a new army recruit and issuing a set of standard drab fatigues. Freshmen at most universities are assigned email addresses like **bronson.b.rumson@stateu.edu**. A student who has an unlucky name like Fred Smith might be assigned something like **fred.smith23@stateu .edu** because there are twenty-two other Fred Smiths who also need unique digital identities. Although my email address has been **rad**[3] since the first email systems were built in the 1970s, my official Georgia Tech email address is **rd122@GTBUZZ.cc.gatech.edu**. Logging into a course management system might mean using a student ID like **338440933** or **br2871**, and because FERPA prohibits the release of identifying information, an especially diligent professor might assign still another arbitrary number to indicate which lab station was occupied on the first day of class.

A freshman whose Facebook friends know her as **borntoskate** is out of luck if she wants to remain connected to old teammates and coaches. And students with complex online profiles that reveal casual, intimate, inscrutable, professional, or even anonymous identities to different friends, professors, merchants, and family members finds that all of those associations are immediately meaningless.

Because freshmen at UMW are expected to have digital identities when they arrive, "UMW students can choose domain names[4] that they can keep for life," says Groom. "It belongs to them. We will host their domains if they want, but UMW really encourages students to create their own domains of one. They bring their digital identities with them, and manage them while they are here. They create, share, and export while they are here. Whatever they want to do with their individual domains is fine with us." Jim Groom's domain of one strategy gives every John Smith or Evelyn Jones who enters UMW a domain name like **johnsmith.com** or **evelynjones.org**—digital identities that they will keep for life.

The subversive Edupunks at the University of Mary Washington have constructed a kind of intellectual way station in the life of a student—the exact opposite of a one-size-fits-all, faculty-centered, efficiently run educational factory. Students arrive at UMW bringing with them all of their prior experience. They spend a few years creating, learning, and building new networks of friends, teachers, and collaborators. And if everything goes according to plan, the graduates of UMW never really leave, because the university lets them keep their unique digital identities. Those identities are so tightly linked to the university that they will carry both with them forever.

MOOCs and Moodles

Paul Erdös was a wandering minstrel, a lyric poet of mathematics who came as close to what I imagine Peter Abelard might have been like as anyone I've ever met, although, by all written accounts of Abelard's physical appearance, the two bore no physical resemblance to each other. Abelard was tall and strikingly handsome. Some say he was "distinguished in figure and manners";[5] Erdos was a small, slight man, with a shuffling gait, who wore large tortoise shell glasses that gave him an owlish look. On the other hand, it could be said of either man that he was often

seen surrounded by crowds—it is said thousands—of students, drawn from all countries by the fame of his teaching, in which acuteness of thought was relieved by simplicity and grace of exposition.[6]

Erdös was famous not only for his mathematics, but also for his eccentric, nomadic lifestyle that brought him into contact with thousands of other mathematicians. He was a giant, and his influence on the course of mathematical history in the twentieth century is hard to overstate. For most of his later years, Erdös had no fixed residence—although Bell Labs mathematician Ronald Graham acted as a sort of home base for Erdös, collecting expense checks and honoraria and generally keeping Paul out of trouble with banks, credit card companies, and the IRS.

Paul Erdös was a prolific mathematician, and his visits to university campuses and industrial research labs invariably caused a flurry of publications coauthored with local scientists. He never really distinguished between students and his more senior colleagues. They were all mathematicians. When he walked into a room, announced "My brain is open," and began solving problems, irrelevancies like age and seniority took a back seat.

It became common for mathematicians to imagine that there was a hubs-and-spokes map of the mathematical world in which two mathematicians were connected if they had jointly authored a technical article, and they assigned a number—called the Erdös number—to every mathematician depending on how far they were from Erdös in the map. If Alice had actually coauthored a paper with Paul, her Erdös number was one. If Bob had coauthored a paper with Alice but not with Paul, then his Erdös number was two. Those with small Erdös numbers also tend to be hubs. As far as we know, Erdös collaborated with 511 people, bestowing on them Erdös number 1. These 511 collaborated with 8,167 others, who therefore have Erdös number 2.

My own Erdös number is 3, so I belong to a much larger group, but I was lucky enough to meet with him on many occasions, and occasionally I would drop in on one of his talks. Erdös did not lecture so much as let you listen in on a conversation. Talks would invariably begin like this: "Let M be a large prime and let f(M) be . . ."—no introductory remarks or review of prior results.

Everyone who knew him seems to agree that he would have been a terrible classroom teacher because he always talked about something new, and students had a very difficult time keeping up with him. It was, of course, impossible to plan to study under him anyway because he was always moving from place to place. It is entirely possible that he thought *everyone* was in such constant motion: no matter how long he had known you, he would ask "Where are you now?" Erdös was like a university that came to you on an unpredictable schedule with no particular result guaranteed or expected, but he may have been the purest teacher of the twentieth century.

Thousands of students would drop in, spend a few hours or days with "Uncle Paul," and absorb as much mathematics as they could handle. It might take them years to digest it all, but that was fine because it might be years before they had another chance to attend his continuing, wandering course in combinatorial mathematics.

Open-ended college courses are uncommon, but not for any pedagogical reason. There is no theory that dictates how college degree programs should be chopped into courses or how many semesters there should be, except that everything should work out to be just long enough to fit the required number of credits. Many institutions offer "Maymester" terms that fit between spring and summer and last two or three weeks. Advanced material is sometimes taught in small recitation groups and is spread over several semesters because there are as of yet no textbooks in the field and therefore no natural course boundaries. The length of a college course is a number that is chosen arbitrarily, and it varies from place to place.

Attendance is also a loosely defined idea for most college courses. In Europe, where completion of course requirements is determined by final examinations, attendance has no meaning at all, and students feel free to drop in when it suits them. Even in American classrooms, instructors rarely take attendance, and the only evidence that regular attendance affects learning is purely anecdotal.

There is no scientific reason that universities have not organized their curricula around Erdös-style open-ended courses. In 2008, George Siemens, a professor at Athabasca University—the Canadian version of Britain's Open University—and a research scientist for the Canadian National Research Council named Stephen Downes decided to offer a course on a theory of learning that they call Connectivism and Connective Knowledge, or CCK.[7] CCK is a long tail concept, a pedagogical theory asserting that learning takes place as students discover how to navigate the interconnected networks across which knowledge is distributed. Their course was about CCK and simultaneously used CCK as the primary teaching method. It was offered again in 2009, and eventually attracted several thousand students.

Not all of the students were actually enrolled in the course. In fact, people were encouraged to take the course for free, contribute to the discussions, and add whatever material they thought might be appropriate. But in order to receive credit from the University of Manitoba, a paid enrollment—in return for which a student would complete assignments and receive personal feedback—was required. The course, which Siemens had advertised as Mega-Connectivism was quickly dubbed a *Massively Open Online Course*—or MOOC—by Edupunks and their colleagues.

The same community that invented MOOC has also adopted an open source CMS called *Moodle*. Moodle has been licensed to forty-six thousand sites and claims to have more than thirty-two million users, making it a rival for Sakai and Blackboard, but its real purpose is to support the constructionists' learning approaches that emphasize teaching methods and an Exploratorium-like system of navigation through course materials. That has made it a favorite of online universities like OU, and—because its stated philosophy is to support social, constructivist theories of learning—has sometimes put Moodle on a collision course with OBA advocates in accreditation organizations.

Moodle designers were not interested in factory automation, and the system shows it. Moodle is an open system: blogs and RSS feeds from any source can be linked directly into a Moodle installation, and PHP scripting is the primary means of extending Moodle features. It would seem that by simply adopting MOOCs and Moodle, a university might be able to test the waters of long tail instruction on a small scale, but most mainstream institutions would find it difficult to also wholeheartedly embrace the concepts, because they come bundled with CCK, and the very idea of CCK carries baggage of its own.

Connected constructivism lives on the fringe of traditional learning theory, and sweeps an enormous number of Internet age ideas, from hub-and-spoke laws to modern theories of media and knowledge, into a set of core principles,[8] many of which are not acknowledged by mainstream behavioral and cognitive learning theorists. According to CCK, "learning is a process for connecting specialized nodes or information sources," and "learning may reside in non-human appliances."[9] George Siemens says that "Classrooms which emulate the 'fuzziness' of this learning will be more effective in preparing learners for life-long learning."[10] An educational reformer who wants to throw out a traditional classroom curriculum in favor of a MOOC based on CCK has to be willing to accept much at face value.

The most troubling consequence of taking CCK too literally is that it moves the teacher neatly to the side of the learning equation, replacing a *mentor* with a learning *process*. In a twenty-first-century university that uses open content and iTunes U, masterful teachers are essential.

In late 2009, two emails from my colleague Richard Lipton arrived. "Hit nine thousand page views today!" said the first one. A few hours later: "We were number 20 on WordPress!" Lipton is a computer science professor and mathematician, a member of the National Academy of Engineering, and well known among his colleagues as a prolific collaborator, although his network of collaborators is not as large as that of Paul Erdös. But Lipton is still in his early sixties and has many productive years ahead of him.

In January 2009, Lipton began blogging pure math on a site he calls Gödel's Lost Letter:

I have worked in the area of theory of computation since 1973. I find the whole area exciting and want to share some of that excitement with you. I hope that these blogs inform and entertain you. I hope that you not only learn some new ideas and hear some interesting open problems, but also get some of the history of the area. One of the things I think people sometimes forget is that research is done by people. One of my goals—perhaps the main one—is to get you to be able to see behind the curtain and understand how research works.[11]

This is not exactly the stuff you would expect to be in the top 0.0007 percent of all of those late 2009 blogs about Michael Jackson, death panels, and the 2016 Olympics, but some of his posts, like "Reasons for Believing P = NP," have been exceptionally popular, drawing hundreds of comments from experts, novices, interested amateurs, and a few cranks. His posts range from informal observations about the nature of research to highly technical research articles that break new scientific ground, always in a conversational, engaging way. Here is a fragment of the online conversation generated by a posting called "Cantor's Non-Diagonal Proof."

timur   I may be missing the obvious, but shouldn't the sequence r_{1}, r_{2}, \dots be allowed to be a sequence of real numbers?

Anonymous   I dont see any deference [sic] between two proofs, just the second one has the unimportant details removed. Think of fixing digits as restricting the final real number to the interval of reals starting with those digits. Thus I dont think this can be of any help.

IlyaRazenshteyn   This proof resembles the proof of Baire's theorem ([0, 1] is not a first category set).

Anonymous 2   I agree with Anonymous, above. Can you elaborate on what you think the essential difference is?

Anonymous 3   I don't actually think the EP is any more specific to the real numbers than the usual presentation of diagonalization is. In both cases, you need some principle that says the diagonal real number exists. . . . The ultimate version of this is priority arguments, where not only are the choices not independent, but in fact the dependencies sometimes force you to go back and change previous choices.

This conversation is not so very different than the conversation that would be overheard outside Lipton's office. He is a prolific researcher, but he is also a gifted teacher, and there is little difference between how he engages with students online and in the real world. He is tall, but not intimidating. His once-red beard is now gray, but he still speaks rapidly and with enough enthusiasm to raise the total energy level of any room that he happens to be in. Ideas tumble out. A large measure of Lipton's success as a teacher can be seen in the emotional response that some of his readers have with this most left-brain of academic pursuits. Madhu Syamala wrote:

Your posts are just too good. And I like the way you write too. Very hard to find that combination in many tcs blogs. Do keep posting them. Keeps people like me who once had a brief glimpse of tcs want to keep reading.

How many students will Lost Letters reach? Like the iTunes U statistics, it is hard to interpret usage statistics, but in a three-month period ending in April 2009, 258 comments were posted in response to 7 articles. During the month of April, the number of views varied from 1,000 to more than 5,000 per day. The most popular articles have attracted almost 10,000 viewers. In general, a Lipton posting is viewed about 2,000 times. The top articles have been viewed 14,723 times.

In all the years I knew him, I never saw Paul Erdös near a computer, so even if he were living today, I do not think he would have turned his Massively Open Course into a MOOC. I am certain that he would not have much interest in CCK. But Paul spent much of his life in motion in order to reach as many other minds as possible, so he would have understood immediately the role that the Lost Letters blog plays in expanding Lipton's seminars.

Lost Letters is more than ten or fifteen graduate students crowded around a whiteboard. However, it is interactive, so it is not an iTunes video, either. It is a MOOC, a continuing conversation between a teacher and his students. This is what a university is like when the technology enables a classroom of nine thousand students, and when there are abundant choices, students will choose this.

16   The Process-Centered University

It is time for American universities in the Middle to take the mentor-protégé relationship seriously. Since the time of Peter Abelard, the role of the instructor has been to offer expertise and inspiration while students offer an audience and a kind of immortality. The role of the university as an institution in this relationship has been debated for hundreds of years. That role has oscillated wildly between loose associations—based on nationality and self-interest—and today's corporate enterprises. Exactly where that oscillation should stop is a debate that occurs only rarely, and the outcome of that debate is not yet decided.

One obvious answer is that universities offer diplomas. In his reporting about Edupunk professor David Wiley's 2008 online course at Utah State University—which came complete with a handmade certificate of completion—*Chronicle of Higher Education* reporter Jeffrey Young had the presence of mind to ask: "When Professors Print Their Own Diplomas, Who Needs Universities?"[1] Universities long ago gave up their stranglehold on certificates. A sufficiently talented mathematical collaborator might earn a small Erdös number. A student blogger's comments are enshrined in a MOOC's archives. Professional associations, fraternities, and business groups hand out prizes, plaques, and framed certificates of achievement. A cynic might observe that many of these recognitions are meaningless, but it turns out that universities routinely offer an array of certificates that have no academic meaning whatsoever, but that students accept and proudly include in their resumes.

University administrators answer that, above all, the universities also offer branding, facilitation, and access. A formal institution can provide learning environments and experiences that individual professors are in no position to duplicate. A university, it might be argued, packages knowledge and provides oversight and structure that channel resources. It keeps everyone on track. This is a dangerous position for a university in the Middle.

As resources get tighter, it raises questions about exactly how universities provide value. It also raises a third possibility besides faculty- and student-centered institutions—a possibility that is most destructive to the competitive value of American universities. It is the one that is invoked more often than any other, because it reinforces the factory model. It is the process-centered university: the well-oiled machine.

Beware the Well-Oiled Machine

Linda's first challenge when she was named department head was to reform the curriculum. Students were required to take the introductory courses in her department that were appropriate for their majors. This requirement meant that the instructional workload for the introductory teachers amounted to thousands of credit hours per year—many more contact hours than would be consistent with effective mentoring. Over time, the department had figured out how to cope with such a high workload: they decided to become a sort of factory.

Part-time instructors—usually retired professionals—were handed an hour-by-hour lesson plan and a large stack of overhead transparencies for recitation to a hundred freshmen. Projects were carried out in smaller groups under the supervision of teaching assistants, many of them undergraduates themselves. Capable and revered instructors—teaching awards had been named in honor of their inspirational careers—had devised the system, but by 2000, all of them had retired. Tenure-track faculty members had virtually no contact with freshmen, and there was no faculty supervision of the introductory course sequence. A Student Service organization staffed by nonfaculty academic professionals and advisors oversaw the entire operation, which consumed a sizeable fraction of the department's operating budget.

By 2002, the results were indisputable. A cheating scandal was exposed to the glare of national media. Lab assignments and projects—designed as a rite of passage by upper classmen and graduate students—required an unreasonable amount of time to complete and were wildly out of sync with the academic goals of most students. Business, science, and engineering students, for example, were barred from using tools that the instructors did not like, even though familiarity with those tools would be required in later courses on campus. Student complaints far exceeded any other unit on campus and the attrition rate for students in Linda's department was well above 50 percent.

Even worse, the introductory courses alienated female students. Male teaching assistants assigned project tasks by gender. Women were assigned writing and documentation tasks; men were assigned leadership roles. Female enrollment was a full ten points lower than the national average and twenty points below the levels of other departments in the university. Open-ended comments from students confirmed that there were few mature guiding hands in the introductory courses.

Linda's first step was to hire Mark, a respected senior professor who had a reputation as a turn-around expert, to guide the reorganization of Student Services. Mark began to review operations of the Student Services organization, but long-time staffers immediately warned him that he should not mess around with how things were currently being done because "it's a well-oiled machine."

It was a revelation. Even the support staff thought of themselves as workers on the factory floor, and the learning spaces reflected it. Students hung out on long wooden benches in large lobby area with a shabby green carpet. To get to instructors' offices, students had to pass under a hand-lettered sign that said "SWAMP." This was a remarkably effective setup for the students who chose to remain, but students—on campus and off—were choosing other paths in increasingly large numbers. Students liked but did not respect the instructors, and their ratings of the instructors were alarmingly low.

Despite a public scandal, an alarming retention rate among the best students, an increasingly hostile environment for female students, and poor ratings from students and faculty members in other departments, Student Services staff members received consistently high marks from their supervisors during annual performance reviews. It did not take Mark long to figure out why the supervisors loved the well-oiled machine. The cost of instruction for the introductory courses was low, and advisors effectively moved the few students who chose to remain through the program without a lot of hassle. Accreditation teams routinely approved the curriculum without requiring much from the department. Best of all, the tenured faculty members were rarely bothered by undergraduates.

While students, alumni, and an alarmed public were letting Mark know that the well-oiled machine was not doing its job, the department's research reputation continued to rise in national rankings. In the strange accounting of the Middle, things were going well.

Press Here to Talk with a Human

In a university, a CMS is a course management system, but for most of the commercial world, the initials "CMS" have another meaning: *customer management system*. Attracting, understanding, and retaining customers—particularly high-value customers—has become such a competitive differentiator for companies that there is an entire industry devoted to managing customers. A consumer might see the effects of technology advances in retail sales.

Online stores remember loyal customers and helpfully offer discounts, advice, and help based on past purchasing patterns—and they never close. In many traditional stores, mobile, handheld computers are the new cash registers, so that customers, who are immediately paired with a sales expert, do not have to wait in long check-out lines. Some retail Web sites have a **press here to talk with a human** button for customers to click for help with problems.

Completely hidden from the customer in the best of these systems are the back office databases and systems that make this kind of technology such a good investment. A company that can easily acquire new customers, determine which products they would like to buy, make the purchasing process hassle-free, and quickly correct problems when they occur is more likely to operate a successful, profitable, growing business. While universities in the Middle were concentrating their CMS investments on the well-oiled machine, disruptive institutions were investing in customer management, trying to understand what their students wanted in a university experience.

Just finding a university means navigating a haphazard maze of impenetrable catalogs, ratings, and sometimes incomprehensible Web sites. There is an institutional uniformity to the marketing of higher education that makes it hard to tell when a university is actually advertising its strengths to potential students. It is even harder for universities to find the right students. Except for athletic scholarship candidates, colleges and universities have few tools for identifying potential stars. The disruptive institutions are the ones who rely on a unique combination of value and brand. They are in demand, but it takes work to keep the demand high.

California's Harvey Mudd College (HMC) is small (730 students), so its president Maria Klawe has to worry about filling only two hundred freshman openings every year—a job that is made easier because of Harvey Mudd's unique value proposition and its high ranking in reputational surveys. "The driving rationale for Harvey Mudd College's taking a liberal arts approach to STEM education was the desire to produce STEM leaders who would understand the impact of their work on society," Klawe told me. They compete for the best students, but even with a compelling value proposition, brand recognition is a problem. According to Klawe, "Harvey Mudd's chief competitors are (in order) MIT, Caltech, and Stanford. Our biggest issue in competing for students is the much greater level of name recognition of these institutions."

It would make life easier for Maria Klawe if HMC had a graduate program to help attract students, but that would diffuse the college's undergraduate focus. But HMC is not interested in chasing the institutions that are higher in the pyramid. Klawe is determined to set her own ground rules for success. Rather than sacrifice core values, HMC capitalizes on its strengths by building a reputational network of influencers. Klawe says, "Our primary approach to building our brand is by building relationships with individual leaders, companies, and organizations in science and technology fields. Each semester, we run a public lecture series that brings leaders on campus for a day. We find that once someone spends a few hours with our students and faculty, they become a Mudd advocate." According to Klawe, influencers, industry partners, and agents are key components of this network: "Their responsibility is to introduce the school to people who should know about us. It's a slow process but it's gradually making a difference."

Without a brand or value advantage, marketing might boil down to old-fashioned recruiting from the right neighborhoods. According to Arizona State University president Michael Crow, "The best predictor of success in being accepted at the university of your choice is zip code. That's because high-income zip codes have the best high schools, and the best high schools prepare students to be accepted at selective universities. However, the data also says that coming from a high-income family is no predictor of future academic success." Universities in the Middle climb the academic hierarchy by becoming more selective, leaving behind many students who should be admitted but will not survive the grueling and impersonal application process.

Applying for admission to a university in the Middle is not a pleasant process. It is a stressful, uncertain time for high school seniors, and the application process does not help. On-campus tours showcase campus life and are designed to elicit applications in large numbers, but a name tag at an orientation meeting might be the pinnacle of personalization that a college can hope to achieve. Overwhelmed college admission offices do their best to sort the applications into the *yes*, *no*, and *maybe* bins so that admissions officers can concentrate on the high-value prospects, but students can wait for months with no feedback at all about their status. They are not individuals; they are simply applications.

Financial aid is another faceless application process. It is simultaneously confusingly specific because each institution offers its own programs and impersonal because they all use an emotionless, consolidated application Web site that simply calculates a dollar amount that a student is eligible to receive with the same precision that a bank might use to qualify a first-time home buyer for an FHA loan. Even after acceptance and enrollment, it is the well-oiled machine that dominates a student's life.

Students who need to take a summer job have to be mindful of the university calendar, because they can only begin classes at the start of the semester. Working parents cannot necessarily take classes at times that minimize day care expenses, because class scheduling does not take student availability into account. Furthermore, classrooms fill up, so a section of a class that is needed for graduation may not be available until the next semester. Graduation dates are determined by the university calendar, not by a job that is currently available but that might be filled by someone else if graduation is delayed.

To a mainstream university, the job market is something separate, distant, and essential to their students, but disconnected from almost everything else on campus. There are counselors, seminars, and job fairs in which dozens—perhaps hundreds—of potential employers set up their booths to meet with graduating seniors, but universities do not take a direct role or responsibility in placing their graduates in suitable positions. Traditional universities merely act as facilitators because no one has the responsibility for ensuring that students find jobs.

Courses have a maximum size, so students who are slow to register are sometimes turned away from a class simply because they lost a footrace. When finances are tight, universities cut the number of sections of popular courses, so there is no guaranteed roadmap from the start to the finish of an academic program. Access to university resources is determined by the faculty, not by student needs. A student who needs to meet with a professor has to realize that he might not be available on research days and that rigidly enforced office hours may mean an extra commute to campus during rush hour traffic. It is usually a surprise when a student decides to leave the program, because the factory has no idea who is unhappy; even though students give warning signs that things are not going well, there is no one assigned to help retain students.

For-Profit, online, and distance education universities rise or fall on recruiting, enrolling, funding, and placing students. They may be businesses, but they are not factories. Disruptive growth from the bottom in higher education does more than threaten the Middle. It attracts investment in technology and services that matter to students. Novak Biddle Venture Partners—the same firm that funded the Blackboard CMS—now includes in its portfolio companies that specialize in long tail, online education. Some, like Maryland startup 2tor, seem to have been founded on disruption. 2tor asks its clients "What If Online Education Were Great?"[2] and provides

Internet-based tools for recruiting, retention, and graduation services. Not surprisingly, the startup market for higher education is the hottest in countries like India.

In the four-year period ending in April 2009, Indian venture and private equity firms invested more than $300 million in higher education, a quarter of which has funded companies that specialize in online learning. Growth in the Indian market attracts investment from the West as well. 2tor investor Novak Biddle is also an investor in a company called Educational Initiative, which promises to improve learning in Indian schools.

Online universities spend a lot to attract and retain good students. In its 2009 third quarter, the University of Phoenix spent nearly $244 million on marketing and sales,[3] and that does not include the fee for naming University of Phoenix Stadium, the home field for the Arizona Cardinals professional football team. The emphasis on effective recruiting is not limited to for-profit institutions. The University College of Engineering in Burla, India, signs up online recruiters on its web page to help it increase its prestige among Indian technical universities.

Smarter recruiting is not a game reserved for online universities. Many universities in the American Middle are trying to climb the reputational ladder by becoming more selective, but casting a *wider* recruiting net may be a competitive differentiator. Michael Crow thinks that the best students may well be in the "next tier who would not be accepted by MIT or Berkeley." Arizona State under Crow refuses to rise in the hierarchy by becoming more selective. "We want to be more successful," says Crow, "and that means accepting good students who apply. Our admission standards are basically what they were at Berkeley twenty years ago. Berkeley is now trying to match the Ivy Leagues in selecting its students. We are not. We know that there are diamonds in the solid students who come to us with solid B averages, and we won't turn them away. They are our success stories."

Universities that are interested in attracting good students know how to personalize the experience. Recruiting prospects at online universities go through the same application process as students at mainstream colleges, but—sometimes within minutes of submitting an application—they are contacted by a human, whose job it is to guide them into successful enrollment.

Working to hold onto students is also important, and that includes making sure that students who want it get financial aid. For-Profit universities account for a disproportionately large number of federally backed student aid packages. Thirty-eight percent of entering students at For-Profits receive federal grants, compared with 27 percent at public universities and

28 percent at traditional private universities. For-Profits rely on federal Pell Grants for up to 85 percent of their total revenue.

Presidents of traditional universities view this situation with alarm and have called for additional regulation to make sure that the reliance on federal funding is capped at 90 percent of revenue. Presidents of For-Profit universities see it differently: they think that their success in seeking grants for entering students is a result of spending more money on their recruiting process.

For-Profits admit a larger proportion of at-risk students than their campus-based counterparts, which helps to account for a graduation rate of less than 27 percent—much lower than the 51 percent graduation rate for their public counterparts, but also much higher than public community colleges, which graduate only 20 percent of their entering students. Nevertheless, executives at For-Profit universities understand the role of retention in improving their brands, and they are prepared to introduce tools and programs to improve retention rates, even if it means a slight decrease in enrollments.

In its 2009 earnings conference call, the University of Phoenix announced a program to allow new students to take a free three-week orientation program prior to enrollment:

It combines stronger commitment of time and energy from students up front, with more help and assistance from us prior to their formal enrollment and receipt of Title IV loans. In its current format the program requires prospective students at selected campuses who have less than 24 credit hours to take a free, three- week orientation program prior to enrolling. Now we're still in the test and evaluation phase of the program. However, as expected, it is having some impact on our new enrollment growth.[4]

Other universities assign a retention team to each student—a group of academic counselors, customer advocates, and academic advisors who have overall responsibility for identifying and removing roadblocks to graduation.

This kind of operational infrastructure is not the exclusive realm of online universities. Mainstream institutions that follow the path toward highly specialized majors like Threads may find themselves forced to handle levels of complexity that far outstrip their existing capabilities, even in the classroom. A classroom instructor in the Threads program manages as many as thirty-six different degree students in a single section. When class projects are assigned, the instructor should assign students to groups in a way that recognizes their individual needs and goals. In fact, to effectively teach a threaded curriculum, instructors have to adjust classroom activities like homework and oral recitation to match the needs of the students in front of them. Trying to manage written exercises, teaching assistant staffing, and instructor calendaring in that that kind of environment can quickly overwhelm pencil-and-paper methods of course management. Heavyweight course management software systems are far too cumbersome to handle that kind of operational flexibility.

Threads also changes the traditional role of academic advisors. In most degree programs, professional advisors have to be familiar only with programmatic requirements—details of academic disciplines hardly ever enter into interactions with students and their advisors, especially during early years of undergraduate programs where students generally proceed in lockstep through fixed core curricula. A student entering a threaded curriculum, however, has a sometimes bewildering array of choices to navigate.

Although many Threads students do not decide on curriculum details until their second or third year, a Threads freshman may have many questions about course content and prerequisites that require subject matter expertise. Expert systems like the one developed by Gradiance that use advanced artificial intelligence techniques or even good commercial customer management systems that track product preferences would help, but these are not the technologies that are preferred by campus IT departments.

The key to successful change in the Middle may lie in the way online universities manage day-to-day instruction. One advantage to online instruction is that lockstep classroom instruction is not necessary, so classes are never full, and the university calendar is not a slave to the demands of campus-based instruction. Western Governors University (WGU) is an accredited online university that was founded by the governors of nineteen Western and Mountain states to increase access to higher education by minority and disadvantaged students. WGU caters to nontraditional students, but its orientation is upmarket. It advertises itself as a high-quality gateway to professional success, but it also puts a premium on flexibility. At WGU, a semester begins every two weeks, and students are given not only a detailed timetable for completion of degree requirements, but also a commitment by the university that the timetable can be met.

The "start anytime" promise is one that pervades online universities, but student-centered universities tend to be agile in many dimensions. Many For-Profits also have bricks-and-mortar campuses where degree students take some of their classes, but unlike most institutions in the Middle, the class scheduling maximizes convenience for students. Classes that start and end to avoid rush hour traffic are common; because nontraditional students have a hard time commuting to campus during normal working hours, evening and weekend classes are also common.

Evening classes are not unusual in adult education, but even in this well understood market, For-Profit and online universities tend to create their own competitive advantages. American Public University offers sixteen- and eight-week options for its online semesters, and registration remains open until a week before the semester starts. The University of Phoenix allows students to take five-week intensive courses so that students who need to devote their full attention to a subject can still fit three courses into a fifteen-week semester, and by attending class year-round, complete baccalaureate requirements in four years.

If something is not going well, For-Profits do not have to wait for faculty committees to decide on a course of action, and—unlike accreditation-driven campuses—For-Profit universities know a lot about what is happening on their campuses. That data helps the business of running the university. The hundreds of millions of dollars in cash that proprietary universities have on hand is plowed back into experimental programs that are designed to improve outcomes for students, but they are also used to fund graduate programs designed to raise reputations.

It is no accident that residential student housing for so many For-Profits is located close to on-campus housing for mainstream universities that offer competing programs: proprietary universities know that word-of-mouth testimonials from smart, satisfied students are just as important in marketing their programs as slick media advertising. As tuitions rise and reputations erode at traditional universities, the For-Profit students who complete on time and find jobs awaiting them may be the best sales force. Universities in the Middle may find that it is not even a level playing field for traditional measures like brand and academic quality.

Social Capital

Mainstream American colleges and universities are preoccupied with aspects of academic life—classrooms, curriculum, and standards—that they think they can control, and they always appear to be shocked that students find value elsewhere. It was disruptive to higher education when, in the nineteenth century, American students looked to athletics and extracurricular activities for motivation outside the classroom, which they found to be increasingly irrelevant. It is disruptive today that the value of an MIT education does not lie in the lectures and textbooks.

Social capital defines the value of an MIT education. How does a university in the Middle compete with that? It is true that the most immediate way to experience a physical community is to live within it, but—as UMW's Jim Groom discovered—it is not the only way, because social networks also generate social capital.

The technology of social networking and online communities extends the reach of physical communities. The power to connect people who share common languages, values, and interests but who may be scattered around the world was recognized early in the development of the Internet when role-playing fantasy games connected virtual adventurers in continuing stories of mysterious cities, dragons, and dungeons. By 1995, the Internet had spawned MUDs (Multi-User Dungeons) and MOOGs (Multi-User Object Oriented Games), as well as MUSEs, MUSHs, MUVEs, MUXs, and VEEs. Edupunks are direct descendents of these early social networkers, which accounts for whimsical names like MOOC and for their chaotic anarchy.

Behind all this play, online communities were building value. Above all, a social network is a real network with components like people, groups, and self-defined relationships. People who share relationships—like "Alice is Bob's friend" or "Charlie belongs to the same group as Alice, but Bob does not"—talk to each other and buy things from each other. They are influenced by other members of the group. Social networks are hub-and-spoke networks, and capital concentrates at the hubs, because in a social network the most valuable people are the ones who have the most influence.

Anticipating the explosive growth of the Internet in the late 1990s, networking pioneer Robert Metcalfe in 1980 predicted that the value of a network to an individual member should be related to the number of other members of the network. Metcalfe was probably thinking primarily of telephone networks, but the reasoning behind his prediction is as solid for today's Internet as it was for the old-fashioned phone network of 1980: if you lived on a primitive planet and owned the only working telephone in the world, you would probably say that the value of the telephone network is zero—it does you no good at all because there is no one to call.

On the other hand, if Alice and Bob also have phones, you can call either Alice or Bob. Alice can call you, but she can also call Bob directly, and similarly, Bob can call both you and Alice. Three separate calls are possible, and if Charlie gets a phone then six separate calls can be made. With a hundred phones, more than five thousand distinct calls are possible. The number of possible calls is much larger than the number of people with telephones, and as the number of telephones grows, the overall value of the network grows still faster. If we all agree that the value of the telephone network is somehow related to the ability of its members to make calls to each other, the relationship between the value of a network and the number of members looks like the curve in figure 16.1.

Internet visionary George Gilder called this observation that the value of a network is a quadratic function of the number of members *Metcalfe's Law*.[5] Metcalfe's Law has been used and misused to justify the sometimes unreasonable growth of the Internet economy. Because it is possible to connect hundreds of users at the same time, there is some disagreement about the exact shape of the value curve, but even the most severe critics[6] of Metcalfe's Law acknowledge that the value of a social network is a *nonlinear* function of the number of participants in the network. What holds for telephones also holds for fax machines, email, blogs, Twitter, and Facebook, and a new generation of social networking sites aimed specifically at value outside the classroom.

Unlike Lost Letters, OpenStudy.com is an online educational platform that connects students and educators in a give-help-get-help community. It enables students to ask questions and reach out to others studying the same things at the same time, regardless of school, expertise, or location. It provides collaboration tools so users can give and get help in real time. It is in effect a geographically distributed Hole-in-the-Wall that reaches far beyond a single course, classroom, or university.

OpenStudy.com is not a CMS. It began life as an outgrowth of research that artificial intelligence professor Ashwin Ram carried out with Emory

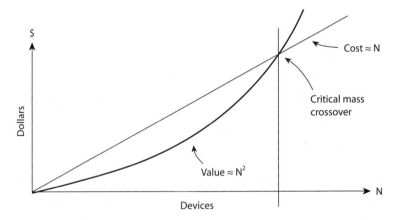

Figure 16.1
Metcalfe's Law of network value.
Source: Reconstructed from fragments of undated archived images of Metcalfe's talk at an IEEE workshop on networking.

University's Preetha Ram. OpenStudy was originally geared toward students who complained about trudging across campus to meet with study groups or keep appointments with faculty during office hours. With funding from NSF, GRA, and NIH, OpenStudy gradually added audio and video capabilities, a people discovery engine, and peer recognition for students who provide help to others. According to Ashwin Ram, we should think of OpenStudy.com as "a community of students who provide real-time help to each other so they can collaborate and study more effectively. Think of it as a social network where the point is to trade study help and answers, not pictures and jokes."

It is not accidental that social networks are so well adapted to producing value in higher education. The hubs and spokes of social networks reflect the long tail effects that influencers have on learning. On a small scale, Mitra discovered that learning communities apparently form spontaneously around leaders independent of any top-down direction or formal authority figure. Why this should be so is not completely understood, but it is partially explained by theories of social impact. In 1981, the social psychologist Bibb Latané published a theory of social impact in which influence in a group is a multiplicative effect of strength, immediacy, and number of people affecting any given individual.[7]

According to Latané, a group of individuals evolves over time, and the course of this evolution tends to have four effects on the group. The first three—consolidation, clustering, convergence—explain how majority views are formed. The fourth—survival of diverse opinions—explains how long tail views migrate to the spokes of hub-and-spoke networks. If Latané is right, then social networks are destined to be dynamic entities in which value is passed from node to node as its members cooperate, collaborate, and share.

This kind of dynamic behavior helps to explain the apparent effectiveness of social networking sites like Lost Letters and OpenStudy.com and almost certainly gives social networks an edge over, say, high-cost, low-benefit group interactions like large lecture hall classrooms. Classroom instruction is a solitary activity. At its best, there is value in the information that flows from teachers to pupils, but, as we have seen, that value can be easily duplicated by online lectures and open content—and virtually all technology innovation in the classroom is aimed at making the one-way flow of information more efficient. There is nothing to offset the inevitable erosion of value in the classroom—no Metcalfe's Law at work to increase the value of the group—because the classroom network looks like the broadcast network shown in figure 16.2 and not like the network in figure 16.3, which

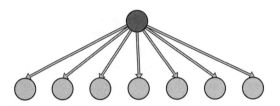

Figure 16.2
A broadcast network.

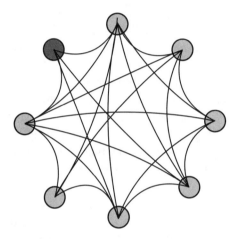

Figure 16.3
A network with rich connections.

is rich in interactions and opportunities for teachers and students to collaborate, cooperate, and generate more value for all participants.

Social networks in physical communities accumulate capital because neighbors do things for each other, they contribute to a common enterprise, and the capital is spent when members of the community need services, support, and information. As noted by Clay Shirkey:

Individuals in groups with more social capital are better off on a large number of metrics, from health and happiness to earning potential, than those in groups with less social capital.[8]

In a large lecture hall, there is little give-and-take. Something that one student knows cannot be efficiently passed along in return for social capital. Social networking sites may have an edge because their interactions create social capital in a way that is hard to duplicate in the real world.

Social capital is an important factor in OpenStudy's success, and Ashwin Ram has a theory about why. "In other social networks, it is a badge of honor to be 'mayor' of a restaurant, have the most viewed video, be invited to the best guilds or create your own, or have more followers than the number of people you follow," Ram told me. In social networks like OpenStudy, social capital is a significant motivating factor for many to submit quality answers or spend time helping their peers. As Ashwin Ram describes it, "The world is one large study group. When a student helps another learn, everyone wins."

This "win" results in the same social capital that drives online reputation systems. In online communities, the greatest incentive besides monetary compensation is an online reputation, especially if that reputation can benefit the individual in the nonvirtual world. Ultimately, the value of social networks in education may lie in the human connections they create. As Jeff Cole pointed out to me, "What appears to be a solitary activity—staring at a screen and tapping on a keyboard—is just part of a more complex world that blends virtual and real interactions." In a social network, giving help has as much value as getting help, and that gives it an advantage over a one-way flow of information, like a lecture.

It is as true in economic networks as it is in neighborhoods: when communities of entrepreneurs cooperate to generate social capital, the rate of innovation, investment, and wealth increases.[9] It is also true in higher education, and that is a lesson for universities in the Middle that want to replace the eroding value of passive classrooms. Embracing large-scale social networking increases the value of the university community by increasing capital in social networks.

17 Hacking Degrees

There are two ways to look at the future that I have sketched in this book. The first—which I do not advocate—is that universities in the Middle had better pay attention to online instruction and other delivery technologies because they will have an impact on cost, access, and bottom-up choice. I discount this point of view because it places no burden on institutions. It is an approach that has been tried over and over again with dismal results: automating the production of things that are not sought after is a path to becoming an effective producer of obsolete products and services.[1]

There is another way to look at the future. Institutions in the Middle do not have the brands and ready capital that allow them to set global agendas. The For-Profits have already figured out how to profitably reach an increasingly larger share of the market that the Middle used to own. The flood of new universities promises students even more value at lower cost. The Middle desperately needs a new way of doing business that can navigate these waters. Technology cannot come to the rescue, but without new technology change may be impossible. Technology may lie on every road to the future, but only for those universities that can explain why they should survive.

Nowhere is this contrast more evident that in the apparently top-down, process-centric concept of *certification*, because as the future unfolds—as students choose their own curricula, universities deskill delivery, and open course content levels the playing field—there is no room for authority-based accreditation. That sounds like a chaotic future, a higher education bazaar in which diploma mills and storefront colleges compete with respected educational institutions for both students and dollars. How, for instance, would an employer know how to evaluate a job candidate who claims to have acquired valuable skills at an unaccredited university? Who provides certifications that can be trusted, and how can universities afford what would undoubtedly be an explosion in accreditation and certification agencies?

In 1990, I had a similar discussion with senior technologists at Citigroup. Citibank was the originator of electronic banking in the early 1980s, but a decade later the research group was wrestling with the problem of providing ever-increasing levels of automation to retail banking customers. In 1990, automated teller machines (ATMs) were common, but not ubiquitous— in part because every ATM had to be connected to a centralized Citibank computer through a private, secure network. There were a few specialized applications like Quicken and Checkfree that automated bill payment and check writing, but when I asked the Citibank engineers whether they foresaw Internet connections to consumers using personal computers at home, they were very pessimistic. They told me in effect that open networks were not suitable for the demands of the banking industry. If everyone were able to join the network, nobody would know who to trust.

But that was before the invention of web browsers and the layers of security that make online banking feasible. In less than a decade, the retail banking and financial services industry transformed itself from a paper-oriented business in which all important transactions began and ended with a form signed and countersigned by human beings to a set of Internet-based services. Ten years later, when I visited Citibank in my corporate role for Hewlett-Packard, the banking executives were not concerned at all about whether the Internet could handle the rigors of their industry. They were concerned with how to use the Internet to further enhance their ability to decrease costs and enhance customer services.

What happened in those ten years is a model for how to deal with the certification problem in higher education. The banking industry, like many others, adopted a set of conventions and protocols that—when adhered to—establish a trust network. Banks essentially tell their customers that when they agree to conduct business online, they are joining a cluster of other customers who mutually share the risks associated with online banking. The banks, for their part, join other networks that reinforce the customer trust networks.

It is not a perfect system, and there are occasional breaches of security, but the vulnerabilities in online banking have little to do with the clusters of trust relationships surrounding specific financial institutions. In fact, we know today that there are far greater vulnerabilities in generic IT problems, like the weak identity management systems that facilitate identity theft, or in underlying economic assumptions that nearly led to a global banking collapse in 2008.

This kind of clustering in social impact networks gives rise to what is probably one of the most surprising answers to how twenty-first-century universities might certify students: diplomas might be cobbled together using rules that are transparent and are agreed upon by clusters of trusted institutions.

The Cape Town Declaration

In cyberculture, "hacking" means two things. One meaning is unpleasant: computer criminals *hack into* systems by breaking security features, stealing passwords, or by launching simultaneous virus attacks on thousands of computers. Software engineers, on the other hand, use the term to describe what happens when an expert computer programmer pieces together an especially elegant software solution to a difficult problem using bits of code from open source repositories and some handcrafted code invented just for this task. When an expert hacker is finished, peers applaud, and the hacked solution becomes part of the design vocabulary of all software engineers. Hacking means changing, dissecting, and combining old tools to get a new tool that is better and more effective than any of the old ones. The interests of the disruptive global forces in higher education might be best served by *hacking diplomas*.

In 2007, a small group of educational anarchists, including Brigham Young's David Wiley and representatives from Creative Commons and the Wikimedia Foundation, met in Cape Town, South Africa, to discuss how to promote open resources in education. The result of the meeting was a declaration of principle, the Cape Town Open Education Declaration, which says in part:

This emerging open education movement combines the established tradition of sharing good ideas with fellow educators and the collaborative, interactive culture of the Internet. It is built on the belief that everyone should have the freedom to use, customize, improve, and redistribute educational resources without constraint. Educators, learners, and others who share this belief are gathering together as part of a worldwide effort to make education both more accessible and more effective. . . . However, open education is not limited to just open educational resources. It also draws upon open technologies that facilitate collaborative, flexible learning and the open sharing of teaching practices that empower educators to benefit from the best ideas of their colleagues. It may also grow to include new approaches to assessment, accreditation, and collaborative learning. Understanding and embracing innovations like these is critical to the long term vision of this movement.[2]

The Cape Town Declaration has been signed by two thousand educational leaders from around the world, including Creative Commons cofounder Larry Lessig and Internet archivist Brewster Kahle. The declaration has been endorsed by two hundred organizations, including iTunes U and universities on every continent except Antarctica. No mainstream American university is a signatory to the Cape Town Declaration.

The Cape Town Declaration is a direct assault on the rationale for centralized accrediting agencies. Built on the process-centered factory model, accreditation has in recent years expanded in both cost and scope to encompass more than what was intended by Andrew Carnegie when he called for a standard unit of credit that would allow fair comparisons between colleges and universities. In American higher education, accrediting agencies conflate two concerns—one relevant to their certification mission, the other an encroachment on institutional prerogatives. The Cape Town Declaration, if widely adopted, would forever separate those concerns. In doing so, it would make the former self-regulating and the latter unnecessary.

There are many in the academic world—professors, deans, provosts, and presidents—who are deeply resentful of the role that accrediting agencies have chosen to play in quality improvement: requiring that certain data be gathered and examining how the data are being used to make programs better. They are afraid to speak up, but in private they argue that it is neither in the best interests of institutions to expose their internal improvement processes to external review and comment, nor in the core competency of accreditation bodies to pass judgment on how institutions decide to improve their programs. High-performing programs find themselves burdened by bureaucratic accreditation requirements that only slow them down. Low-performing programs spend precious resources on sometimes meaningless lists of requirements that could be better spent on actually improving their programs.

The purpose of accreditation is to verify that the educational content of degree programs meets minimal requirements, that the credits granted for completing courses can be fairly compared by different institutions, and that instructional faculty and facilities meet guidelines consistent with quality education. If institutions insisted that accrediting limit itself to these goals, would the current, closed, bureaucratic approach to accreditation still be necessary? There might be a better, cheaper, more effective, more open certification method.

In a 2009 blog about open accreditation, David Wiley points out that "accreditors are interested in transparency and accountability," and then asks a startling question:

Can you think of a better way to create and facilitate transparency and accountability than putting all of your department's courses in OCW and taking [a] pro-open stance on other department output like research publications and policy documents?[3]

Open accountability takes the question of whether an institution is teaching accredited material out of the hands of a centralized authority and separates the powers of accrediting agencies. Open accountability would make it feasible for any institution to piece together highly specialized degree programs from open content course materials, and in effect, to hack accredited diplomas.

Canadian educational consultant Tannis Morgan proposed two alternatives to current accreditation models.[4] The first is to accredit self-access centers, the repositories where OCW materials and other online resources are kept, an approach that many think is unlikely to succeed. It is open to question whether agencies would agree to accredit a free-floating entity like a self-access center. The second is to encourage interinstitutional shared course components and publish the institutional clusters that result, effectively encouraging the improving programs to aspire to join a cluster that is led by a program with a higher reputation.

The second proposal can be implemented without centralized certifying bodies, and there are already functioning systems to use as models: interinstitutional agreements to accept transfer credits. Universities routinely review the courses and curricula of cooperating institutions to determine whether to allow the transfer of credits. Accreditation plays no role in this process. In fact, there are many examples in which courses completed at one accredited institution are not allowed to count for transfer credit at another institution.

Interinstitutional shared components are also common aspects of degrees that are offered jointly by two institutions. To agree on a joint curriculum, universities have to share their course materials and answer questions about course contents and credits posed by their partners, but once established, a joint degree is a common statement of program quality.

When three or more universities are involved in offering several joint degrees, the overhead involved in comparing courses can be overwhelming, so universities in the European Union and the United States often agree to common frameworks. Like a treaty, a framework places the burden on an institution not only to comply with the requirements, but to make available to institutional collaborators all evidence of compliance.

In 1987, the European Commission, faced with an increasingly mobile university student population and a complex, costly web of interinstitutional agreements, agreed on a program called the *Erasmus*[5] framework. By

2006, more than one hundred and fifty thousand students were involved in Erasmus exchanges. In 2004, an international version, *Erasmus Mundus*, was established leading to joint master's degrees across Europe, North America, India, and China.

There are other frameworks that require the cooperation of participating universities. European institutions transfer credit hours under an agreement known as the European Credit Transfer and Accumulation System. Incompatibilities between differing curricular models are minimized by the Bologna Process, which establishes compatible academic degree and quality assurance standards for the forty-six participating countries.

The worldwide experience with self-access centers, frameworks, and other transparent ways of sharing course materials is that clusters and networks of clusters of cooperating institutions form automatically. Like other networks, these clusters accumulate social capital as mature and experienced institutions share their resources with newcomers.

Everything we know about social networks says that, inevitably, leaders and influencers will emerge in these clusters, and as predicted by Bibb Latané, we should expect influence in a group to be a multiplicative effect of strength, immediacy, and the number of partners affecting any one institution. In higher education, influence is correlated with reputation: the members of a cluster with the highest reputations will dominate the rest of the cluster's beliefs about quality.

Hacking Reputation

It is only speculation at the moment that reputation hacking can be a long tail alternative to authority-based reputations, but it is particularly intriguing that online reputation management in the commercial world rejects most of the assumptions of the one-size-fits-all factory floor.

We began this book with a look into reputation-based rankings from the 1925 rankings of graduate programs and the 2009 THE rankings of international universities. Unless we were to specifically inquire about it, we would not know, for example, whether the top-ranked institutions in Slosson's 1910 list were accredited by some body that made outcome-based assessments (they were not), but it did not matter much because there was already a cluster of opinion about the quality of the top universities.

What about the local branch campus of any large public university system in the United States today? Let's call it Local State College (LSC). There is almost certainly a cluster of opinion regarding the quality of LSC's programs, but it seems like an impossible task to determine how much trust to place in that cluster. How about India's Jagand Nath University or Korea's Woosong University? India alone has chartered more than fourteen thousand colleges and universities—many of them with little or no reputation outside a small group of faculty, administrators, and financial backers (who sometimes have a social ax to grind). These reputational clusters—when they exist—are small, easily steered, and not useful to either prospective students or employers.

Reputations are not established by magic. They involve history, performance, and the kind of transparency that shared information provides. California State Polytechnic University (Cal Poly) is located in San Luis Obispo, in California's inland Paso Robles wine country. Cal Poly accepts 36 percent of its applicants, so its eighteen thousand students tend to score higher on the SAT and be near the top of their graduating high school classes. The highest degree that Cal Poly offers is a master's, so it is grouped with similar institutions for reputational ranking purposes. USNWR, for example, calls Cal Poly a *Western* college; for sixteen years, Cal Poly has ranked in the top ten Western colleges that do not grant doctorates. The Cal Poly endowment is currently valued at $116 million. It is a university that is solidly in the Middle.

When I was working for Hewlett-Packard, I was surprised in 2001 to receive an invitation to share the stage at Cal Poly's Centennial Founder's Day Ceremony with Caltech president and Nobel Laureate David Baltimore and NSF director Rita Caldwell. As HP's CTO, I often received university speaking invitations, but I declined most of them due to constraints on my time. I was flattered that Cal Poly president Warren Baker would want to include me on the program with the youngest Nobel Laureate in history and the first woman to head the National Science Foundation, but I had no connections that I knew of to Cal Poly. I was sure that there were other industry executives who were more suitable choices, so I asked my assistant to send my regrets to the president. Then the email started.

My inbox was stuffed with dozens of messages from HP employees urging me to accept the invitation. They were not all alumni. I got messages from donors, parents, and—most significantly—managers and coworkers of Cal Poly alumni within HP. All of them said the same thing: strong ties to Cal Poly—a university in the Middle—were very important to the Hewlett-Packard Company. A few days later, my assistant tracked me down because Marilyn Edling—a senior HP executive—was trying to reach me. Marilyn was a friend, but she was also very persistent. "What are you doing, Rich?" she said when I returned her call. "You can't turn Warren down. Cal Poly is our single largest source of business school graduates."

Could this be true? My office was literally next door to Stanford and was just down the road from Cal Berkeley—two of the Élites. How important could Cal Poly be? Very important, as it turned out. The email just skimmed the surface of Cal Poly's extensive reputational network. Graduates of Cal Poly's Orfalea School of Business were steeped in what former dean Bill Pendergast called "hands-on learning" that made them particularly well-suited to HP's collaborative culture. Business students interacted with engineers and designers, and Orfalea graduates were well known within the company for being able to add immediate value to project teams. I did not know it at the time, but Cal Poly's program was a sort of Threaded curriculum that students could tailor to suit their own aspirations. I accepted President Baker's invitation and arranged for a gift of a hundred and fifty HP computers to reoutfit Orfalea's aging instructional laboratory.

Cal Poly is a member of an invisible reputational network that links together campuses that have become important suppliers of graduates for corporations and governments. These kinds of invisible reputational networks are so common that the idea of large, persistent, stable reputational networks that emerge spontaneously from social interactions became the main thesis of James Surowieki's *The Wisdom of Crowds*:

> The market . . . satisfied the four conditions that characterize wise crowds: diversity of opinion (each person should have some private information, even if it's just an eccentric interpretation of the known facts), independence (peoples' opinions are not determined by the opinions of people around them), decentralization (people are able to specialize and draw on local knowledge), and aggregation (some mechanism exists for turning private judgments into a collective decision). If a group satisfies those conditions, its judgment is likely to be accurate.[6]

As recently as 1997, it was unclear whether reputation and trust networks would emerge in online marketplaces where there is clearly no one in charge. eBay, the online auction and marketplace, faced this problem from its earliest days. An eBay buyer had no particular reason to trust that a seller would deliver merchandise as advertised, and an eBay seller could not be sure that a prospective buyer would actually pay. Many innovations grew from this basic dilemma, but key to eBay's success was the appearance over time of a reputation system that allows buyers and sellers to rate each other.

Many of these ideas came from a line of research—originally called "social recommendation" or "social filtering." In the early days of the Internet, social scientists hit upon the following idea: because there will be many customers searching for videos, auto parts, or shoes, maybe the technology can be used to help customers help each other find things. Study after study showed that actual preferences were highly correlated with the preferences predicted by social recommenders. MIT professor Pattie Maes summed up the impact of social filtering in the seminal paper in the field:

One observation is that a social information filtering system becomes more competent as the number of users in the system increases.... As the number of user scores used to generate a prediction increases, the deviation in error decreases significantly. This is the case because the more people use the system, the greater the chances are of finding close matches for any particular user.[7]

Social filtering is a hubs-and-spokes concept, and the clusters of similar institutions that result would be hard to identify were it not for the scale and diversity of opinion that the Internet enables. The use of reputational clusters as an alternative to central arbiters of reputation is attractive in many other respects. Reputational clusters, for example, bypass the *beauty contests* that figure so prominently in current approaches to judging quality. As I have already discussed, there is no general agreement on what measurements to make in judging an institution's quality, so reputation is frequently established by decree: everyone agrees to take the subjective judgment of an authority figure. But purely subjective judgments are limited on one side by the immediate experience of the authority—a considerable limitation as the amount of specialization increases—and the notoriously inaccurate effect that public accolades have on steering reputations:

The problem, of course, is that the reverence for the well known tends to be accompanied by a disdain for the not so well known. The physicist Luis Alvarez summed up this point of view decades ago when he said: "There is no democracy in physics. We can't say that some second-rate guy has as much right to opinion as Fermi." While this approach makes sense in terms of economizing your attention . . . it has a number of dubious assumptions built into it, including the idea that we automatically know who the second-rate are, even before hearing them.[8]

V   The Long View

18   The Laws of Innovation

When it is written, the story of American colleges and universities in the twenty-first century will note that they became strong at a time when there were comparatively few choices in higher education. When faced with competition, some institutions reinvented themselves, but most of them clung to the belief that change, if it came at all, would be gradual. They seemed to be helpless bystanders as their value was quickly eroded by newer—often more agile—institutions. It is not a new story.

The pattern repeats throughout history: institutions that become inwardly focused, self-satisfied, and assured of their central role in society are easy prey for innovative experimenters who tap into the needs of students, places, and times. Universities that want to escape this fate have to understand the laws of innovation.

The forces shaping higher education—curriculum, a faculty-centered culture, reliance on simple fixes, unexamined assumptions, and the inherent advantages of disruptors—are strong. There are incentives to solve big problems, but higher education is a massive system, and the ability of an individual institution to change is often masked by complexity. How many university presidents would turn their attention from solving immediate, near-term problems to charge into a battle where the stakes were high and the likelihood of prevailing depended on so many different factors? But change in higher education does not necessarily need a massive influx of funding or wholesale policy changes. Not every innovation requires that a university overthrow its curriculum or abandon all of its current infrastructure. Universities in the Middle that want to make it to the end of the twenty-first century should look again at the historical arc. They should take the long view.

It has been a hundred years since Slosson ranked American universities by reputation. The population of the United States had not yet reached one hundred million, and less than a million students enrolled in universities.

Private universities and public institutions shared the academic stage. The first of the great wealth-producing academic patents had not yet been written. A university in today's Middle might want to speculate about the world that higher education might serve a hundred years from now, because innovation is possible for those institutions that take the long view.

Asia can afford to take the long view of just about everything. For 1,820 of the last 2,000 years, India and China alone were responsible for most of the world's goods and services.[1] Therefore, to many in Asia, the dominance of Western economic power seems recent, temporary, and reversible. It is a view that is reinforced daily by the pace of change in China, Singapore, and Korea, countries that have a single-minded focus on innovation. Each has taken a different approach, and the story of how Asian universities have responded to their national aspirations has a message for the American Middle.

China is vast and complicated, and so is its approach to innovation. Even the Chinese term for innovation—*zizhu chuangxin*[2]—is complex, a combination of words whose English translation involves original invention, novel uses of existing inventions, and improvements on innovations that were made elsewhere.

Zizhu Chuangxin

In 2003, the Institute of Higher Education of Shanghai Jaio Tong (SJT) University in China set out to gather information on the performance of Chinese universities relative to the world's greatest universities using quality indicators that would be recognized internationally. It was a bold step for the Chinese. SJT had to be aware that any ranking of world universities would expose glaring weaknesses in China's system of higher education, but the national will to improve was strong. The SJT researchers knew that the first step toward improvement would be an honest assessment of the current state of affairs. They had no way of knowing how influential the SJT rankings would become. Their first innovation was to bypass subjective judgments. Public acclaim had to take a backseat to quantifiable measurements. Only the measurable output of a university was important to SJT. The choice of what to measure is an exercise in *zizhu chuangxin*.

Input measures like selectivity—which figure prominently in reputational rankings in America—are meaningless in countries like China, which are trying to build their capacity in higher education. University enrollment in China jumped in five years from 3.4 million to 13.4 million, and the percentage of college-age students enrolled in Chinese colleges and universities grew from 3.7 percent in 1990 to more than 21 percent today.

Output measures like student satisfaction play virtually no role in determining institutional quality in China. University students learn between five and ten thousand Chinese characters, a requirement that can be satisfied only by rote memorization. Chinese students are accomplished and accustomed to hard work, but there is little to suggest that their satisfaction with the pace and style of classroom instruction plays any role at all in assessing a university's quality.

The SJT designers chose objective performance criteria, and because half of all Chinese undergraduate degrees are earned in science and technology fields, there is a noticeable bias toward research universities with strong technical programs. Institutions are rated on the number of prestigious international prizes that faculty and students win, the number of highly cited researchers, and the number of articles in the journals *Nature* and *Science*.

The *USNWR* rankings have a large subjective component, but the SJT rankings to do not. The SJT does not attempt to measure the quality of education or the impact of an institution. Stanford is ranked second in the world by SJT, but there is nothing to reflect Stanford's role in catalyzing innovation in Silicon Valley, which in 2008 was responsible for more than half of all venture capital investment in the United States. There is nothing to indicate how a university has helped the city in which it is located or affected its nation's economy. For the Chinese, innovation in higher education is *yinjin xiaohou xishou zaichuangxin,* the kind of *zizhu chuangxin* that depends on assimilation, and—because pure research output and impact are the aspects of academic reputation that SJT prizes most—the SJT encourages Chinese institutions to reward the publication of large numbers of articles in scientific journals that are likely to be cited by large numbers of other researchers.

The top-ranked SJT universities are not Chinese and, by and large, they are not Asian. Fifty-seven of the top one hundred are American research universities that are also highly ranked by domestic reputational surveys. There are five Japanese universities among SJT's top one hundred, and two among the top twenty-five. No business school from the Asia-Pacific region ranks among the top twenty. Beyond the top one hundred SJT uses tiers, as opposed to strict numerical rankings. Seoul National University is in the 152–200 band, and two other Korean universities are in the 201–302 tier along with Nanjing University, the top-ranked Chinese institution.

Assimilation is not always easy, so Chinese institutions that chase the SJT's quantitative criteria sometimes find themselves encouraging a culture that values productivity over all else. Chinese Ministry of Science officials, investigating academic standards, found that more than a third of all PhD candidates admitted to plagiarism, bribery, or other behavior that would be grounds for dismissal in the United States. In 2006, concern about adherence to international standards of academic conduct prompted a hundred and twenty Chinese scientists residing in the United States to send a letter to the Ministry urging action on reported cases of misconduct. But these cases are relatively rare.

If the SJT rankings have exposed any trend at all, it is the large-scale deployment of Chinese scientists into leadership positions in Western scientific and technological circles. Former Bell Labs vice president Bob Lucky, who studies global trends in engineering technology, estimates that 70 percent of all papers submitted to the journals of the Institute for Electrical and Electronic Engineers are authored or coauthored by Chinese scientists, and China is on the verge of surpassing American universities in patent production. The SJT game is one that the Chinese know how to play, but in Asia, there are many paths to innovation.

Singapore, Inc.

Singapore is tiny and corporate. At one time, Hewlett-Packard had substantial manufacturing and engineering facilities in Singapore, and every government briefing I attended began with an historical timeline that tied important national milestones to the history of HP. I soon discovered that there was a briefing like that for every major international company in Singapore. In those days, even casual visitors sensed that Singapore's economic strategy was built on the assumption that it would continue to be the dominant innovative force in the region. Though today Singapore looks over its shoulder to the east and sees new competition from Hong Kong and Shanghai, it remains a nation that never strays too far from a strategy that aligns academic, government, and industry around a few, easy-to-explain goals.

Elsewhere in Asia—more frequently in areas where universities were historically training grounds and not venues for independent inquiry—universities search for a model that will allow them to claim international success. The Malaysian peninsula has generated its own approach to innovation by parceling out responsibility for improvement in higher education to government agencies that resemble nothing so much as corporate enterprises. Higher education in Singapore rests in the ministries of education and economic development, the often-warring offices of a government that does not tolerate controversy.

Driving west along the island's southern coast, it is impossible to miss the cities of shipping containers that line Singapore highways. Until it lost the title in 2005 to Shanghai, the Port of Singapore handled more cargo than any other shipping port in the world. It is small wonder that, like Venice a thousand years before, Singapore views its importance to the world using terms like "gateway." *Gateway* is also the name of Singapore's strategy for keeping its competitive position in Asia. Singapore is a small island, but it is home to hundreds of multinational corporations that want to stand at the crossroads between East and West. Gateway is a strategy aimed at a future when Singapore's shipping industry does not have to carry the burden for economic growth because the magnetic appeal to the world of entrepreneurship, the arts, and education are as irresistible as the hundreds of shipping berths were a generation ago. Singapore is a Western enclave in Asia, but it is also Asian, and any company that wants to build a bridge from East to West discovers that it takes an understanding of both cultures to be successful.

To grow its economy at the nearly 10 percent per year rate to which it has become accustomed, Singapore needs tens of thousands of highly skilled workers. The entire university population strains to reach fifty thousand, so Singapore needs to double the number of university students, and that can only be done by attracting foreign students in large numbers. Singapore needs to become Asia's educational gateway.

To the west are Indian coastal states; to the south and east are growing economies in Vietnam and Indonesia. Singapore is surrounded by Asian students who cannot afford to attend foreign universities, but in order to compete for those students, the reputation of Singapore's local universities needed to be burnished with international star power. The Ministry of Education knew how to attract stars. Lee Kuan Yew, Singapore's first prime minister, began in the 1980s to plan for growth beyond industrialization, a program of investment in cutting-edge life sciences, media, and computer facilities continued by his successor and, most recently, by his son, Hsien Loong. Singapore offered a hassle-free environment for scientists and engineers from the best American, European, and Pacific universities. University professors came in large numbers to sample the offerings of the most research-friendly government on Earth.

A biomedical researcher who left one of the top American labs to join a well-funded Singapore research institute told me that the offer was too good to turn down. "When I was in the United States, there was a dramatic change in the way funding was done. When I was starting out as an assistant professor, we had tremendous flexibility in deciding what we wanted to do with a lot of funding. By 2003, 90 percent of my funding came from DoD. I was basically forced to do research in a particular area that I was not particularly keen to do." Singapore was able to create a research environment that even the most elite program could not match.

As frightening as that vignette is for American universities, the story of how Singapore views factory-based undergraduate education should set off alarms in the Middle. Central to the government's Gateway strategy was the Economic Development Board (EDB) program to build a higher education hub. Its goal was to double the number of foreign undergraduates attending college in Singapore by 2015, an impossible task given the capacity and interests of local universities.

The EDB needed international brands that would attract foreign students but would not compete with the aspirations of the National University of Singapore to move into the top one hundred in the SJT rankings. It would have been a risky partnership for any international university, but precarious ties to untested growth plans made it especially worrisome. Johns Hopkins University was an early partner, but by 2007 that relationship was in shambles amid accusations and counteraccusations involving financial commitments.

The EDB was offering cash to compensate for risks, and—on the promise of optimistic enrollment projections—deals were struck with a number of universities for permanent campuses subsidized by hundreds of millions of dollars in EDB investment. Foreign universities that asked to see the research behind rosy market forecasts were rebuffed. Requests to meet with executives of the Singapore-based offices of the foreign companies that would hire the graduates of the new programs went unanswered.

Nevertheless, a number of universities signed agreements with EDB to open ambitious campuses, taking on enormous risks if student demand did not materialize. One of the first foreign partners was Australia's University of New South Wales (UNSW), which in early 2007—with an investment of almost $20 million and a goal of enrolling fifteen thousand students by 2020—opened the initial stages of a comprehensive international campus near Singapore's International Plaza and planned to borrow an additional $150 million to continue building.

Within two months of its grand opening, UNSW announced that it was shutting down its Singapore campus. Enrollments had fallen far short of projections: only 148 students had enrolled and 100 of them were native Singaporeans. The projected losses for UNSW would have been $15 million in the first year alone, a financial burden that the university called unsustainable.

Other Western universities are waiting in line for the privilege of being the outsourcing contractor for Singapore's ambitious growth plans, but of course they do not look at it that way. Many of the universities that are being courted to fill in for UNSW are farther down the reputational hierarchy. They are briefed on the research institutes and the opportunities for collaboration with local industry, but they are not told that Singapore's research partners have already been selected. The institutions that are jockeying for position in Singapore's race to create an education hub are interchangeable commodities. They do not know it yet, but it is not a race to the top.

Axiomatic Design

Like Singapore, South Korea is corporate, but it is complicated, too. It is a small country where innovation is tied to the industries that fuel its economic growth, and where the process of innovation has been reduced to three laws.

South Korea has prospered by reinventing its manufacturing capabilities and aligning its national focus with economic advances. Korean automobiles and consumer electronics now compete successfully with other global brands. The largest companies like Samsung and Daewoo—despite considerable turmoil in senior management ranks—have also surged in heavy industry as suppliers of technology infrastructure. The effects of this reinvention are evident to any visitor: in the years since Korea's emergence from third-world status and nondemocratic strongman rule, the country has helped define modern culture for the rest of the world.

It is among the most connected societies on the planet. It is impossible not to notice the ubiquitous smartphones streaming video to commuters on gleaming public transportation systems. Some of my slightly embarrassed Korean friends have told me about an obsession with cleanliness—a sign of emergence into first-world status—that led in part to a national initiative to renovate public lavatories and toilets. Public restrooms are a source of pride to Koreans—they are not only sanitary marvels, but also showcase Korean technology.

Koreans are very serious about innovation. Like Singapore, their national ministries remind Western visitors of corporate boardrooms. Like China, innovation in Korea is results-driven, and international scientific reputation is a source of national pride. When, in 2007, a respected professor at Seoul National University was found to have fabricated stem cell research results, there were reverberations through all levels of South Korean society. From 1962 until the financial crisis of 1998, the Korean economy grew from

$2.3 billion to $442 billion, and per capita income grew more than a hundredfold. Korea is today the thirteenth largest economy in the world.

Now well into his seventies, Korean Advanced Institute for Science and Technology (KAIST) president Pyo-Nam Suh remains a formidable figure, and—much like presidents of American universities—he knows how to get his own way, even when the forces deployed against him seem overwhelming. His remarkable career spans two continents. He retains a chaired professorship in mechanical engineering at MIT, his alma mater and an institution where he has spent forty years, and for two years, he was head of all engineering research at NSF. He is an entrepreneur and advisor to governments. The Korean Five-Year Plan of the 1980s that led directly to the national innovative surge in the 1990s bears not only his name, but also the imprint of an intellect that rejects most of the complexity of Asian economics in favor of simplicity of design.

There is no Korean version of *zizhu chuangxin,* because the Korean innovation system is a model of simplicity. Suh is the creator of an engineering theory called *axiomatic design,* a phenomenally successful method for designing complex systems of all kinds. Axiomatic design is at its best when it is applied to existing systems to expose mistaken assumptions and flaws in the original designs. One of the consequences of axiomatic design theory is a precise way of choosing among competing designs: once a designer has properly exposed all of the requirements that a system is supposed to satisfy, removed all the redundant ones, and is convinced that each requirement can be satisfied without affecting the others, the proper design is the one with the least information content. In other words, when presented with competing designs, a decision maker should choose the one based on the most general principles.

Suh's three laws of innovation are the embodiment of axiomatic design when applied to the future economic health of South Korea. The first law is a technical one that sets up an axiomatic design for a system of innovation. The second and third laws describe how an innovation hub is needed to attract the critical mass of ideas and funding that are needed to ignite and sustain innovation. There are no secondary indicators needed because the system will perform if it is properly designed. There are no problems arising from cultural barriers because the principles governing innovation are the most general ones possible.

KAIST is an institution that is already well regarded globally for its undergraduate programs, but it is a university in the Middle. Like many Korean universities, KAIST is struggling to transform itself into a leading research institution, and its story—a story that has virtually nothing to do with classrooms of the future or online education—shows how a vision can set in motion a set of disruptive initiatives and events.

Suh's 2006 address was one of the rare aspirational presidential inaugurals:

Our long-term vision . . . is no less than achieving the following ultimate goal: KAIST will become one of the best scientific and technological universities in the world, and, as such, the region around KAIST will become a major hub for high technology industries in Korea and the world.[3]

Nam Suh wanted KAIST to be a disruptive force in higher education, and his vision for how to do that was based on a script taken from the three laws of innovation:

I believe there are three major goals for KAIST. The first is to produce the next generation of leaders for society, industry, and academia. The second is to build the knowledge base and create technologies that will shape the future of humankind. The third goal is to provide public service that will change our world for the better.[4]

But to implement his vision, Suh had to reverse KAIST's long cultural drift toward a factory model and away from real innovation. KAIST inherited its internal culture from a broader Korean culture that had over decades become attuned to the goal-measure-control discipline of the manufacturing floor pioneered by Japanese industrial planners.

There is no figure in U.S. history comparable to Korean president Chung-Hee Park. Park ruled from 1961 until his assassination in 1979. He set in motion most of the economic forces that are responsible for Korea's current prosperity—and many of the country's social flaws. Educated in Japan, he made economic growth the focus of public and private life in South Korea:

This Japanese experience was a vital component in the character of Park's future rule. Not only was he exposed to Japanese planning, but he and his fellow Korean officers were imbued with the Japanese attitude of placing the interests of the group and nation before personal or family interest.[5]

The principles of Japanese planning also had an impact on Korea's universities. Research universities in particular adopted management styles that focused on quantitative processes and measurable outcomes. These were success criteria that were much more closely aligned with the SJT criteria, but to Suh, they were irrelevant. The criteria for hiring, promotion, and tenure were not based on externally meaningful measures of quality.

Research productivity, for example, was evaluated by counting publications. But Korean tenured professors set the standards for journal quality. Articles in Korean journals—written in Korean and unlikely to be read outside Korea—were given the same weight as articles in prestigious international publications. Government funding for university research in science and engineering increased dramatically, but an increasingly centralized bureaucracy for setting research priorities that demanded efficiency and measurable output from its investment adopted methods of Japanese quality control. The Koreans were emphasizing the kind of predictability and uniformity that actually decrease the likelihood of breakthrough research.

Korean was the classroom language for most institutions, which was a barrier to foreign instructors, internationally acclaimed textbooks, and the easy exchange of students that have become the hallmark of Western universities. Japanese planning implies a division of responsibility that undermines industry-university collaboration, so universities that aspired to research excellence were not inclined to mine their research results for intellectual property. Without a university-based engine for innovation, venture capital was not attracted to South Korea in sufficient amounts to make a difference in how research was conducted.

High Risk, High Reward

This was the status of Korean higher education when Nam Suh ascended to the presidency of KAIST. Although KAIST undergraduates were among the best in the world at "core" science and technology disciplines, and with increasing frequency won scholarships and fellowships to prestigious graduate programs in Europe and the United States, no Korean research universities were scored highly in international rankings based on reputation.

Suh created a national stir by announcing in 2007 that instruction in English would be required at KAIST by 2010. All of the interests that had been aligned with Korean language instruction were vocal in their opposition, but the impact of the announcement at KAIST was immediate. KAIST began attracting faculty members from the United States, particularly in areas of strength like robotics and device physics. Nearby institutions that also adopted English-only instruction—like Woosong University's Graduate School of Business that had recently appointed Georgia Tech sociologist and economist John Endicott as president—saw their international enrollments begin to surge.

Suh had an even more profoundly disruptive idea: stop counting publications as a criterion for promotion and tenure. In its place, KAIST began demanding evidence of the impact of research when measured against international norms.

Koreans conduct business meetings around long, low coffee tables. The host sits in a throne-like armchair at one end of the table and the other participants gather around. There are clues to the status of the host. For example, a long, ornate table indicates an important meeting. In 2008, I was seated next to Suh, while an impossibly large number of KAIST deans and department heads crowded around the intricately carved table that dominates his large office. Always the MIT professor, Suh was quick to point out that the "big chairs and tables, including my desk, in my office are the ones I inherited from the previous president, Bob Laughlin, and they were purchased by his predecessor. I am not sure if they were Bob's favorite furniture, knowing Bob's sophisticated taste."

Suh was explaining to me the reasoning behind his reforms, but his staff leaned in, straining to hear every word. It was as if they needed to hear it one more time from the boss's mouth to understand what was about to happen. "Look," he said, "most universities put most of their effort into incremental research because that's how you can generate the most journal articles." In Suh's view, incremental research is aimed at other faculty members and an impact in the medium term. He drew the diagram in figure 18.1.

Suh went on to say, "But really great universities put most of their effort into having either an immediate impact or into research that will change the way people will look at the world." For a technological university, immediate impact means immediate economic impact and a renewed emphasis on patents and the creation of new, exciting businesses—the kind of innovation that Stanford and Imperial College are famous for. Long-term impact means swinging for the fences. It fosters an environment

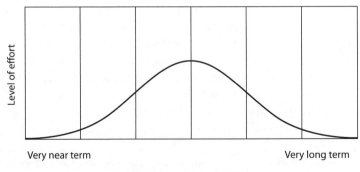

Figure 18.1
Incremental impact.

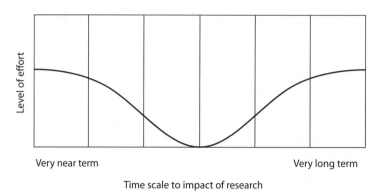

Figure 18.2
High impact.

of fearlessness and risk-taking that encourages the best minds to attack the most difficult problems. It is the kind of research that creates new fields and wins international prizes.

Suh said, "Great universities make their investments like this" and drew a diagram like the one in figure 18.2. It was true. Great universities did not put much effort into incremental impact. They aspired to change the world, and they either demanded immediate impact or big-bet generational impact. In great universities, there are rewards for taking big risks.

True to his inaugural promise, Suh was in the process of redesigning KAIST to be an innovation hub—a hub that either immediately changed economic life in Korea or changed the world in a generation or two. In other words, KAIST was to be an institution focused on the least predictable—and least controllable—aspects of university research.

The only way to reach this vision was to change the rules to encourage extraordinary performance from the best KAIST faculty and attract a new generation of scientists and engineers—people who have aspirations to change the world. There is no room on the factory floor for "swinging for the fences," so if Nam Suh's vision for KAIST is going to be successful, South Korea has to abandon the controlled approach to its public institutions that is deeply ingrained in its culture. It is an approach that leaves some professors behind. In the first year of the reforms, a third of the faculty candidates for tenure were turned down, despite publication records that would have made them shoo-ins under previous administrations.

Suh understands that KAIST is only a part of an innovation continuum. The first of his three laws says that all of the necessary steps have to be in place, and Suh believes that Korean public education has to produce graduates who can think great thoughts, not just score well on entrance exams. Parents spent $16 billion in 2007 to supplement what had already been taught in public schools. Suh says the results are questionable: "Public schools are a failure. Korean parents spend an obscene amount of money on tutors. For what? So they can take exams and get into KAIST. We're going to stop accepting simple exam results. To get into KAIST, you have to write something substantial in English."

Since its founding in 1971 as the Korean version of MIT, students have attended KAIST tuition-free, but in a move sure to create even more controversy, Suh will change that as well. "Students can still attend tuition-free," he said, "but they have to earn Bs or better or else they will start paying tuition." The fees will be substantial, but they are designed to motivate students, not line the pockets of the university. Suh is aware that his vision for KAIST is an experiment that may not succeed. After all, his predecessor was Nobel laureate Robert Laughlin. Laughlin stumbled by pulling KAIST too far and too fast from its historical roots. "My Korean is better than his," jokes Suh, but there is an underlying message in that joke. Nam Suh's tenure at KAIST is not motivated by change for its own sake. At its core, KAIST's transformation is about the future of Korea: "Korea's GDP won't continue to double forever," Suh pointed out. "The country has to do something different. EEWS—energy, environment, water, and sustainability—these are the areas where we think we need to be good."

Culture change in most universities is difficult, but KAIST has a special place among South Korea's technological universities, and the path to changing the culture cannot be to simply abandon the school's traditional value proposition. Suh knows that there are many Koreans who are already upset that longstanding traditions have been overturned. "I have two years to go, and there are people who are counting every minute," he says with a smile. In its pursuit of an international reputation, KAIST cannot simply walk away from its uniquely Korean role. The Korean bureaucracy, employers, and the public who have long regarded a KAIST education as a gift to the next generation would block that path.

Ocean Science

South Korea is the world's largest ship builder by a wide margin. Ship building is an economic lynchpin, and Korea's status in the industry was achieved by a planned evolution of heavy manufacturing technology that, despite extraordinarily high labor costs, keeps Korean ships among the most price competitive in the world. Ship builders like Daewoo rely on mechanical engineering graduates from KAIST to maintain their global position. This creates a problem for Nam Suh, who must continue to hire world-class research faculty for his mechanical engineering department. Top academic mechanical engineers do not care about ship building.

Suh is a mechanical engineer with superb international credentials, so he knows what he is talking about when the subject turns to engineering research. "There are no good research problems in ship building," Suh told me. We already know what counts as a good research problem for Suh: it is one that has the potential to transform the ship building industry either in the short run or the long run, and his estimation is that most of the mechanical engineers who work on ship building are pursuing incremental research—not an area in which KAIST will be making massive investment. "It is hard to build an elite university around ship building," he said. But this is Korea, so "the university cannot suddenly declare its intention to de-emphasize ship building in order to build an elite department of mechanical engineering. KAIST would need another kind of research to enhance the university's international reputation."

Nam Suh's solution to this problem was to push the value of mechanical engineering at KAIST farther out on the long tail. He wanted to encourage research that would simultaneously train ship builders and open a new research front by focusing not on the ships themselves, but on the environment in which ships operate. Suh felt so strongly about this that he filed an international patent for a Mobile Harbor,[5] and at one time even considered creating a new field of study, called Ocean Science. "There are a lot of very hard unsolved problems that involve ships if you concentrate on the environment in which ships operate," Suh explained to me. "And the beauty of it is that students learn the same skills that the ship builders need. We can attract MIT graduates to work on ocean science but not ship building."

What kinds of research problems would ocean scientists work on? One of the bottlenecks in international shipping is the relatively small capacity of deep-water ports. International shipping tends to be concentrated in ports where access is limited and ships must maneuver with precision in order to avoid collisions. But ships are designed for the open seas. Bringing a large number of vessels into a small area necessarily slows things down as ships move in and out. Then there is the bottleneck caused by loading and unloading the ships. As shipping containers are moved between storage areas and the ships themselves, the entire capability of a port's berth is occupied. Without automation, most of this time in port is dedicated to waiting, but even with automation, only one ship at a time can be serviced. In essence, most of the time a ship spends in port is spent waiting in line while the ships ahead of her load and unload their cargo. Increasing the number of ships does not increase the flow of goods because ports are bound to service them serially. But Nam Suh asks, "Why should ships come into a harbor? What if ports could go to the ships?" Imagine a port with many high-speed mobile harbors. "A mobile harbor is an automated vessel, with shallow draught," Suh explained, "that would pull alongside big ships while they are in open water, offload containerized cargo, and move it rapidly to on-shore locations." A port with a capacity for a dozen vessels could in this way multiply that capacity by a factor of ten or more by investing in virtual ports, according to Suh. "A stable platform would eliminate the need for cranes. One design could handle 1,250 containers." Suh sees potential for the harbor in Africa, Malaysia, the Middle East, and the shallow Yellow Sea between Korea and China.

The fact that virtual ports are not yet possible is good evidence that there are some difficult engineering problems to be solved. Energy-efficient, high-speed movers capable of deep-water navigation would have to be strong and lightweight and would therefore certainly require new materials and design principles. New robots would be needed and would have to be an order of magnitude lighter and cheaper than existing cargo movers and more capable of operating safely and autonomously.

Ocean science could be KAIST's version of Threads, a long tail specialization that balances the value of a KAIST mechanical engineering education with the need to attract top-ranked research faculty to raise the university's international reputation. It is not a candidate for distance education because proximity to the world's largest ship building industry is a necessity. It is too early to tell whether ocean science or, indeed, whether any of Nam Suh's initiatives to redefine the value proposition for Korean higher education will work, but it has already had an effect on how South Korea interacts with universities around the world.

Nucleation

Ocean Science is just one of the ideas that Suh threw onto his ornate conference table that morning. They are ideas that are rooted in Korea, but have international appeal. Suh wants KAIST to establish itself in the environment and sustainability field, a perfect fit for a university in a country where half of all exports consist of automobiles and trucks. The other large segment of Korea's economy is electronics and communications. A quarter of all KAIST graduates are hired by electronics giant Samsung, so the online electric vehicle—an effort to marry the digital age with sustainable transportation technologies that use recharging roads might also be strategic for both KAIST and Korea. KAIST engineers decided that "lithium batteries are not the best way forward because of cost, weight, and limited supplies of lithium." according to Suh. "A road that involves burying power strips so that vehicles suck up power from the strips without ever coming into direct contact," would, Suh explained, "allow for smaller batteries and extended range."

These are inherently cross-disciplinary adventures. Collaboration between experts in such far-flung fields as artificial intelligence and fluid dynamics is required to make them successful, but Suh also knows that the farther out you are on the long tail, the more collaboration plays a role in gathering a critical mass of ideas together. A program that is focused only on local problems cannot acquire a reputation on a global scale, and because KAIST's ambition is to solve problems of global significance, partners and collaborators have to view the university as a peer.

Even in the toughest of fiscal times, ideas that converge around projects aimed at making Korea a better, more competitive place give university innovators a seat at the table. In early 2009, Korea passed a supplementary budget to deal with the economic crisis. I asked Suh how Korean higher education had fared. He told me, "During the deliberation for the supplementary budget, I convinced President M. B. Lee of Korea to include R&D projects as part of the budget so as to create jobs for scientists and engineers." Lee allocated a small fraction of the 2009 supplementary budget to support science and engineering projects, and KAIST was able to secure $50 million of the supplementary budget to undertake the Mobile Harbor and On-Line Electric Vehicle projects. Suh says that, "both projects are going ahead fast." He is using the economic downturn as a time to "see if we can create new technologies and new industries. Good research and development does not have to take years. My colleagues, researchers, and students worked literally day and night to demonstrate the feasibility of these two ideas since January 2009." Nam Suh is clearly convinced that the future of South Korea and KAIST are inextricably linked.

It is not an accident of planning that these ideas all converge at KAIST. KAIST's president is very clear about his aspirations: "I think Korea needs to have a very different kind of education where we produce more people who can think, who can lead by conceiving solutions to problems that humanity has to solve in the twenty-first century." Suh is trying to affect the nucleation rate for innovation. He enjoys the metaphor of water condensing around a particle to accelerate the formation of water droplets, as the energy in an innovation system favors the ideas that form around existing innovations. "It is difficult to nucleate an innovation hub with only a limited number of innovations. It is much easier if there are hundreds or thousands of ideas available for innovation."

19 Just Change My Title to "Architect"

For three spring days in 2009, Nam Suh and Arizona State University president Michael Crow sat shoulder to shoulder at a conference table in the village of Glion, perched above the Swiss resort town of Montreux, and considered their respective roles on the global academic stage. They were among the twenty academic and industrial leaders who had been invited to attend the 2009 Glion Colloquium on Higher Education. The topic was "Universities and the Innovative Spirit,"[1] a good match because they are both innovative men, and like innovators everywhere, they are not afraid to take risks.

Suh's plan for the Korean Advanced Institute of Science and Technology was set. He had a palpable conviction that the axioms he is using to redesign higher education in Korea are the right ones. The future was uncertain, but South Korea was in the midst of a continuing economic expansion, and his role was to dream up ways for KAIST to help continue that expansion by igniting the country's innovation engine.

Crow was probably happy to take a break from Arizona politics. The state had sliced his budget by 21 percent, a cut that threatened ASU's plan to create the New American University and prompted an extraordinary open letter questioning by name the commitment of state legislators to higher education. Like Suh, Crow wears his conviction on his chest, but he is not an engineer, and his conviction is not one that comes from axiomatic deductions. It is the result of deep reflection on the complexities of the forces shaping higher education in the United States. He does not expect to fail, but he also understands that he is working without a net and that failure is always possible.

Remarkably, these two men talk about success in exactly the same way. They talk about intellectual fusion and knowledge entrepreneurship. They also both speak with passion about where their universities are rooted. To be successful, they have to connect with where they are—what Crow calls "leveraging place"—and they have to take responsibility for transforming society. For Nam Suh, this means reengineering the nuts and bolts of how a Korean university operates. For Michael Crow, it means reconceptualizing what it means to be a public university in twenty-first-century America. Crow knows that being a university in the Middle, like KAIST or ASU, is dangerous because of the incredible global forces shaping education. Institutions that do not evolve are fated to a future of irrelevance and maybe extinction. "This is, for both of us," he says calmly, "an experiment in genetic engineering." That makes Arizona State a rare institution, because in the last half of the twentieth century, experimentation was almost nonexistent in American higher education.

Where Are the New American Experiments?

Competitors almost killed off tiny Williams College in 1821, when it was barely thirty years old. Williams was only the second college in Massachusetts when it was chartered in 1793, and like most of the twenty other American colleges, it mixed fundamentalist religion with the classical European curriculum. Almost everything else about Williams—from its inhospitable location to its decision to send missionaries overseas—was an experiment, including its lack of formal ties to a Protestant denomination. Williams was dependent on state appropriations and tuition, but the exploding number of denominational colleges strained Williams's claim on state funding. Nathaniel Hawthorne once observed that the Williams students were local boys, limited in their ability to support the college financially:

Country graduates—rough, brown-featured, schoolmaster-looking. . . . A rough hewn, heavy set of fellows from the hills and woods in this neighborhood; unpolished bumpkins, who had grown up as farmer-boys.[2]

When President Zephaniah Swift Moore decided to move the college to Amherst, the remaining Williams students and faculty were left with nothing of value except the loyalty of the alumni and the dedication of the new president, Edward Dorr Griffin, to an independent brand of religious conservatism that was not under the control of any sect. Alumni formed an association dedicated to the future of Williams College—the world's first alumni association—and Griffin personally raised funds from private sources, often by standing on street corners and soliciting gifts from strangers.

Although Williams was not on firm financial ground until the turn of the century, it was enough. Williams began to innovate. They adopted academic regalia to hide class differences among students. They rejected the compulsory classical curriculum, but not course requirements. They also rejected the barren lectures and rote memorization common in nineteenth-century classrooms and adopted the more personalized Oxford tutorial system of instruction. While other colleges chased university status, Williams focused on its students. Williams College survived and became a model for undergraduate liberal-arts education, but it was not the only American experiment. By the turn of the century, England had only eight universities; America had hundreds. But, by the 1950s, the construction of new American universities slowed dramatically. Without new universities, experimentation stopped.

I visited Michael Crow in the spring of 2010 to ask him how the ASU experiment was going. His office was large, but most of it had been taken over by stacks of papers and books that document the state of American higher education. Unlike Nam Suh's office the small sitting area in Crow's office was informal and intimate. He began by pointing out "America stopped building higher education capacity in 1960." In the intervening fifty years, the number of students enrolled in American colleges and universities has more than quadrupled, but the number and kind of universities they attend have not changed substantially. The design of modern American higher education uses assumptions that were formulated while China was an economically insignificant Asian power, before the personal computer and the Internet were invented, and before commercial air travel made it possible to reach virtually any spot on the globe in twenty-four hours. Crow is incredulous that higher education in the United States has not tried to keep pace: "Where are the new Williams Colleges," Crow asked me. "Where are the plans for significant expansion of our major research universities? Where are the experiments in institutional form?"

When it comes to remaking an entire institution, Crow is right. The United States has produced only a handful of new universities since 1960. However, there have been some recent experiments. California's Harvey Mudd College is barely fifty years old, but it successfully competes with MIT, Caltech, and Stanford by charting a unique course: science and engineering graduates who understand the impact of their work on society. HMC has a core curriculum, but students are required to take 30 percent of their coursework in the humanities, social sciences, and the arts. Harvey Mudd president Maria Klawe left her position as Princeton's dean of engineering in 2006, vowing to continue a tradition of liberal arts values in every one of HMC's seven hundred science and engineering students. "Faculty, students, and staff choose to be at HMC because they deeply believe in our mission," Klawe told me. The college recruits only two hundred new students annually, a number that is small enough to allow collaborative relationships between faculty and students.

HMC's size and focus lend themselves to experimentation that would be impossible in a larger school. "We regularly try new approaches," Klawe said to me in early 2010. "For example, we are about to launch a revised core curriculum that implements writing in the technical disciplines for first-year students." This is not a minor tweak. It requires professors who are not only experts in their fields, but are also tuned in to how communication skills are taught in the classroom. It is a hands-on project: "About forty percent of our math, science, and engineering faculty are taking a workshop on how to teach writing," she said.

On the other hand, the new Williams College might be the Franklin W. Olin College of Engineering—Olin College, as it is known locally. Chartered by Massachusetts in 1997, Olin is small—current enrollment is 317—and as dedicated to a single educational principle as Williams was: Olin reverses the first-theory-then-practice model of education in science, technology, and math. Students start to work on projects their first day on campus, and continue—using Threads-like project books to guide their coursework—combining disciplines throughout their academic programs. There are no departments. Faculty members do not have tenure. Some Olin courses are taught on other campuses as part of a cooperative network of nearby universities in Boston so that Olin faculty can focus on their core mission: to foster creativity and risk taking.

Another experiment is the University of California at Merced, the first new American research university of the twenty-first century. Like KAIST and ASU, UC Merced is planted in a place. Its goal is to attract half of its students from California's Central Valley. That makes it different from Berkeley, San Diego, and UCLA, because the only way to be successful in the Central Valley is to be as diverse as the people who live there. On the day it opened its doors, Merced's students were 37 percent Asian American, 25 percent Hispanic, and 6 percent African American. Half of the entering students were the first in their families to attend college. Caucasians are in a minority at UC Merced.

The socioeconomic distribution of students at UC Merced is deeply disturbing to some. Former Princeton president William G. Bowen's book *Crossing the Finish Line: Completing College at America's Public Universities* systematically analyzes massive amounts of data to understand "the dramatic slow-down in the building of human capital over the past 35 years."[3] Bowen lays the blame squarely at the feet of public universities, where—outside a few "flagship" institutions, like Berkeley and Michigan, whose selectivity in admissions allow them to compete effectively with private universities—according to Bowen, a flawed culture allows low graduation rates to flourish. It is a culture, as Bowen argues with pages of data and statistics, that is tied to the socioeconomic status of its entering students.

Michael Crow is also concerned with graduation rates, but he thinks that Bowen's data are measuring something else entirely: the relationship between selectivity and performance. In Crow's view, a data-driven analysis like Bowen's can be used like a hammer to pound universities in the Middle into a kind of submission to the demands of the Carnegie hierarchy, where the way to succeed is to imitate the institutions at the top, to be as exclusive as they can be, and in the process sacrifice the diversity that might have made them great.

When the 2009 California state budget crisis began to threaten funding for the flagship universities, the drumbeat started immediately to protect the most selective institutions by cutting funds at Merced, where performance would have lagged anyway. Berkeley, San Diego, and UCLA would need funds to continue to attract the smartest applicants in order to produce the smallest possible entering class yields—exactly the opposite of what a great public university should be doing, according to Michael Crow. "That's Caltech's mission," he says, referring to the small, private university that houses a dozen Nobel laureates and is among the most selective institutions in the world. Crow does not believe it is fair to beat up every public university in the country because they are not graduating as many of their students as the most selective institutions. "They are not a hand-selected class where you can predict graduation rates. At a place like Princeton, the probability of graduation is one hundred percent, barring sickness," Crow, who spent a large part of his career at highly selective Columbia University, told me.

Michael Crow wants Arizona State University to be one of the great experiments, a university that measures itself by who it includes, not who it leaves behind, a New American University built on challenges and assumptions of the twenty-first century. He wants to avoid what he says would be the supreme disaster in higher education.

Avoiding the Supreme Disaster

Clayton Christensen is seldom mentioned by name in books about the future of universities, but the *Innovator's Dilemma*[4] is nevertheless on the minds of presidents of public universities. When a university president is measured on admission rates, dollars spent per student, and research income, it takes an act of faith to choose a different path. Most presidents do not choose any path at all, choosing instead to manage the processes that they have inherited. It is one of the reasons that I was unable to find inaugural addresses during the last century that recognized the forces of change and defined aspirational goals. Presidents are trained early in their careers that change of that magnitude is not good stewardship. To abandon a strategy of improving what has made them great would be irrational, but presidents also know that conditions change, that disruptors are not bound by incremental rules, and that the rules of the game may be rigged. They know that innovation might require them to be irrational.

The dissonance is paralyzing. Former University of Michigan President Jim Duderstadt knows the danger of incremental approaches in times of immense change:

Institutions all too frequently choose a timid course of incremental, reactive change because they view a more strategically driven transformation process as too risky. They are worried about making a mistake, about heading in the wrong direction or failing . . . many mature organizations such as universities would prefer the risk of missed opportunity to the danger of heading into the unknown.[5]

But the pressure to continue along the current path is so huge that Duderstadt even coined the term "logical incrementalism" to describe his approach: be incremental except in those cases where it is logical to deviate from the path. The supreme disaster for universities in the Middle is that their incremental paths lead to collapse. That is the future that the New American University is trying to avoid.

Most universities are organized around *envy models*. Public universities envy Berkeley and Michigan; private universities envy Harvard and Princeton. Technical institutes envy MIT. Universities in the Middle wait in line to chase one of those institutions, hoping to become one of them. If that were a wildly successful model, there would be no current debate over the value and cost of public higher education. But in order to pursue higher-ranked institutions, a university has to become more selective, more elite, and more disconnected from its community.

The 2006–2007 AAU summary of baccalaureate degrees awarded to black students[6] shows what a university in the Middle has to be prepared to sacrifice to become as selective as their objects of envy: diversity. They have to be prepared for graduating classes with very few black students, for instance. Black students received less than 5 percent of the undergraduate diplomas awarded at more than half of the AAU universities.

As admission standards go up, so does average family income. The supreme disaster is that a public university—convinced that it can only be a certain size—becomes so selective that the average family income of applicants who can be accepted rises, and thus universities become vehicles for socioeconomic class separation. There are some who think this is the path to excellence for public universities.

It is not the path to excellence for Michael Crow's Arizona State: "Everyone waits in line hoping to become Michigan, rather than thinking I am the best in my region or at my specialty, so how do I make that available to every single kid? You have to rethink everything. I am not talking about a social agenda. It's an access agenda. For talent to access a great university you have to design the university differently." That may involve understanding how a university succeeds where it is located.

In Arizona, as in much of the country, universities have been resoundingly silent on their role in transforming society. There are education departments everywhere. They produce the bulk of the K–12 teachers, but there are few that have taken responsibility for the state of public education, many choosing instead to argue that it is a matter of money flowing into public education. Rather than measure success by admission selectivity, ASU wants to have an impact on the way that science and math are taught in Arizona public schools. "We are producing teachers who are trying to teach math and science and are not doing a very good job; why isn't a quarter of the engineering class putting a teaching certificate in their pockets?" asks Crow. "A few of them will become teachers, and they all have the potential to become teachers."

It is hard to imagine how an incremental strategy would result in a plan to make sure that engineering graduates are capable of walking into any classroom in the state. Presidents who simply oversee processes are unlikely to end up with such a simple, fundamental change because it involves a redesign of the university. That is why Michael Crow refuses to see himself as a mediator, as a caretaker for processes that won't evolve: "You can just change my title to architect," he says. "My job is to design so that the university can be the knowledge enterprise that is the most effective here. Most presidents are not designing, or, if they are, they are designing to chase someone else."

We Don't Have a Ministry of Education

There is no Ministry of Education in America. There are enough forces resisting change in higher education, from the inward looking culture of faculty-centered universities and the homogeneous, envious culture of university leadership to the inevitable distractions of their vast constituencies; the burden of a process-centered model that overly values the methods of the factory floor; and a seeming disdain for the marketplace lessons of the innovator's dilemma: institutions that continue to expand beyond the value their customers are willing to pay for eventually find themselves at the mercy of disruptive forces that will soon demonstrate their value. As an enterprise, higher education has become a victim of its own success. Universities have become rigid and self-satisfied. They are walled gardens, convinced that, like Oxford and Cambridge, they can hold outside forces at bay and retain what they've had in the past.

It is their fate that they are subject to disruptive forces, but institutions are still free to choose different paths, to differentiate themselves, to define their own value in their own way, and to define their own challenges. The number of new universities being built outside the United States is staggering. There are almost none being built inside the United States. But that does not mean that individual institutions cannot experiment. The New American University is an experiment, but it also aims to be a comprehensive mainstream university that is competitive and successful. It is in their strategic plan: "Establish national standing in academic quality and impact for colleges and schools in every field." Faculty members are self-conscious about how they will achieve that, but they tend to agree that their standing in the eyes of their peers is very important. If there is a perception that they are chasing fads or are trying to avoid hard work, they will not succeed, but they are adamant about setting the bar for themselves.

Rolling back admission standards to a level that is comparable with those of Berkeley in the 1950s probably means another forty or fifty thousand students. Most universities in the Middle would give up on such an aggressive growth plan, but that would run afoul of another part of the strategic plan: "Access and quality for all."

To be successful, Arizona State has to give up institutional envy, because the rankings are rigged to favor universities that spend a lot of money per student. ASU cannot compete if the measure of success is cost per student, because that cost is passed along in the form of tuition increases and decreased public support. They would much rather compete on outcomes like the number of Fulbright, Truman, or Marshall fellows, Peace Corps volunteers, or students that go on to graduate school. They want to be judged on their success in attracting and retaining minorities or helping the Arizona desert to sustain the urban growth it will experience over the next generation. The leadership at ASU knows that in order to do that, it will have to spend money carefully, investing in parts of the educational experience where the investment might matter and taking unnecessary cost out of other parts. Michael Crow realizes that will require not only new ways of teaching, but entirely new models for colleges and universities. Some of the cost savings will come from online courses. In a memo to the Arizona Board of Regents,[7] he noted that ASU planned to offer approximately eight hundred courses online in the fall of 2010. Although this is only 10 percent of course offerings, he says that it is a "simple notion that we can dramatically increase our efficiency and effectiveness with changes like on-line learning." He calls new information technologies transformational "enablers of universal customized learning" and believes they will "unleash a new type of intellectual liberty."[8]

He maintains a more cautious view, however, regarding the kind of ubiquitous deployment of online courses that are used in proprietary universities. He cautions that for "immersion learning universities" like Arizona State University, online courses are not a substitute for other ways of teaching. They are an "augmentation of the learning environment," he told me. He draws a sharp distinction between large for-profit institutions that offer "episodic learning environments," which he defines as "isolated, single classes from non-academic professionals as teachers," and research universities that are charged with a "fundamentally different process for imparting knowledge and instilling critical thinking and advanced learning."

Nonetheless, Crow favors efforts to lower the cost of delivery of general education requirements. When I asked him how he would do that, he responded, "If a student can demonstrate that he already has the skill set, then why does he have to take the class?" It is a better use of scarce resources to concentrate on the more specialized courses, where an instructor has a better chance of having an impact. Not all of the cost savings come from online courses. Some come from technology that gives faculty members more tools to deal with size and complexity. ASU foresees a day when freshman chemistry laboratory exercises can be carried out in virtual laboratories. They are investing in artificial intelligence systems to aid human advisors. A system called e-advisor allows students to map their courses and their pathway to a degree—a process that does not require human supervision.

I had the impression that deans and department heads had been given a business problem—how to spend less per student and still outperform their peers on important success metrics—and that they really did not know at the outset what kind of technology would be important. I asked engineering dean Dierdre Meldrum what technologies she thought would help, and she immediately listed the most popular handheld devices, but was clearly more interested in talking about effectiveness. She told me, "We are actually thinking about entirely different ways of educating students." Meldrum views technology as a tool for delivering highly personalized undergraduate courses that have been boiled down to units with specific inputs and outputs, so that mastery of specific topics can be guaranteed. She explained that "the means for delivering the modules will vary from in-person one-to-one interactions to online instruction lectures by the best professors to self-paced interactive learning." Her prime concern is the effectiveness of the technology so that "we are certain that a student is proficient in the areas they set out to learn."

Arizona State believes that it can afford to take the long view. Not everything has to be done now because its strategy will unfold during the next hundred years. Thirty years ago, the sponsored research programs brought no significant income to the university. Today, the institution generates almost $400 million in funded research. "A hundred years is long time," Crow told me. "All we know for sure is that the evolutionary forces are unbelievable." He knows that it took a hundred years for Williams College to crawl from the brink of financial ruin to its current position as the most sought-after liberal arts college in the nation. "Where were Stanford and Chicago a hundred years ago?"

Michael Crow's core belief—the principle that guides the New American University—is that in order to be valuable, a public university has to be the place that captures talent, wherever it comes from. He does not believe that universities are at an evolutionary dead end. As we sat in his office overlooking the modern administration buildings of Arizona State University, Crow looked at me intently and repeated what he has said many times to his faculty: "This is very serious business, this reconceptualization of what a public university is supposed to be."

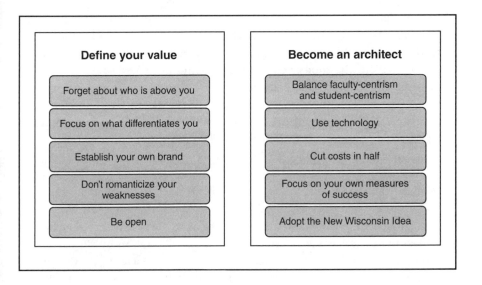

An American university is an institution that conjures images as individualized as the experiences of the students who pass through its classrooms. As I write this, I am looking at a print hanging in my study, Marisa Range's 250 Scenes of Princeton in Blair Arch. It is a composite image of smaller photographs: a satellite dish here, a porticoed entry there, and in the middle, a stained glass rendering of the university flag and shield above a scroll bearing the Princeton motto: Dei sub numine viget ("Under the protection of God she flourishes"), which is a fitting motto for the birthplace of atomic energy, the computer age, and intercollegiate football, and a campus where Einstein took his afternoon walks, Jeff Bezos invented the world's largest bookstore, and John Nash became the hero of A Beautiful Mind.[1] I had such images in mind when in 2002 I left my position as chief technology officer at Hewlett-Packard to return to my alma mater as dean of computing at Georgia Tech—an institution that I thought could achieve greatness.

But the vast majority of universities bear no resemblance to Princeton—or to Georgia Tech for that matter. The *Blair Arch* images probably mean little to the three hundred million students who will attend India's twenty-seven thousand new universities. There is no *Blair Arch* photo of the online university that offers a teaching certificate to Shannon, a part-time student in Marietta, Georgia, who prefers the personal attention that she receives from her web-based team of teachers to the anonymity of the three-hundred-seat classroom at a nearby campus-based university. Nor is there a picture of a baker from San Diego, who downloads free MIT physics classes from iTunes U simply because he likes the idea of "looking at the world through physics-colored glasses." Nowhere in *Blair Arch* are any of the scholars in the thousands of urban classrooms where students—perhaps the first in their families to attend college—work their way into professional careers. The institutions that survive from semester to semester on uncertain income from ever-rising student fees or steadily declining state subsidies are more concerned about accreditation than architecture. The *Blair Arch* images are from a different world.

Images from the Middle

In early November 2009, the University of California at Berkeley—the top-ranked public university in the country—raised its tuition by 32 percent, prompting massive student protests of increases that have tripled the cost of university education during the past decade. For the placard-carrying students, who think they have been locked out of public education in California because they cannot afford it, the university experience has changed. The Berkeley laboratories where Nobel Prize winners once conducted research are now dirty and decaying because budget cuts have made it impossible to properly maintain them. These are images that prompted the *New York Times* to write:

Among students and faculty alike there is a pervasive sense that the [tuition] increases and the deep budget cuts are pushing the university into decline.[2]

Most American colleges and universities—the two thousand or so institutions that are virtually anonymous but that enroll 80 percent of the nation's college-age students—are not like Princeton, and they are under even more intense pressure than prestigious Berkeley.

The future looks very different for most American colleges and universities. Asia's thousands of new universities, Apple's iTunes U, and the hundreds of virtual universities that offer online courses are vanguards of a virtual explosion in global higher education—a market that is desperately trying to keep up with the raised expectations of the half of the world's population that has joined the free market economies in the last generation and wants access to education to improve lives and create wealth. Higher education is, suddenly, a rapidly growing marketplace with many alternatives. There are thousands more institutions of higher learning in the United States than can be supported. Many will not be able to compete with cheaper, nimbler, and frequently more effective alternatives.

A key economic lesson of the last decade—that compelling value is needed in order to prosper when there are abundant inexpensive choices—has not been internalized by American institutions, which for the most part continue making investments to climb academic hierarchies in a costly, rigged game that they cannot win. In the name of excellence, they become more isolated from the needs and expectations of the communities they depend upon for support. Inward-looking, they focus on their own needs and rewards and try to defend the status quo by erecting impenetrable barriers and exclusionary standards.

There are, in the United States, seventy or so Élite institutions that have sufficient resources to establish their own agendas. These are universities that have amassed more than a billion dollars in endowment and a billion dollars in research funding. They are the most selective, and most of them are able to keep their enrollments small. The Élites continue to prosper by attracting the hottest research professors, who in turn attract the most desirable students in a virtuous cycle that drives enhanced reputations and therefore attracts the best new professors.

At the other extreme are For-Profit institutions that eschew traditional measures of reputation but enroll the largest fraction of undergraduates in the United States. Some are so profitable that their cash reserves rival the spending power of the Élites. They are the least selective. In fact, their strategy is to grow to be as large as possible because their delivery technologies do not penalize them for reaching huge numbers of students.

The private Élites tend to believe that their reputations are secure and that they are therefore immune from whatever disruptions await the expanding higher education market, although history indicates otherwise. The public Élites are slightly more vulnerable, but the hundreds of public and private universities in the Middle who find their value eroded as costs soar and bread-and-butter students choose other alternatives are at the greatest risk. That is their fate.

It is the fate of universities to be shaped by political, economic, and social forces, but each institution remains free to choose the road it wants to travel—to choose its own destiny in the twenty-first century. Everyone who has a stake in this story of American higher education should demand a better outcome than a long, slow slide to the margins. This book is filled with examples of universities that changed history by changing course. Some have realized that it is far easier to experiment than to tread furiously to stay put, all the while drifting and sliding toward irrelevance, watching values and reputations erode while new global rules for higher education are being decided elsewhere. Any university in the Middle can choose a different path if it prepares itself now, if it defines a compelling value proposition and then imagines an institution that is capable of delivering that value. Prosperity even for these institutions is not guaranteed, but we—the parents, government officials, employers, students, and alumni—who are the real stakeholders in American higher education should demand more than survival. There are ten rules for the twenty-first century, and we, the stakeholders, should demand that our institutions follow them. Like the experimenters, visionaries, and troublemakers who came before, we should demand that presidents and provosts, deans and professors, trustees and chancellors get on with reconceptualizing what an American university is supposed to be. As Michael Crow says, "This is very serious business."

Define Your Value

1. Forget about who is above you.

William Bowen's thesis is that large public universities, with the exception of the most selective ones, are not doing their job because they are not graduating enough students. Bowen was president of Princeton University—a university of less than eight thousand students whose 10 percent acceptance rate makes it second only to Harvard in Ivy League selectivity. But Princeton's performance has virtually nothing to do with the performance of an institution like Berkeley that enrolls thirty-five thousand. Berkeley, ranked #21 by USNWR, has a 22 percent acceptance rate. Public Berkeley is more selective than private Carnegie Mellon University (CMU), which has a total undergraduate enrollment of six thousand students and is ranked #23 by USNWR. Berkeley graduates only 44 percent of its students; Carnegie Mellon's graduation rate is nearly 90 percent. It makes no sense for CMU to chase Berkeley because it is more selective and ranked higher, nor does it makes sense for Berkeley to chase CMU's graduation rate. They are as different from each other as they are from Princeton.

The images in Blair Arch are not interchangeable, and no university in the Middle can define its value by comparing itself to Princeton. Institutional envy is not the basis for a winning value proposition because academic hierarchies are useless for an institution that has not yet figured out how to define its value. Forget about who is above you; they are playing a different game than you are.

2. Focus on what differentiates you.

It is a competitive world for universities in the Middle, and the sudden availability of cheaper, better, more flexible alternatives—many enabled by technology—threatens institutions that cannot articulate what makes them different. I do not mean generic marketing phrases, like "nurturing environment" or "helping students acquire essential skills." A desire to be excellent does not make you stand out from the crowd. Williams College is competitive in part because of paths that it did *not* take: Williams chose not to become a university. But Williams also held a core belief that *tutoring* provided a better path to a liberal arts education. Harvey Mudd College also has a central value proposition. It stands virtually alone in focusing on how to provide a liberal arts education in math, science, and engineering. Many institutions have made choices to stand out from the crowd. Olin's sleek, efficient approach to combining disciplines is hard for ponderous, faculty-centered institutions to duplicate. Western Governors' online curriculum starts a new semester every two weeks.

The forces promoting uniformity in traditional higher education are enormous, which means that American higher education is lacking for experimentation at the very time when experimentation is most needed. There is no other way to find out what differentiates you in an abundant marketplace where the disruptors do not mind taking risks.

3. Establish your own brand.

Reputations are always subjective. Even the reputational rankings that have the trappings of objectivity have assumptions built into them. The SJT rankings are based on publication counts, but there is a web of subjective judgments that undergirds the numbers. It is a matter of judgment, for example, whether to include or exclude a given journal in the count, and little assumptions like that have big consequences on rankings.

If, in a crowded marketplace, the only things that matter are brand, value, and price, why would an institution turn the job of establishing its reputation over to an agenda-driven authority figure?

Jim Groom's University of Mary Washington wants to be "known as a kick-ass place," and knows how to use its Edupunk credentials to shoulder its way into the consciousness of digitally connected liberal arts students. Cal Poly focuses on turning out managers who are so tuned in to technology markets that companies like Hewlett-Packard make them their number one recruiting stop.

Most of the globally recognizable brands in higher education were established a hundred years ago, when the number of students attending college was one-twentieth of today's enrollment, and multiversities had not yet made their appearance. No one knows what the landscape will be like in another hundred years, but I am certain that the leading brands will not be self-satisfied, inwardly focused institutions whose reputations have been established for them by a centralized authority.

A reputation is a brand—one of the three essential components to success in the new marketplace for higher education. The universities that prosper in the twenty-first century will not be the ones that let bureaucracies and competing institutions define their reputations for them.

4. Don't romanticize your weaknesses.

Everyone who has conducted a job interview knows to watch out for this exchange:

Interviewer: Tell me your biggest weakness, Bob.
Bob: I work too hard.

Universities play this game in reverse, with virtuous legends and romanticized histories to explain why their weaknesses should be viewed as noble. Anything that makes your institution slow to move, inflexible, and disconnected from its stakeholders is a weakness that will eventually work to the benefit of newer institutions who compete for the same students, tuition dollars, and brand recognition. Here are some examples:

• Tenure may be a necessary safeguard for academic freedom, but it is also a weakness. It is widely misunderstood outside academia, and it creates peculiar conflicts in motivations. Twenty-first-century institutions have to figure out how to balance these inconsistencies, and that will be hard to do if tenure is romanticized as an essential part of professorial life.
• A spirited eighteenth-century defense is easy to mount for a bloated, inflexible core curriculum, but institutions in the Middle are so diverse that a one-size-fits-all curriculum is easily undermined by newcomers. The classical core curriculum is romanticized as the common learning experience of all educated people when there is no agreement whatsoever about what is common to all educated people.

• A dark, crowded lecture hall engenders a one-way flow of information that is no match for a flawless online performance, particularly when there is a phalanx of professional coteachers who stand ready to help out. The lecture hall, in fact, is romanticized as part of a "personal learning experience."
• An ivory tower can be both a monument and a barrier; and like many features of daily life on a university campus, has no relationship to the value of the institution. It is dangerous to romanticize the inapproachability of the university as historical legacy when it actually disconnects the institution from the community it needs to thrive.

5. Be open.

It has been nearly four hundred years since the Jesuit Father Nicholas worried aloud that if the university were to use a particularly popular textbook, it might lose its value. It is still unsettled today among many in the Middle whether the greatness of a university is defined by how tightly it hangs on to knowledge or who it excludes from its classrooms. Even basic questions about the value of a university education remain unsettled. Questions like these pose no dilemma to disruptors above and below—to be successful, a university needs to be democratic. A university needs to be open in all senses; it needs to embrace the widest possible community and use technology to open its classrooms to hundreds or even thousands of students. It needs to abandon the business model that overly values classroom attendance. It needs to step back from the role that intellectual property and a culture of ownership plays in determining what is done and what is excluded. The Middle must abandon the very idea of a vertically integrated business model.

Democracy means more than publishing open content. It means using it and, therefore, having to add real value in the classroom. It might also mean throwing out technologies that are aimed at guarding the gates in favor of simpler, open technologies. It might mean open-ended, online courses that resemble more than anything else a continuing dialog. It might mean combining forces with peers who would otherwise be competitors.

Become an Architect

6. Balance faculty-centrism and student-centrism.

Universities in the Middle need to find a new way to balance the faculty-centrism that dominates American higher education. The word of a university faculty is important, but—as institutions from medieval masters universities to Clark Kerr's postwar multiversity have found out—it is not necessarily the last word. A university that focuses too intently on the needs of its faculty eventually becomes ossified and bloated as it finds that more and more of its time is devoted to the minutiae of the profession. It is human nature that decisions in a faculty-centered university—even those framed in moral terms—reflect personal self-interest.

As more alternatives become available and students are presented with better choices, bread-and-butter students will flee. An institutional architect has to put students, alumni, and the needs of the larger community into the design equations. The marketplace will sort out generic marketing platitudes about student-centered learning experiences from a real commitment to an educational enterprise that is as dedicated to stimulating its students as it is the preservation of the status quo for its faculty.

7. Use technology.

This rule has some conditions, however. It is a mistake to assume that technology will alter the landscape without fundamental institutional change. Technology does not drive this kind of change; it enables it. And the technology has to focus on value creation.

The historical arc from Abelard to Apple is a hub-and-spoke story, where innovation enables universities to provide the education that is needed, not the one that is required by the expediencies of the factory floor or the demands of a central bureaucracy. A university in the Middle can use its technology investments to create a walled garden, or it can reinvent itself, using lightweight, sharable technology to enable specialization and networking.

Electronic textbooks, open seminars with thousands of students, and semesters that expand or compress based on the desires of individual students would be impossible without web-based tools. Meme-like specialization and highly individualized tutoring would be out of reach for most institutions in the Middle but for the adoption of technology that has been tried out in the commercial marketplace. Open content clearinghouses create clusters of institutions that will all share materials, freeing universities to concentrate resources on producing value for their students. Open source communities can alter the relationship between universities and authority-based arbiters of reputation and quality.

8. Cut costs in half.

Educational quality has too long been associated with spending, when there is evidence that access, flexibility, and performance are not affected by per-student expenditures. Serious institutional design needs to include getting costs under control.

Half of the cost of general education requirements at most universities can be eliminated by adopting better technology and curriculum reform. It is not even a stretch for most institutions to reach this goal. Colleges have been giving credit for high school Advanced Placement courses for many years now; with the availability of open courseware and other open materials, high-quality online courses, and standard frameworks for credit sharing, extending these programs to all entering students reduces the load on introductory classrooms dramatically. Even when courses are required, a portfolio of methods for satisfying course requirements can bring down costs substantially.

Where do the cost savings go? In some cases, they go toward making a college education more affordable. Even more importantly, costs saved in easily replicated parts of a curriculum can be better applied in more specialized, advanced courses, where small class sizes and specialized equipment are often the dividing line between educational excellence and mediocrity.

Cross-subsidies with athletics, technology licensing, research, and other services that do not contribute directly to education bloat expenses. Teaching loads at most universities in the Middle have been creeping down for decades—virtually without challenge by arbiters of academic quality—in the mistaken belief that time spent in the classroom hinders research. In fact, universities that receive substantial external research funding often find that grants come with hidden strings. Highly productive, mobile professors levy surcharges on their institutions as the price for retaining their services—many times with the cooperation of federal agencies that refuse to pay the full cost of research.

9. Define your own measures of success.

And while we're at it, let's take spending out of the picture altogether as a measure of success. A university in the Middle needs to focus on measures that mean something to the university. A strategy of focusing on outputs, not inputs, can have wide-ranging impact, not only on how universities are operated, but also on how well they perform. Reputational rankings of American universities put more weight on input measures like selectivity and dollars spent per student, and relatively little weight on objective measures of performance.

In 2008, the Center for College Affordability and Productivity[3] (CCAP) developed a ranking based in equal parts on student satisfaction and professional honors earned by alumni,[4] ignoring input measurements altogether. Half of the top ten research universities and six of the top ten liberal arts colleges are in the top ten of the CCAP rankings, but the exceptions are interesting. The result of ranking universities on student satisfaction alone is even more interesting. Boston College (ranked #35 by *USNWR*) is top ranked by CCAP. Samford University (ranked #118 by *UNSWR*) is ranked in the top ten by CCAP. On the average, liberal arts colleges perform much better than research universities, and public research universities drop out of the top twenty-five altogether.

There are dozens of "me-too" success metrics that are virtually meaningless for the average institution. A university in the Middle can spend millions of dollars annually on an office like Technology Licensing that returns very little value to the institution. John Preston, former head of the Massachusetts Institute of Technology's technology transfer office and now a senior lecturer at the school's Entrepreneurship Center, bluntly says, "Royalty income is such a horrible means of measuring success. Schools should instead focus on wealth and job creation, economic development, and corporate goodwill."[5]

Nam Suh's insistence that KAIST faculty members concentrate on demonstrating the impact of their publications was a dramatic shift in an academic culture that had drifted toward easily quantifiable—but easily achieved—success measures. Michael Crow chose to define success for Arizona State not in terms of low acceptance rates, but in terms of the number of "gems" that would be reached. There are stories everywhere of colleges and universities that defined for themselves what it means to be successful, and then designed their institutions to reach those goals.

10. Adopt the New Wisconsin Idea.

On June 17, 1877, John Bascom, president of the University of Wisconsin, gave a baccalaureate sermon entitled "Education and the State." Bascom's vision of a nonsectarian public university in the service of its community— a vision that the new universities of the American West had to tie their success to society—had such a profound impact on the course of higher education that it has become known as the Wisconsin Idea:

All inquiry, all truth must be passed over to the community by school and college, by pulpit and press, as a community possession; and as a supplement to this, every citizen must have the means of instruction so open to him that he shall be brought in living contact with this knowledge.[6]

It is not a badge of honor for universities in the Middle that the Wisconsin Idea seems to have been abandoned in a headlong rush to carve out segments of society for exclusion. So deep is the disconnect between mainstream universities and the communities in which they are rooted that no leader of traditional higher education could admit, "The reason the

University of Phoenix exists at all is that all of those various universities . . . did not provide access to a large number of students who are capable and wanted access to higher education."[7]

Some universities that aspire to academic greatness have campuses in neighborhoods and cities that are in disrepair, blighted in many cases by forces that the university is in a position to do something about. Others establish foreign outposts to extend their reach but have no stake in the future of the local countries and regions. Universities have seen an influx of students in recent years who—unlike their counterparts of a decade ago—want to apply their skills to help solve social problems but find that learning how to do that is not part of an accepted curriculum.

It is the New Wisconsin Idea, but it is also as old as the first American colleges and as universal as Nandan Nikekani's plea to return to his country's "most enduring legacy." Charles Vest and the remarkable universities that make their materials freely available to everyone are committed to the New Wisconsin Idea.

There are dozens of examples of universities in the Middle that have made a commitment to this modern renewal of John Bascom's vision. They are working to tie success to their cities and towns, the communities where their students and alumni live, and to society which—like the American West of 1877—depends upon them for teachers, engineers, and educated citizens.

The Banner Year

1852 was a banner year for liberal art colleges in the United States. Amherst was barely thirty years old, a product of a merger between a secondary school that had been established some years before and Williams College president Zephaniah Swift Moore's group of pilgrims, who were convinced that the inhospitable environment at Williamstown was not suitable for the founding of a proper university. Both schools were tested and ultimately prospered, but at the time they were bold experiments. Others must have been watching, because in 1852, a dozen colleges, all of them devoted to the liberal arts and many with ready-made constituencies, followed suit.

Mills College was founded in 1852 as the Young Ladies Seminary. In 1851, Susan and Cyrus Mills bought the college and moved it from its home in Benicia to Oakland, California, where it survived elimination of seminary classes, the introduction of graduate programs, and an attempt in 1990 to admit men, which led to a two-week strike that shut down operations and forced the trustees to reverse their decision to create a coeducational institution. It is today a campus of fifteen hundred students, and one of the premier liberal arts colleges west of the Mississippi. Its endowment tops $300 million, a stable financial base that it uses wisely. Mills students and alumni understand the value of their degrees, and the college remains a single-sex institution at the undergraduate level. Only the graduate programs admit men.

Tufts was also founded in 1852 as a liberal arts college. It has Unitarian roots and a bias toward public service. Unlike Williams, Tufts began a post–Civil War transition to university status that culminated in the 1970s with its emergence as major research university. Tufts' billion-dollar endowment and reputational ranking mark it as one of the Élite. The same year that Tufts was founded, Wartburg College was founded in Saginaw, Michigan, by Bavarian Lutherans. They were undoubtedly influenced by the German academies where they had been educated. Wartburg moved several times before finding a permanent foothold in Waverly, Iowa. It enrolls fewer than two thousand students and has a $33 million endowment, small by most standards. It does, however, have a hefty $36,000 yearly tuition. Wartburg—like Mills and Tufts—has managed over the last century and a half to stay focused on core values.

In 1852, Massachusetts educator and reformer Horace Mann also founded a college. Mann was the brother-in-law of Nathaniel Hawthorne, an admirer of Williams College. It is not known what effect Hawthorne's opinion of Williams had on Mann. Mann showed no particular interest in higher education until his appointment as secretary of the newly created Massachusetts School Board in 1837. Mann was progressive even by Massachusetts standards and became a controversial spokesman for the role of public education in creating informed citizens. Although it earned him a place in the history of American education, Horace Mann's philosophy was not popular at home, so it must have seemed like a miracle when he had a chance to lead a new college in Yellow Springs, Ohio, named after the ancient Greek city of Antioch.[8]

Mann presided over Antioch College with single-minded intensity for a theme that had occupied him since his undergraduate days at Brown University: The Progressive Character of the Human Race.[9] He hired the first female professors and was devoted to the idea that an Antioch education should serve the greater good. He beat John Bascom by a quarter-century with his admonition to every graduating class: "Be ashamed to die until you have won some victory for humanity."[10]

Antioch College was a twentieth-century beacon of progressive thought, "a laboratory in democracy,"[11] according to alumna Coretta Scott King, but although black students had been admitted prior to the Civil War, Antioch remained racially segregated well into the twentieth century. In 1940, *The Antioch Program for Interracial Education* began to recruit nonwhite students and give them full scholarships. Coretta's older sister, Edythe Scott, was also an Antioch student, the "first African American to attend Antioch on a completely integrated basis."[12] Eventually, African American students constituted 25 percent of Antioch's enrollment.

Civil rights was not the only activist cause that flourished at Antioch. In the 1960s, the free speech and antiwar movements had firm hold on students, faculty, and administrators in seemingly equal measure. The Antioch experiment in democracy drew students who reflected Horace Mann's humanistic ideal and needed a college with Antioch's high tolerance for diversity, dissent, and protest.

In the fall of 1969—at the height of political turmoil over the Vietnam War—I was on a cross-country road trip and stopped for an afternoon at Antioch to soak up what I would later discover was the last of the 1960s counterculture. Antioch's enrollment had soared to almost twenty-five hundred, and although it lacked the scale of Wisconsin or Berkeley, it was exciting to be there. There seemed to be a seamless confluence of liberal thought among faculty, students, locals, and stray visitors. There was no hint of the deep cultural and political divisions that would in few months tragically provoke armed troops to fire on students at Kent State University, a mere two hundred miles away.

For almost forty years, I had barely thought of Antioch College at all until a June 2007 *New York Times* op-ed piece masquerading as an obituary caught my attention: *Where the Arts Were Too Liberal.*[13] Antioch, the first coeducational college in the nation, the university that was unafraid of controversy, was suspending operations. Antioch College had died.

By the time Antioch College shut down, there were fewer than two hundred students enrolled, and its endowment had shrunk to $5 million. College operations would have been impossible. Some years before, Antioch College had been absorbed by Antioch University, a largely online university whose five national campuses enrolled thousands of students. Antioch University had also adopted Horace Mann's vision of the liberal arts in the service of democracy, so Antioch College became a small component of a larger, proprietary university dedicated to the same ideals. Antioch University, whose online undergraduate and nonresident graduate programs continued to grow, was largely unaffected by the shutdown of its famous sibling.

Antioch College faculty were laid off, some within weeks of arriving on campus. This was a clear financial exigency—one of the two valid reasons under AAUP guidelines for dismissing a tenured professor—but the faculty members who were let go nevertheless filed a grievance with the AAUP, an organization that had failed in previous years to gain much support at Antioch.

In their letter of complaint, Antioch College faculty members cited "the administration's failure to consult significantly with the faculty both before and after the June 2007 declaration of financial exigency and asserting that the university system had a 'well-established pattern' of 'neglecting consultation with the faculty or with the Administrative Council (AdCil) about the financial well-being of the college.'" The AAUP had investigated Antioch on prior occasions and found "concerns about apparent departures from AAUP-supported principles and procedural standards related to sound government."[14]

The faculty of Antioch College had designed and implemented a strategic plan that included a new curriculum. Critics would later sarcastically charge that Antioch faculty were "so hip, so politically active, so relevant,"[15] implying that they were interested only in students who reflected those values. The AAUP found fault with college governance, faculty participation in budgeting and program-cutting decisions, and the manner in which the administration executed the new strategy. The investigative report was silent on the role that the strategy itself played in driving away students and donors. Although the immediate cause of Antioch's death might have been a massive failure in governance, it was not the root cause. Even as the online programs at Antioch continued to grow, influence at Antioch College coalesced around ideas that had little value to students looking for a liberal arts education, and the diversity of ideas that should have migrated to Antioch's long tails never emerged. The institution that had made its reputation on diversity became a smaller and smaller haven for intellectual orthodoxy and conformity. As the number of entering freshmen dropped below a hundred, then twenty, the faculty at Antioch still managed to convince themselves that process was the culprit. Even as the college was shutting down, they planned to resurrect Antioch College in its old image by 2012. They were convinced—as the online university flourished—that they could sell an Antioch education to students who were not interested and to donors who failed to see the value.

In March 2010, Dana College, a small liberal arts college in Blair, Nebraska, announced that it was being sold to a for-profit corporation that promised to return the school to solvency and double enrollments. This followed by only a few weeks the announcement of the sale of Iowa's Waldorf College to the For-Profit Columbia Southern University. It was only a year before that Portland State University in Oregon announced that after forty-five years it was closing its certification program for teachers of blind and disabled children due to decreasing enrollments and rising costs. Portland State was losing students in a booming market. Special needs teacher certification is one of the most popular online curricula.

Epilogue

The Antioch College story came up at dinner one evening. I was visiting the chair of a well-respected department at a large land-grant college in the Middle—near the top of the Middle, but struggling like most public universities with budget cuts that threatened to reverse gains in research stature made during the last ten years. At the end of the story, he said, "That's not our problem. We are at capacity. There is no way we can absorb more students." I asked if there were more students that could be admitted, and he said, "Sure, but they will go somewhere else." "Where?" I asked. He thought for a minute, and then recited a list of alternatives. Some were above his institution in the reputational pyramid, some were competitors, and some were in China and India. Then he said, "A lot will get [an online] education."

"So you're getting a smaller share of a growing number of students," I said, and he was quick with his reply: "Those are students we don't want. You don't understand, Rich. We have no more capacity." We went on like this for a little while, and finally I asked why they were not figuring out how to give those students access. "What happens in a growing market when you are losing market share to your competitors who are building capacity?" He stopped. I pressed him. "Where will those students go in a hundred years? What will the universities that have the capacity for the students you turn away look like?" He realized I was asking him what the university of the twenty-first century would look like. After a long pause, he said "It will not look like us."

Notes

Prologue

1. Committee on Prospering in the Global Economy of the 21st Century: An Agenda for American Science and Technology 2007.

Chapter 1

1. Manning 2000.

2. Kerr 2001.

3. Rudolph 1990.

4. Gilman 1885.

5. The Morrill Act of 1862 7 U.S.C. § 304 and the Morrill Act of 1890, also known as the Agricultural College Act of 1890, 26 Sta. 417, 7 U.S.C. § 321.

6. Letter from Vannevar Bush to President Harry Truman, July 25, 1945.

7. Congressional Budget Office 2007.

8. Kerr 2001, 14.

Chapter 2

1. American Association of University Professors 1940.

2. Although professors who are denied tenure at one institution frequently lose their jobs as a result, "firing" in academic circles is not what most people imagine when they hear, "You're fired!" When a professor is denied tenure, many months or years can pass before the position is actually terminated. Sometimes the intervening time is used to try again, but more often than not there is a slow and many times quite congenial parting of the ways during which the faculty member searches for a new position, oftentimes with the help of his or her former colleagues.

3. American Association of University Professors 1940.

4. Theodore Herfurth 1949. Available online at <http://www.library.wisc.edu/etext /wireader/Contents/Sifting.html>.

5. ibid.

6. Georgia Humanities Council 2002. Available online at <http://www.georgia encyclopedia.org/nge/Article.jsp?id=h-594>.

7. Ibid.

8. Ibid.

9. Ibid.

10. Thomas 2005.

11. Committee on Gender Differences in Careers of Science, Engineering, Mathematics Faculty 2010.

12. Rothman, Lichter, and Nevite 2005.

13. Kerr 2001.

14. Rudolph 1990, 271.

Chapter 3

1. New York Times 1996.

2. Office of Research Integrity 1996.

3. Baltimore 2003.

4. "Baltimore to Retire as Caltech President" 2005.

5. Kirp 2003, 54.

6. Kerr 2001, 209.

7. Ibid., 22.

8. Christensen 1997.

9. Bethel 2009.

10. Kerr 2001, 116–117.

11. Ibid., 136.

12. Ibid.

Chapter 4

1. Friedman 2006, 315.

2. THE Times Higher Education 2009.

3. QS Top Universities 2010.

4. Center for World-Class Universities and Institute of Higher Education Shanghai Jiao Tong University, China 2009.

5. Presidential Initiative: Oscar Arias Sánches, *Conceptual Document: Peace With Nature*, Republic of Costa Rica, 2006. <http://www.pazconlanaturaleza.org/admin /descargas/upload/CONCEPTUAL_DOC.pdf>.

Chapter 5

1. Jones and Wellman 2009, 1.

2. Ibid., 1.

3. Slosson 1910.

4. Hughes 1925.

5. Terrell 2009.

6. Endowment amounts are quoted for the year 2007 in U.S. dollars. The steep decline in stock markets that began in September 2008 also eroded the value of most college and university endowment funds.

7. AAU Membership Policy, January 1, 2002.

8. Nilekani 2009.

9. Neelakantan 2004.

10. Nilekani 2009.

11. Fogel 2010.

12. *Sindh today.* "Over 27,000 Institutes of higher learning needed: Sibal." November 7, 2009. <http://www.sindhtoday.net/news/1/68995.htm>.

13. Ministers of European Higher Education Area 2010.

14. Denholm 2009.

15. Bureau of Labor Statistics 2010.

16. Pope 2006.

17. Berg 2005.

18. Caplow and McGee 2001.

19. Ibid., xxiii.

20. Suskind 2008.

21. Dunn 2008.

Chapter 6

1. The name SGI is famously ambiguous in supercomputing circles. The company known today as SGI is actually the renaming of a company called Rackable that purchased the original SGI in April of 2009 for $25 million. SGI is also the name of one of the first supercomputing companies and held a significant share of the high-performance computing market until the late 1990s.

2. Roland and Shiman 2002, 288–289.

3. Karin 2010.

4. *Field of Dreams* 1989. Directed by Philip Alden Robinson and distributed by Universal Studios.

Chapter 7

1. Cohen, Boyer, and Helling 1973.

2. Reimer 2003.

3. Diamond (Commissioner of Patents and Trademarks) v. Chakrabarty, 447 U.S. 303, 206 USPQ 193 (United States Supreme Court, June 16, 1980).

4. University and Small Business Patent Procedures Act (Bayh-Dole Act), 35 U.S.C. § 200–212.

5. Feldman, Colaianni, and Liu 2007, 1799.

6. Ibid.,1800.

7. Johnson 2005.

8. Jelinek and Markham 2007, 257.

9. Heller 2008.

10. Ibid.

11. Testimony of R. Stanley Williams before the Subcommittee on Science Technology and Space of the United States Senate Committee on Commerce Science and Transportation, September 17, 2002.

Chapter 8

1. Yale University, n.d.

2. Rudolph 1990.

3. Ibid., 433.

4. Ibid., 437.

5. Ibid., 434.

6. Lombardi 2000.

7. Grileches 1998.

8. Higher Education Statistics Agency 2010.

9. White House Office of Management and Budget, Circular A-21 (revised August 8, 2000).

10. Family Educational Rights and Privacy Act (FERPA), 20 U.S.C. § 1232g, August 21, 1974.

11. American Association of Universities (AAU) 1998.

12. Rudolph 1990, 439.

Chapter 9

1. Knight Commission on Intercollegiate Athletics. Quantitative and Qualitative Research with Football Bowl Subdivision University Presidents on the Costs and Financing of Intercollegiate Athletics: Report of Findings and Implications. Art&Science Group, 2009.

2. Johnson 1989, 3.

3. Ibid., 10.

4. Blumenstyk 2008.

5. Arizona State University 2009.

6. Except for scholarships and endowments, which fell by 35%, and spending for auxiliary services, which rose by 6% at public research universities.

7. National Center for Public Policy and Higher Education 2010.

8. National Center for Public Policy and Higher Education 2006.

9. Immerwahr, Johnson and Gasbarra 2008.

10. Ibid.

11. National Center for Public Policy and Higher Education 2010.

12. Ibid., 12.

13. Christensen 1997, xix.

14. Knight Commission on Intercollegiate Athletics 2009.

15. National Center for Public Policy and Higher Education 2010.

16. Immerwahr, Johnson, and Gasbarra 2008, 14.

17. Kirp 2003, 241.

18. Christensen, Horn, and Johnson 2008.

19. Blumenstyk 2009.

20. Crow 2009.

21. Lewin 2009.

22. Davis 2008.

23. Immerwahr, Johnson, and Gasbarra 2008, 24.

Chapter 10

1. Rait 1918. 111.

2. Boyer and McKeon 1976.

3. Abelard 1922.

4. History taken from Rait 1918.

5. University of Bologna Statutes, 1405.

6. Rait 1918, 21.

7. Ibid., 102.

8. Grendler 2006, 1.

9. Carlsmith 2002, 215–246.

10. West Texas A&M University, "Strategic Plan 2009-2014."

11. Rudolph 1990, 127.

12. Ibid., 156.

Chapter 11

1. Image created by Matt Britt, December 2006: "I created this small partial map of the Internet from the 2005-01-15 data found at <http://www.opte.org/maps> using a slightly different rendering technique. . . . Each line is drawn between two nodes, representing two IP addresses. The length of the lines are indicative of the delay between those two nodes. This graph represents less than 30 percent of the Class C networks reachable by the data collection program in early 2005. Lines are color-coded according to their corresponding RFC 1918 allocation as follows:.

- Dark blue: net, ca, us
- Green: com, org
- Red: mil, gov, edu
- Yellow: jp, cn, tw, au, de
- Magenta: uk, it, pl, fr
- Gold: br, kr, nl
- White: unknown."

2. Pine 1993.

3. Alma Laurea 2009.

4. International Center for Educational Statistics 2008.

5. Rudolph 1990, 287.

6. Ibid., 126.

7. Ibid., 125.

8. "Addresses at the Inauguration of Charles Wilson Eliot as President of Harvard College." October 19, 1869. Cambridge, Mass. .

9. Lewis 2007.

10. Ibid.

11. Ibid.

12. Christensen 2000.

13. Dawkins 1989.

14. *The Blair Witch Project*, 1999. Daniel Myrick and Eduardo Sanches, dirs. Hexan Films.

15. Zero Wing. 1991. Sega Game Corporation.

16. Sandoval 2006.

17. Stephenson 1992.

18. Benitez 2001, 29–31.

19. Heylighen 1996.

20. Kauffman Panel on Entrepreneurship Curriculum in Higher Education n.d.

21. National Commission on Service-Learning n.d.

22. Ministry of Knowledge Economy 2004.

Chapter 12

1. Stephenson 1992.

2. The Computing Research Association (CRA), a Washington-based association of academic and industrial computing research organizations, extensively documented enrollment changes in computer science programs, conducted extensive public education campaigns, and promoted curriculum changes to attract undergraduates. The best source of data on enrollment trends is available from CRA online at <http://cra.org>.

3. Lohr 2005.

4. Frauenheim 2004.

5. Seidman 2004.

6. Pink 2005.

7. Friedman 2006.

8. Lohr 2005.

9. Friedman 2006, 1.

10. In particular, the IGERT (Integrative Graduate Education and Research Traineeship) program sponsored by NSF.

11. Finkelstein 2004.

12. Between 2000 and 2007, McKinsey & Company conducted extensive Indian economic growth surveys and found that employability of graduates of Indian universities chronically low (e.g., 10 to 15 percent for business school graduates and 26 percent for engineers in the technology services industry). Summaries of these data are contained in a report that McKinsey prepared for NASSCOM in April 2007 entitled *Perspective 2020: Transform Business, Transform India* (McKinsey India 2007). The following TATA Institute of Social Sciences report surveys these and other data: R. C. Datta, Sony Pellissery, and Paul G. D. Bino. *Employability: Concept, Indicators, and Practices*, ATLMRI Discussion Paper (Mumbai: TATA Institute of Social Sciences, 2007).

Chapter 13

1. Rimer 2007.

2. University of Texas Austin, *Center for Instructional Technologies*. <http://wlh.web host.utexas.edu> (accessed June 13, 2010).

3. *Academic Earth*. <http://academicearth.org> (accessed June 13, 2010).

4. Kakalios 2005.

5. Ibid., 153.

6. Vest 2007, 96.

7. Carlsmith 2002, 215–246.

8. MIT News Office 2001.

9. GNU is actually an acronym invented to describe Stallman's open source operating system. It stands for the phrase "GNU's Not Unix!" It is somewhat of a programmer's joke because the acronym appears in its own definition.

10. Vest 2007, 156.

11. Vise 2008.

12. Vest.2001.

13. Vest 2007, 156.

Chapter 14

1. Wheeling Jesuit University, *The Center for Educational Technologies*. <http://www .cet.edu> (accessed June 15, 2010).

2. Mayo Clinic, *Classroom of the Future*. <http://www.mayoclinic.org/feature-articles /levine-classroom-future.html> (accessed June 15, 2010).

3. Cooperstock 2001, 688–692.

4. *Good Will Hunting*. 1997. Gus Van Sant, dir. Miramax, New York.

5. Mitra and Rana 2001, 221–232.

6. Swarup 2005.

7. Ting and Jensen 1974.

8. I was a somewhat unwilling participant in this experiment. Between 1970 and 1972, the ALF project recruited graduate students to record lectures and simultaneously write longhand notes that could be displayed on an ElectroWriter. The

resulting lectures were then replayed to live classes so that data could be gathered to assess the effectiveness of the technology. I was one of those graduate students.

9. Cole 2009, 17.

10. Hsi 2003, 308–319.

11. Woolley 1994.

12. Abowd 1999, 508–530.

13. Carr 2004.

14. Plymale 2005, 60–61.

15. Educause, *Educause*. <http://www.educause.edu> (accessed June 15, 2010).

16. Christensen, Horn, and Johnson 2008.

17. Allen 2004.

18. Fendrich 2007.

19. Woolston 2008, S4G-3.

20. EDUCASE Web site, <http://www.educause.edu>.

Chapter 15

1. Kamanetz 2009.

2. *WordPress*. <http://www.wordpress.com> (accessed June 15, 2010).

3. I selected my email handle "rad" in 1975, and I have managed to keep my **rad @xyz.gov**, **rad@abc.edu**, and **rad@lmf.com** identities through jobs in government, education, and industry by befriending, cajoling, and sometimes losing my temper with IT managers.

4. Domain names are the basis for identification on the Internet. They allow people to use easily recognizable and easy to memorize names in place of the strictly numeric Internet addressing system that computers and networking hardware rely on. Based on the Domain Name System (DNS), domain names are used to identify generic categories with top-level domains like *.com* or *.edu*, but they are also used as identifiers for individual Web sites, company data, host computers, and other resources that are meant to be publicly accessible. Assigning a domain name to an individual gives that person a permanent Internet identity around which all blogs, email, webcams, and other aspects of online life can be organized.

5. George Croom Robertson, M.A., Professor of Mental Philosophy and Logic at University College, London, 1867–1892, was editor of *Mind*. His articles have been republished under the title of *Philosophical Remains* (Bain and Whittaker 1894).

6. *Encyclopedia Britannica*, 11th ed., sv "Abelard, Peter (1079–1142)."

7. Siemens 2006.

8. George Siemens has organized these ideas in two Web sites. <http://www.elearn space.org> was set up to "explore elearning knowledge management, networks, technology and community." Siemens also maintains a blog site devoted to connected connectivism at <http://www.connectivism.ca>.

9. George Siemens, December 12, 2004, Connectivism: A Learning Theory for the Digital Age. <http://www.elearnspace.org/Articles/connectivism.htm>.

10. Ibid.

11. Richard J. Lipton, *Gödel's Lost Letter and P=NP: A personal view of the theory of computation.* <http://rjlipton.wordpress.com> (accessed June 15, 2010).

Chapter 16

1. Young 2008.

2. 2tor, Great Universities Unleashed. New York, NY.

3. Apollo Group, Inc., Form 10-Q Quarterly Report for the period ending November 30, 2009. United States Securities and Exchange Commission.

4. Transcript of call available at <http://seekingalpha.com/article/181545-apollo -group-inc-f1q10-qtr-end-11-30-09-earnings-call-transcript?page=-1> (accessed July 16, 2010).

5. Gilder 1993.

6. Briscoe, Odluzko, and Tilly 2006.

7. Latané 1981.

8. Shirky 2008, 192.

9. Breznitz and Taylor 2009.

Chapter 17

1. Carr 2004.

2. The Cape Town Open Education Declaration, 2007. The Cape Town Declaration is an evolving, living document. New signatories are added online: <http://www .captetowndeclaration.org>.

3. David Wiley, *Iterating toward openness: Pragmatism over zeal.* March 24, 2009. <http://opencontent.org/blog/archives/tag/accreditation> (accessed June 15, 2010).

4. Tannis Morgan, *Explorations in the Ed Tech Worlds*. <http://homonym.wordpress .com/about/> (accessed June 15, 2010).

5. The Erasmus program and its global counterpart Erasmus Mundus are named after the Dutch academician Desiderius Erasmus of Rotterdam, who studied in various Protestant academies in northern Europe at the same time that Jesuit universities were rising to prominence in the south.

6. Surowiecki 2005, 10.

7. Maes and Shardanand 1995, 210–217.

8. Surowiecki 2005, 170.

Chapter 18

1. Maddison 2001.

2. In Chinese: 自主创新.

3. The complete text of Suh's inaugural address is available online at <http://www .kaist.edu/english/01_about/01_president_03.php> (accessed June 17, 2010).

4. Ibid.

5. Breen 2004, 135.

6. Nam Pyo Suh, "Mobile Harbor for Marine Transportation System." International Patent WO/2009/102107, August 20, 2009.

Chapter 19

1. Weber and Duderstadt 2010.

2. Hawthorne 1900, 192.

3. Bowen, Chingos and McPherson 2009, xiii.

4. Christensen 1997.

5. Duderstadt 2009, 264.

6. University of Florida, n.d..

7. Michael M. Crow, May 4, 2010, memo regarding online courses to Arizona Board of Regents.

8. Crow 2006.

Chapter 20

1. Nasar 1998.

2. Lewin 2009.

3. Center for College Affordability and Productivity 2008. <http://centerforcollege affordability.org/pages/page.asp?page_id=79147> (accessed June 15, 2010).

4. Fifty percent based each on ratemyprofessors.com and on the appearance of alumni in Who's Who in American 2008.

5. American Society for Engineering Education 2006.

6. Bascom 1877.

7. Pope 2006.

8. Located in present-day Turkey, Antioch rivaled Alexandria as the center of the civilized world and nurtured early Christianity as it fought to establish itself among the world's religions.

9. This was Mann's Valedictory Oration at Brown: see Messerli 1972.

10. Mann used this admonition to graduating classes many times. For a complete compilation, see Workers of the Federal Writer's Project of the Works Progress Administration in the State of Massachusetts 1937.

11. Coretta Scott King, *Remarks at 2004 Antioch Reunion.* Videos of these remarks are available online at <http://antiochcollege.org/media/video/969.html> (accessed June 13, 2010).

12. Ibid.

13. Goldfarb 2007.

14. AAUP Committee on University Governance 2009.

15. Wickham 2010.

Bibliography

AAUP Committee on University Governance. 2009. *College and University Government: Antioch University and the Closing of Antioch College. Investigative Report.* American Association of University Professors.

Abelard, Peter. [1922] 1972. *Historia Calamitium: The Story of My Misfortunes*, translated by Henry Adams Bellows. New York: MacMillan and Company.

Abowd, Gregory. 1999. "Classroom 2000: An Experiment with the Instrumentation of a Living Educational Environment." Pervasive Computing.

"Addresses at the Inauguration of Charles Wilson Eliot as President of Harvard College." October 19, 1869. Cambridge, Mass.

Allen, Mary J. *Assessing Academic Programs in Higher Education.* Bolton, Mass.: Anker Publishing, 2004.

Alma Laurea. 2009. "Indagine 2009, Pofilo dei Laureati 2008." Bologna, Italy.

American Association of Universities (AAU). 1998 (January 21). "AAU Summary of College Costs Commission Report." AAU.

American Association of University Professors. 1940. *1940 Statement of Principles on Academic Freedom and Tenure.* AAU.

American Society for Engineering Education. 2006. ASEE Prism, 16(6).

Arizona State University. 2008. "Fiscal year 2009 state budget cuts force ASU to cap enrollment, freshman applications close March 1, five months early." <http://www.asu.edu/budgetcuts> (accessed June 15, 2010).

Bain, Alexander, and T. Whittaker, eds. 1894. *Philosophical Remains of George Croom Robertson (with a memoir).* London: Williams and Northcage.

Baltimore, David. 2003. "SAM—Severe Acute Media Syndrome?" *Wall Street Journal,* April 28.

Bascom, John. 1877 (June 17). "Education and the State." Baccalaureate Sermon. Madison, Wis.: University of Wisconsin.

Benitez, Bribesta Luis. 2001. "Mimetics: A Dangerous Idea." *Asociación Interciencia* 26(1): 29–31.

Berg, Gary A. 2005. *Lessons from the Edge: For-Profit and Nontraditional Higher Education in America*. Westport, Conn.: ACE/Praeger Series on Higher Education.

Bethel, Brian. 2009. "University President Wears Many Hats." *Reporter News: Your Abilene Online*, May 24. <http://www.reporternews.com/news/2009/may/24/university-president-wears-many-hats>.

Blumenstyk, Goldie. 2009. "More than 100 Colleges Fail Education Department's Test of Financial Strength." The Chronicle of Higher Education, June 4.

Blumenstyk, Goldie. 2008. "20 Years Later: How One Flagship Has Changed." The Chronicle of Higher Education, December 12.

Bowen, William G., Matthew M. Chingos, and Michael S. McPherson. 2009. *Crossing the Finish Line: Completing College at America's Public Universities*. Princeton, N.J.: Princeton University Press.

Boyer, Blanche, and Richard McKeon. 1976. *Peter Abelard—Sic et non: A Critical Edition*. Chicago: University of Chicago Press.

Breen, Michael. 2004. *The Koreans: Who They Are, What They Want, Where Their Future Lies*. New York: Thomas Dunne Books.

Breznitz, Dan, and Mollie Taylor. 2009. "The Communal Roots of Entrepreneurial Techology Growth? Social Fragmentation and the Economic Stagnation of Atlanta' Technology Cluster." *Social Science Research Network*, October 2. <http://ssrn.com/absract=1481857> (accessed June 15, 2010).

Briscoe, Bob, Andrew Odluzko, and Benjamin Tilly. 2006. "Mefcalfe's Law Is Wrong." IEEE Spectrum, July.

Bureau of Labor Statistics. 2010. *Occupational Outlook Handbook: Computer Software Engineers and Computer Programmers*. Washington, D.C.: United States Department of Labor.

Caltech Media Relations. 2005. "Baltimore to Retire as Caltech President, Will Remain at Institute as Biology Professor," News release, October 3.

Caplow, Theodore, and Reece C. McGee. *The Academic Marketplace*. New Brunswick, N.J.: Transaction Publishers, 2001.

Carlsmith, Christopher. 2002. "Struggling Toward Success: Jesuit Education in Italy 1540–1600." *History of Education Quarterly* 42(2): 215–246.

Carr, Nicholas G. 2004. *Does IT Matter?* Cambridge, Mass.: Harvard Business School Publishing.

Center for College Affordability and Productivity. 2008. "Ranking Methodology." *The Center for College Affordability & Productivity*. <http://centerforcollegeaffordability .org/pages/page.asp?page_id=79147> (accessed June 15, 2010).

Center for World-Class Universities and Institute of Higher Education Shanghai Jiao Tong University. 2009. *Academic Ranking of World Universities*. China. <http://arwu .org/index.jsp>.

Christensen, Clayton M. 2000 (March 2). "The Required Course Subcommittee: A Sentence from Hell." Case Number 9–600–008. Cambridge, Mass.: Harvard Business School Press.

Christensen, Clayton M. 1997. *The Innovator's Dilemma*. Cambridge, Mass.: Harvard Business School Press.

Christensen, Clayton M., Michael B. Horn, and Curtis W. Johnson. *Disrupting Class: How Disruptive Innovation Will Change the Way the World Learns*. New York: McGraw-Hill, 2008.

Cohen, S. N., Annie C. Y. Boyer, and R. B. Helling. 1973. "Construction of Biologically Functional Bacterial Plasmids In-vitro." Proceedings of the National Academy of Sciences 70(11): 3240–3244.

Cole, K. C. 2009. *Something Incredibly Wonderful Happens: Frank Oppenheimer and the World He Made Up*. New York: Houghton Mifflin Harcourt Publishing Company.

Committee on Gender Differences in Careers of Science. 2010. *Engineering, Mathematics Faculty. Gender Differences at Critical Transitions in the Careers of Science, Engineering, and Mathematics Faculty*. Washington, D.C.: National Research Council.

Committee on Prospering in the Global Economy of the 21st Century: An Agenda for American Science and Technology. 2007. *Rising Above the Gathering Storm: Energizing and Employing America for a Brighter Economic Future*. Washington, D.C.: National Academies of Science, National Academy of Engineering, and the Institute of Medicine.

Congressional Budget Office. 2007. *Federal Support for Research and Development*. Washington, D.C.: Congressional Budget Office.

Cooperstock, Jeremy. 2001. "The Classroom of the Future: Enhancing Education through Augmented Reality." *HCI: International 2001 Conference of Human–Computer Interaction*.

Crow, Michael M. 2009 (January 21). "Proposed Budget Cuts and the Future of Arizona." Arizona State University Office of the President. <http://president.asu.edu /node/602> (accessed June 15, 2010).

Crow, Michael M. 2006. "The University of the Future." *Issues in Science and Technology*. Winter: 5–6.

Datta, R. C., Sony Pellissery, and Paul G.D. Bino. 2007. "Employability: Concept, Indicators, and Practices." ATLMRI Discussion Paper. Mumbai: TATA Institute of Social Sciences.

Davis, Erroll B. 2008. "Colleges Need to Offer Clear Path to Leadership." Chronicle of Higher Education, July 18.

Dawkins, Richard. 1989. The Selfish Gene. Oxford: Oxford University Press.

Denholm, Andrew. 2009. "Universities Will Get Extra Funding to Promote Work-Related Learning." Herald Scotland, February 4.

Duderstadt, James J. 2009. A University for the 21st Century. Ann Arbor: University of Michigan Press.

Dunn, Rachel. 2008. "Congress Reviews Financial Aid Policies." The Daily Princetonian, February.

Feldman, Maryanne, Alessandra Colaianni, and Connie Kang Liu. 2007. "Lessons from the Commercialization of the Cohen-Boyer Patent: The Stanford University Licensing Program." In A. Krattinger, R. T. Mahoney, and L. Nelson, Intellectual Property Management in Health and Agricultural Innovation: A Handbook of Best Practices. Oxford: MIHR, 1797–1807.

Fendrich, Laurie. 2007. "A Pedagogical Straightjacket." Chronicle of Higher Education, June 8.

Finkelstein, Larry. 2004. "Restructuring Academic Programs for a Global Based Knowledge Economy." CRA Snowbird Conference. Snowbird, Utah.

Fogel, Robert. 2010. "$123,000,000,000,000 (China's Estimated Economy by the Year 2040: Be Warned)." Foreign Policy, January/February.

Frauenheim, Ed. 2004. "Students Saying No to Computer Science." CNET News, August 11.

Friedman, Thomas L. 2006. The World Is Flat: A Brief History of the Twenty-First Century (Updated and Expanded). New York: Ferrar, Strauss, and Giroux.

Georgia Humanities Council. 2002. "The Cocking Affair." The New Georgia Encyclopedia. University of Georgia Press. <http://www.georgiaencyclopedia.org/nge/Article.jsp?id=h-594>.

Gilder, George. 1993. Gilder Technology Report. Gilder Publishing and Forbes.

Gilman, Daniel C. 1885. The Benefits which Society Derives from Universities: An Address. Baltimore: Johns Hopkins University Press.

Goldfarb, Michael. 2007. "Where the Arts Were Too Liberal." New York Times, June 17.

Grendler, Paul F. 2006. *Renaissance Education between Religion and Politics*. Hampshire, UK: Ashgate Publishing.

Grileches, Zvi. 1998. *R&D Productivity: The Econometric Evidence*. Chicago: University of Chicago Press.

Hawthorne, Nathaniel. 1900. *Passages from the American Note-Books*. New York: Houghton-Mifflin & Co.

Heller, Michael. 2008. *The Gridlock Economy: How Too Much Ownership Wrecks Markets, Stops Innovation, and Costs Lives*. New York: Basic Books.

Herfurth, Theodore. 1949. "Sifting and Winnowing." <http://www.library.wisc.edu/etext/wireader/Contents/Sifting.html>

Heylighen, Francis. 1996. "Evolution of Memes on the Network: From Chain-Letters to the Global Brain." In *Ars Electronica Festival 96. Memesis:the future of evolution*, edited by G. Stocker and C. Schopf, Vienna/New York: Springer. 48–57

Higher Education Statistics Agency (U.K.), April 2010 *Performance Indicators*. <http://www.hesa.ac.uk/index.php/content/category/2/32/141/>.

Hsi, S. 2003. "A Study of User Experiences Mediated by Nomadic Web Content in a Museum." Journal of Computer Assisted Learning 19(3): 309–319.

Hughes, Raymond M. 1925. *A Study of Graduate Schools in America*. Oxford, OH: Miami University.

Immerwahr, John, Jean Johnson, and Paul Gasbarra. 2008. *The Iron Triangle: College Presidents Talk about Costs, Access, and Quality*. San Jose: National Center for Public Policy and Higher Education.

International Center for Educational Statistics. 2008. *Ten Years after College: Comparing the Employment Experiences of 1992–93 Bachelor's Degree Recipients with Academic and Career-Oriented Majors*. Washington, D.C.: U.S. Department of Education.

Jelinek, Mariann, and Stephen Markham. 2007. "Industry-University IP Relations: Integrating Perspectives and Policy Solutions." IEEE Transactions on Engineering Management.

Johnson, Eldon L. 1989. "Evolution of the State University Idea: Presidential Inaugural Addresses Before 1860." *Education Resources Information Center*. <http://www.eric.ed.gov/ERICWebPortal/detail?accno=ED414831> (accessed June 15, 2010).

Johnson, Wayne C. 2005. *Changing Interfaces Between the Research University and Industry*. Washington, D.C.: Engineering Research Council Workshop and Forum.

Jones, Dennis, and Jane Wellman. 2009. *Rethinking Conventional Wisdom about Higher Ed Finance*. Delta Project on Postsecondary Costs, Productivity, and Accountability.

Washington, D.C.: National Center for Higher Education Management Systems (NCHEMS).

Kakalios, James. 2005. *The Physics of Superheroes*. New York: Penguin Press.

Kamanetz, Anya. 2009. "How Web-Savvy Edupunks Are Transforming American Higher Education." *Fast Company* (September 1).

Karin, Sidney. 2010. "Thoughts, Observations, Beliefs, and Opinions about NSF Supercomputer Centers." *HPCWire*, January 28.

The Kauffman Panel on Entrepreneurship Curriculum in Higher Education. *Entrepreneurship in American Higher Education*. The Kauffman Foundation.

Kerr, Clark. 2001. *The Uses of the University*. 5th ed. Cambridge, Mass.: Harvard University Press.

Kirp, David L. 2003. *Shakespeare, Einstein, and the Bottom Line: The Marketing of Higher Education*. Cambridge, Mass.: Harvard University Press.

Knight Commission on Intercollegiate Athletics. 2009. *Quantitative and Qualitative Research with Football Bowl Subdivision University Presidents on the Costs and Financing of Intercollegiate Athletics: Report of Findings and Implications*. Art&Science Group.

Latané, B. 1981. "The Psychology of Social Impact." American Psychologist 36: 343–356.

Lewin, Tamar. 2009. "State Colleges Also Face Cuts in Ambition." *The New York Times*, May 17.

Lewin. 2009. A Crown Jewel Struggles with Cuts.*The New York Times*, November 19.

Lewis, Harry R. 2007. *Excellence without a Soul: How a Great University Forgot Education*. New York: Public Affairs.

Lohr, Steve. 2005. "A Techie, Absolutely, and More." *New York Times*, August 23.

Lombardi, John V. 2000. *University Improvement: The Permanent Challenge. Arizona State University*. Tempe, Ariz.: Center for Measuring University Performance.

Maddison, Angus. 2001. *The World Economy: A Millennial Perspective*. Paris: OECD.

Maes, Patty, and Upendra Shardanand. 1995. "Social Information Filtering: Algorithms for Automatic Word of Mouth." *CHI Proceedings: Computer-Human Interaction Conference*.

Manning, Kathleen. 2000. *Ritual Ceremonies and Cultural Meaning in Higher Education*. Westport, CT: Greenwood Publishing Group.

McKinsey India. 2007. *Perspective 2020: Transform Business, Transform India*. Bangalore, India: NASSCOM.

Messerli, Jonathan. 1972. *Horace Mann: A Biography*. New York: Knopf.

Ministers of European Higher Education Area. 2010. *Official Bologna Process Website*. <http://www.ond.vlaanderen.be/hogeronderwijs/bologna>.

Ministry of Knowledge Economy. 2004. *2002 Informatization Whitepaper*. Seoul.

MIT News Office. 2001. *Interview with Charles Vest*. <http://web.mit.edu/newsoffice /2001/ocw.html> (accessed June 13, 2010).

Mitra, Sugata, and Vivek Rana. 2001. "Children and the Internet: Experiments with Minimally Invasive Education in India." British Journal of Educational Technology 32(2): 221–232.

Nasar, Sylvia. 1998. *A Beautiful Mind: The Life of Mathematical Genius and Nobel Laureate John Nash*. New York: Touchstone.

National Center for Public Policy and Higher Education. 2006. *Measuring Up 2006: The National Report Card on Higher Education*. San Jose: National Center for Public Policy and Higher Education.

National Center for Public Policy and Higher Education. 2010. *Squeeze Play 2010: Continued Public Anxiety on Cost, Harsher Judgments on How Colleges Are Run*. San Jose: National Center for Public Policy and Higher Education.

The National Commission on Service-Learning. n.d. *Learning in Deed: The Power of Service-Learning for American Schools*. Ohio State University, The Kellogg Foundation, and the John Glenn Institute for Public Service and Public Policy.

Neelakantan, Shailaja. 2004. "India Struggles to Meet Demand for Higher Education." Chronicle of Higher Education, June 18.

New York Times Editorial Staff. 1996. "The Fraud Case that Evaporated," *New York Times*, June 25.

Nilekani, Nandan. *Imagining India*. New York: Penguin Press, 2009.

Norman, Augustine. 2007. *Committee on Prospering in the Global Economy in the 21st Century. Rising Above the Gathering Storm: Energizing and Employing America for a Brighter Economic Future*. Washington, D.C.: National Academy of Sciences, National Academy of Engineering and the Institute of Medicine.

Office of Research Integrity. 1996. "Summaries of Closed Inquiries and Investigations Not Resulting in Findings of Research Misconduct—1996." Washington, D.C.: U.S. Department of Health and Human Services.

Pine, Joseph B. 1993. *Mass Customization*. Cambridge, Mass.: Harvard Business School Press.

Pink, Daniel H. 2005. *A Whole New Mind: Why Right-Brainers Will Rule the Future*. New York: Riverhead Books.

Pope, Justin. 2006. "Q&A with Head of U. of Phoenix." *Belleville News-Democrat,* October 13.

Plymale, William O. 2005. "Pervasive Computing Goes to School." Educause Review 40(1): 60–61.

Top Universities. 2010. *QS Asian University Rankings.* <http://www.topuniversities .com/worlduniversityrankings>.

Rait, Robert S. 1918. *Life in the Medieval University.* Cambridge: Cambridge University Press.

Reimer, Nils. 2003 (April 23). "A Personal History of the Stanford University Office of Technology Licensing." Caramel, Calif..

Rimer, Sara. 2007. "At 71, Physics Professor Is a Web Star." *New York Times,* December 19.

Roland, Alex, and Philip Shiman. 2002. *Strategic Computing: DARPA and the Quest for Machine Intelligence.* Cambridge, Mass.: MIT Press.

Rothman, Stanley, S. Robert Lichter, and Neil Nevite. 2005. "Politics and Professional Advancement Among College Faculty." The Forum. <http://www.bepress .com/forum>.

Rudolph, Frederick. 1990. *The American College & University: A History.* Athens, Ga.: University of Georgia Press.

Sandoval, Greg. 2006 (June 2). "YouTube: Our Humor, Not Our Hack." *CNET News.* <http://news.cnet.com/yourube-our-humor,-not-our-hack/2100-1026_3-6079314 .html>

Seidman, Stephen. 2004. "Software Offshoring—Risks and Opportunities for Computing Programs." CRA Snowbird Conference. Snowbird, Utah.

Shirky, Clay. 2008. *Here Comes Everybody: The Power of Organizing without Organizations.* New York: Penguin Press.

Siemens, George. 2006. *Knowing Knowledge.* Lulu.com. <http:www.lulu.com/product. knowing-knowledge/545031>

Slosson, Edwin E. 1910. *Great American Universities.* New York: The Macmillan Company.

Stanford University News Service. 2008 (March 4). "Stanford to Help New Saudi University with Applied Math, Computer Science." <http://news.stanford.edu/pr/2008 /pr-kaust-030408.html> (accessed June 15, 2010).

Stephenson, Neal. 1992. *Snow Crash.* New York: Bantam Books.

Surowiecki, James. 2005. *The Wisdom of Crowds.* New York: Anchor Books.

Suskind, Ron. 2008. *The Way of the World*. New York: Harper-Collins.

Swarup, Vikas. 2005. *Q & A*. New York: Scribner.

Terrell, Kenneth. 2009. "Harvard and Princeton Top the U.S. News College Rankings." *U.S. News & World Report*, Aug. 19.

THE Times Higher Education. 2009. *World University Rankings*. <http://timeshigher education.co.uk/worlduniversityrankings>.

Thomas, Cal. 2005. "Closing of the University Mind," *Washington Times*, April 3.

Ting, T. C., and A. P. Jensen. 1974. "An On-line Interactive Audiographic Learning System." *Proceedings of the 1974 Annual Conference of the ACM, Volume 1*. Association for Computing Machinery.

University of Florida. "Association of American Universities 2006–2007 Degrees Awarded Black Students." Office of Institutional Planning and Research. <http://www.ir.ufl.edu/minority/dgaabl.pdf> (accessed June 15, 2010).

Vest, Charles. 2007. *The American Research University from World War II to World Wide Web: Governments, the Private Sector, and the Emerging Meta-University*. Berkeley, Calif.: University of California Press.

Vise, David A. 2008. *The Google Story*. New York: Bantam Dell.

Weber, Luc E., and James J. Duderstadt. 2010. *University Research for Innovation*. London: Economica.

Wickham, Henry. 2010. "Antioch College RIP." The American Thinker, April.

Woolley, David R. 1994. "Plato: The Emergence of Online Community." *Computer-Mediated Communications Magazine* 1(3): 5.

Woolston, Donald C. 2008. "Outcomes-Based Assessment in Engineering Education: A Critique of its Foundation and Practice." *38th ASEE/IEEE Conference on Frontiers in Education*. Institute for Electrical and Electronic Engineers.

Workers of the Federal Writer's Project of the Works Progress Administration in the State of Massachusetts. 1936. Selective and Critical Biography of Horace Mann. Amherst, Mass.: Commissioner of Education James G. Reardon.

Yale University. n.d. *Yale Statistics of Enrollment*. <http://www.yale.edu/oir/book _numbers_original/a.pdf>.

Young, Jeffrey. 2008. "When Professors Print Their Own Diplomas, Who Needs Universities?" *The Chronicle of Higher Education*, September 25.

Index